# Regions of the United States

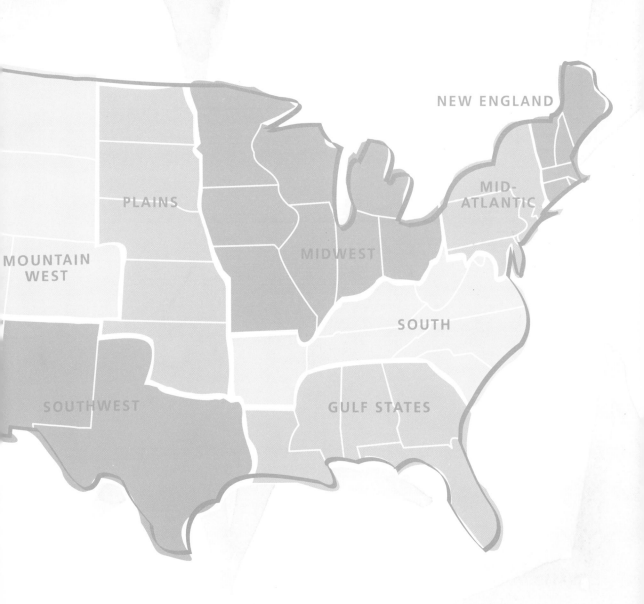

NEW ENGLAND

MID-ATLANTIC

PLAINS

MOUNTAIN WEST

MIDWEST

SOUTH

SOUTHWEST

GULF STATES

# *Simply the Best*
# All American

## Our 250 Regional Favorites
## from Around the Country

**IDG BOOKS WORLDWIDE**
AN INTERNATIONAL DATA GROUP COMPANY
Foster City, CA   Chicago, IL   Indianapolis, IN   New York, NY

IDG Books Worldwide, Inc.
An International Data Group Company
919 E. Hillsdale Boulevard
Suite 400
Foster City, CA 94404

For general information on IDG Books Worldwide's books in the U.S., please call our Consumer Customer Service department at 800-762-2974. For reseller information, including discounts and premium sales, please call our Reseller Customer Service department at 800-434-3422.

**A Word About Weight Watchers**

Since 1963, Weight Watchers has grown from a handful of people to millions of enroll-ments annually. Today, Weight Watchers is recognized as the leading name in safe and sensible weight control. Weight Watchers members form a diverse group, from youths to senior citizens, attending meetings virtually around the globe. Weight loss and weight management results vary by individual, but we recommend that you attend Weight Watchers meetings, follow the Weight Watchers food plan, and participate in regular physical activity. For the Weight Watchers meeting nearest you, call 1-800-651-6000. Or check out our web site at www.weightwatchers.com.

**Weight Watchers Publishing Group**
Creative & Editorial Director: Nancy Gagliardi
Publishing Assistant: Jenny Laboy-Brace
Recipe Editors and Developers: Rebecca Adams, David Bonom, Barry Bluestein & Kevin Morrissey, Jill Van Cleave, Cynthia DePersio, Linda Gassenheimer, Brenda Goldberg, Maureen Luchejkon, Lori Longbotham, Diane Morgan, Deri Reed, Greg Patent, Sarah Reynolds, Tracey Seaman, and Martha Schueneman.
Text: Joanne Lamb Hayes, Ph.D.
Nutrition Analysis: Jeanne Gedson, Antonina Smith
Photographer: Ann Stratton
Food Stylist: Rori Spinelli
Book Designer: Amy Trombat

Library of Congress Cataloging-in-Publication data available from the publisher.

ISBN: 0-7645-6193-6

Manufactured in the United States of America

10  9  8  7  6  5  4  3  2  1

# ★ ★ ★ contents

# Introduction

WHEN YOU THINK OF AMERICAN CUISINE, WHAT COMES TO MIND? Surely, culinary historians can piece together a clearer picture of what constitutes true American fare. But ask a home cook that question. What would she or he reply? Maybe the first question to ask is: Where do you live? For instance, someone born and bred in the Plains states might contend you can't talk about real American food without talking about barbecue. A New Englander might nominate a boiled beef dinner or fish chowder as purely American, while someone from the Southwest would insist you label authentic American cooking with corn and chiles. A Southerner might wax poetic on pecans and peanuts. While one Westerner would mention any recipe that highlights the fine beef from the area's prized cattle, another might say that any dish that features locally grown, farm-fresh ingredients is one that defines real American fare.

The American Dream certainly is alive and well.

Whether it was the nation's first English colonists who settled in Massachusetts or today's global immigrants who leave behind histories and families from around the world, America still is the destination of countless in search of a fresh start in a new land. It is a nation that, to this day, embodies the hope, longing, and promise of a better life.

A better life, however, probably are not the words that came to the minds of those first settlers. Plagued with monumental hardship and obstacles that few today could even conceive of (let alone endure), those pioneers certainly must have been the role models for our much-heralded characteristic of American ingenuity and perseverance. Yet they struggled on and learned to adapt, especially when it came to the food. They made the best use of the New World ingredients they stumbled upon and cultivated, as well as those they were introduced to by Native Americans. And somewhere between the labor, hardship, despair, and adaptation, a cuisine was born.

Our cuisine blends from the cultures and culinary traditions of the countless peoples that have crossed our borders. And in typical American fashion, we also might contend that we've borrowed and blended the best to create a cuisine that escapes definition—yet is utterly delicious.

With *Simply the Best All American* we tried to marry the flavors of the foods found all around the country. In some cases, we've melded the modern with the traditional (like Pecan-Crusted Fish, Corn Timbales with Vegetables and Cheese, Peppered Buffalo Tenderloin Steaks with Merlot and Cherry Sauce, Butternut Squash and Swiss Chard Risotto, and Tropical Coleslaw) while in others, we tried to remain true to the original—but using a lighter touch (such as Yankee Pot Roast, Maine Blueberry-Crumb Pie, Shoofly Pie, Peanut Soup, Jambalaya, or Dutch Apple Pie). We've showcased just some of the regional specialties, with dishes that highlight the foods introduced by the people that settled in an area, as well as the fare that sustains and is indigenous to a region. As always, we've included ideas and ways to get the dish on the table a little easier, as well as some fanciful folklore to give you a greater sense of the dish in terms of the role it plays in the creation of American cuisine, as well as American history.

Nancy Gagliardi
Creative & Editorial Director

*chapter one*
# New England

# Vermont Cheddar Soup

MAKES 6 SERVINGS

*The British brought the art of making cheddar cheese to New England. It shouldn't be surprising, then, that some of the best cheddar in the United States today hails from Vermont.*

2 teaspoons unsalted butter
1 small onion, chopped
1 celery stalk, chopped
1 small carrot, peeled and chopped
3 tablespoons all-purpose flour
3/4 teaspoon dry mustard
1/4 teaspoon ground nutmeg
4 cups low-sodium chicken broth
1 (12-ounce) can evaporated fat-free milk
1/2 pound shredded light cheddar cheese
2 teaspoons Worcestershire sauce
6 slices crusty bread, toasted

1. Melt the butter in a nonstick saucepan over medium heat. Add the onion, celery, and carrot and sauté until softened, 5–6 minutes. Stir in the flour, dry mustard, and nutmeg; cook 1 minute. Add the broth and simmer 15 minutes.

2. Puree the soup in batches in a blender or food processor and return to the saucepan. Stir in evaporated milk and simmer over medium heat 5 minutes; do not boil. Add the cheese and stir until melted and smooth. Stir in the Worcestershire sauce. Serve with the toast.

*Per serving  275 Calories, 10 g Total Fat, 6 g Saturated Fat, 23 mg Cholesterol, 611 mg Sodium, 28 g Total Carbohydrate, 2 g Dietary Fiber, 21 g Protein, 544 mg Calcium.*

*POINTS per serving: 6.*

★ *American Way* To keep the fat down, we use light cheese in this soup; if you prefer to use Vermont cheddar, select an extra-sharp variety and use only 1/4 pound. For effortless cheese shredding, cut the cheddar into chunks and use the cheese-shredding blade in your food processor.

FLASHBACK >> 1978

Alternative businessmen and Vermont hippies Ben Cohen and Jerry Greenfield open the first Ben & Jerry's Homemade Ice Cream and Crepes store in a onetime gas station in their home state.

# New England Clam Chowder

## MAKES 4 SERVINGS

*Creamy white chowders have been a New England staple since at least the early 1700s. In colonial days, chunks of white-fleshed fish, not clams, were the star.*

3 slices bacon, cut into 1/4-inch pieces
1 onion, chopped
3 red potatoes, diced
1/2 cup water
1 (8-ounce) bottle clam juice
1/4 teaspoon dried thyme
2 (6 1/2-ounce) cans minced clams, drained
2 tablespoons all-purpose flour
2 cups fat-free milk
2 tablespoons chopped flat-leaf parsley
1/2 teaspoon salt
1/4 teaspoon freshly ground pepper

1. Cook the bacon in a large saucepan over medium heat until almost crisp, about 4 minutes. Add the onion and cook, stirring occasionally, until soft, 3–4 minutes. Stir in the potatoes and cook 3 minutes. Add the water, clam juice, and thyme; bring to a simmer. Cover and cook until the potatoes are tender, 12–15 minutes. Reduce the heat to low. Stir in the clams and cook until the clams are heated through, about 5 minutes.

2. Combine 6 tablespoons of hot liquid from the saucepan and the flour in a small bowl. Stir the mixture back into the saucepan. Increase the heat to high and bring to a boil. Cook until the soup thickens, 1–2 minutes. Reduce the heat and stir in the milk, parsley, salt, and pepper. Heat gently until the soup is hot, but do not let it come to a boil.

*Per serving* 420 Calories, 18 g Total Fat, 6 g Saturated Fat, 66 mg Cholesterol, 770 mg Sodium, 37 g Total Carbohydrate, 3 g Dietary Fiber, 26 g Protein, 239 mg Calcium.

*POINTS per serving: 9.*

## REVOLUTIONARY COOKBOOKS

Not surprisingly, three of America's earliest and most significant cooking tomes hail from the innovative kitchens of New England. In fact, the very first American cookbook, *American Cookery* by Amelia Simmons, An American Orphan, was published in 1796 in Hartford, Connecticut. In addition to countless European-style recipes like those found in imported cookbooks used throughout the colonies, *American Cookery* helped New World cooks navigate the use of such "exotic" ingredients as corn, beans, squash, and pumpkin.

Exactly one century later, Fannie Farmer self-published the *Boston Cooking School Cook Book*, which taught Americans how to measure accurately (she introduced the concept of using level spoonfuls) and cook scientifically. Although not a bestseller in Europe, the book was a runaway success in America. It went back for several printings in its first year and, in a true test of its longevity, the *Boston Cooking School Cook Book* continues to inspire cooks today.

In 1963, Julia Child introduced the groundbreaking *The Art of French Cooking*. The book, which gained widespread attention thanks to the Boston Public Television series it spawned, introduced home cooks to haute cuisine. Thanks to Child's easygoing, playful manner and relaxed style, serious and complicated French dishes seemed eminently doable to cooks who may have previously found foods like soufflés, chocolate mousse, or coq au vin too fussy and time-consuming to prepare. The success of *The Art of French Cooking* led to the celebrated PBS series, which launched a new era in American cooking. Many food historians credit Childs with spurring the trend (which continues to this day), motivating cooks to experiment with international cuisines, try unfamiliar ingredients, and pair wine with meals.

# Baked Cod with Potatoes

MAKES 4 SERVINGS

*Over 200 years ago, the importance of cod on the New England economy led to the mounting of the "Sacred Cod," a six-foot model of the fish, in the Massachusetts State House and the naming of Cape Cod. This dish showcases a classic cod preparation—a simple mix of cod, potatoes, and bread crumbs—and is as elegant as it is easy.*

2 large baking potatoes, peeled and cut into 1/8-inch–thick slices

2 tablespoons unsalted butter, melted

1/2 teaspoon salt

1/2 cup plain dried bread crumbs

1/4 cup chopped fresh parsley

1/4 cup fresh lemon juice

1/4 teaspoon freshly ground pepper

4 (6-ounce) cod fillets

1. Preheat the oven to 425°F. Spray a baking sheet with nonstick spray.

2. Combine the potato slices with enough cold water to cover in a medium saucepan. Bring to a boil and cook 1 minute. Remove from the heat and let stand 2 minutes. Drain well. Return the potatoes to the saucepan and toss with 1 tablespoon of the butter and 1/4 teaspoon of the salt.

3. Combine the remaining 1 tablespoon butter and 1/4 teaspoon salt, the bread crumbs, parsley, lemon juice, and pepper in a small bowl. Arrange the fillets on the baking sheet. Press one-quarter of the bread-crumb mixture onto the top of each fillet. Arrange the potatoes around the fillets. Bake until the fish is just opaque in the center, 7–10 minutes.

4. Adjust the oven to broil. Broil the fish 5 inches from the heat, until the bread crumbs begin to brown, about 1 minute.

*Per serving* 389 Calories, 8 g Total Fat, 4 g Saturated Fat, 90 mg Cholesterol, 512 mg Sodium, 43 g Total Carbohydrate, 3 g Dietary Fiber, 35 g Protein, 79 mg Calcium.

*POINTS per serving: 8.*

★ *American Way* If you prefer, substitute another thick white fish, such as grouper or striped bass, for the cod.

# Portuguese Fisherman's Stew

MAKES 4 SERVINGS

*Renowned as navigators and fishermen, it makes sense that the Portuguese immigrants of the early 1800s chose to settle in the fishing communities that blossomed along the coasts of Rhode Island, Massachusetts, and northern Connecticut. This dish combines an array of seafood with signature Portuguese flavorings, linguiça, a garlicky Portuguese sausage, and saffron.*

2 red potatoes, cut into eighths

1 medium carrot, peeled and chopped

½ onion, chopped

2 ounces linguiça, chorizo, or reduced-fat kielbasa, sliced

2 garlic cloves, minced

½ pound tomatoes, chopped

1 (8-ounce) bottle clam juice

½ cup dry white wine

½ teaspoon saffron threads, crushed

¼ teaspoon dried oregano

¼ teaspoon cayenne

8 littleneck clams, scrubbed

8 mussels, scrubbed and debearded

¼ pound medium shrimp, peeled and deveined

¼ pound cod fillet

¼ pound sea scallops

1 tablespoon chopped fresh cilantro

1. Spray an 8-quart saucepan with nonstick spray and set over medium heat. Add the potatoes, carrots, onion, linguiça, and garlic; sauté until the onion begins to soften, about 6 minutes. Stir in the tomatoes, clam juice, wine, saffron, oregano, and cayenne; bring to a boil. Cover, reduce the heat, and simmer 15 minutes. Add the clams and simmer, covered, 3 minutes.

2. Stir in the mussels, cover, and simmer 3 minutes more. Discard any clams or mussels that don't open. Add the shrimp, cod, and scallops; cook until the shrimp are pink and no longer opaque, about 5 minutes. Stir in the cilantro and serve.

*Per serving* 277 Calories, 7 g Total Fat, 2 g Saturated Fat, 84 mg Cholesterol, 501 mg Sodium, 25 g Total Carbohydrate, 3 g Dietary Fiber, 26 g Protein, 75 mg Calcium.

*POINTS per serving: 6.*

 *American Way* If you can't find linguiça, Mexican chorizo or Polish kielbasa make fine substitutes.

*Portuguese Fisherman's Stew*

# New England Clam Bake

MAKES 4 SERVINGS

*When the earliest settlers arrived in New England, they observed the Native Americans baking clams and other shellfish in pits over hot stones that had been covered with seaweed. Today, our version uses the backyard grill. Although lobster is a somewhat costly addition to our clambake, the crustacean was so plentiful in New England during colonial times that it was considered a poor man's food.*

4 red potatoes, cut into eighths

4 ears of corn, shucked and halved

1 red onion, cut into 1/2-inch–thick wedges

4 garlic cloves, thinly sliced

1 cup dry white wine

1/2 cup chopped fresh parsley

3 tablespoons fresh lemon juice

2 tablespoons unsalted butter

1 teaspoon hot pepper sauce

4 sprigs fresh thyme, or 1/2 teaspoon dried

1/2 teaspoon salt

1/4 teaspoon freshly ground pepper

24 littleneck clams, scrubbed

24 mussels, scrubbed and debearded

2 (11/2-pound) lobsters

1. Spray the grill rack with nonstick spray; prepare the grill.

2. Combine the potatoes, corn, onion, garlic, wine, parsley, lemon juice, butter, pepper sauce, thyme, salt, and pepper in a large, deep, disposable aluminum pan. Cover the pan tightly with foil and place directly on the grill. Close the grill cover and cook the vegetables 20 minutes.

3. Remove the pan from the grill and carefully open the foil. Place the clams and mussels in a single layer on top. Set the lobsters on top of the clams. Reseal the pan with foil and return it to the grill. Close the grill cover and cook until the potatoes are tender, the lobsters are cooked through, and the clams and mussels have opened, 20–25 minutes. Discard any clams or mussels that don't open.

*Per serving  484 Calories, 10 g Total Fat, 5 g Saturated Fat, 144 mg Cholesterol, 850 mg Sodium, 57 g Total Carbohydrate, 6 g Dietary Fiber, 40 g Protein, 133 mg Calcium.*

*POINTS per serving: 9.*

★ *American Way*  Cooking live lobster is not for the faint-hearted. Try placing the live lobster in the freezer for 10 to 15 minutes to dull its senses prior to dropping it into a pot of boiling water or grilling. Or, buy fresh cooked lobster at the market.

# Cornmeal-Crusted Chicken Pot Pie

### MAKES 6 SERVINGS

*Cornmeal lends an interesting crunch—and a lovely yellow color—to the crust of this traditional comfort food. Early recipes called for fowl that needed to simmer for many hours to become tender, but we can use cooked chicken breast, so the pot pie is cooked in a flash.*

## CRUST

1 cup all-purpose flour

2 tablespoons yellow cornmeal

¼ teaspoon salt

5⅓ tablespoons solid vegetable shortening, chilled

2–3 tablespoons ice water

## FILLING

3 red potatoes, diced

2 medium turnips, peeled and diced

2 carrots, peeled and chopped

1½ cups thawed frozen pearl onions

1½ cups thawed frozen peas

2 cups low-sodium chicken broth

¾ pound cooked skinless boneless chicken breast, cubed

1 tablespoon Worcestershire sauce

¾ teaspoon salt

½ teaspoon dried thyme

¼ teaspoon ground nutmeg

¼ teaspoon freshly ground pepper

1 cup fat-free milk

¼ cup cornstarch

1 tablespoon fresh lemon juice

1 tablespoon Dijon mustard

1. To make the crust, combine the flour, cornmeal, and salt in a medium bowl. With a pastry cutter or 2 knives, cut in the shortening until the mixture resembles coarse crumbs. Stir in the ice water, 1 tablespoon at a time, until a dough forms and holds together when pressed between your fingers. Shape the dough into a disk, wrap with plastic, and refrigerate 30 minutes. Preheat the oven to 400°F.

2. To make the filling, bring a large pot of water to a boil. Add the potatoes, turnips, and carrots; return to a boil and cook 3 minutes. Add the onions and peas; cook 1 minute more and drain. Return the vegetables to the saucepan, add the broth, chicken, Worcestershire sauce, salt, thyme, nutmeg, and pepper. Bring to a boil and cook 1 minute.

3. Combine the milk and cornstarch in a small bowl; stir until the cornstarch has dissolved. Stir the dissolved cornstarch into the chicken mixture and cook just until the sauce begins to thicken, about 1 minute. Remove from the heat. Stir in the lemon juice and mustard. Pour the mixture into a 9-inch, deep-dish pie pan.

4. On a lightly floured counter, roll the dough to a 12-inch circle, pressing the edges of the dough back together if they split. Carefully place the dough over the chicken mixture in the pie pan. Tuck the edges down the sides of the pan. Pierce the dough with a sharp knife in several places. Brush with 1 tablespoon water. Bake until the crust is golden and the filling is bubbling, about 30 minutes.

*Per serving 457 Calories, 15 g Total Fat, 4 g Saturated Fat, 51 mg Cholesterol, 622 mg Sodium, 54 g Total Carbohydrate, 6 g Dietary Fiber, 27 g Protein, 147 mg Calcium.*

*POINTS per serving: 9.*

# Marinated Grilled Quail

### MAKES 4 SERVINGS

*Quail, a New World game bird, is not related to European quail. When colonists discovered a New World bird strikingly similar in appearance to the European quail, they christened it with the same name. Although quail are small (less than 10 ounces), they have a wonderful, intense poultry flavor. The most commonly available quail is the bobwhite, which is found in the wild, as well as being cultivated throughout New England. Quail are available in some fine butcher shops and by mail order.*

2 teaspoons grated lemon zest

1/4 cup fresh lemon juice

4 teaspoons chopped fresh rosemary

4 teaspoons chopped fresh sage

2 large garlic cloves, minced

2 teaspoons honey

1 teaspoon salt

1/4 teaspoon freshly ground pepper

4 quail

1. Combine the lemon zest, lemon juice, rosemary, sage, garlic, honey, salt, and pepper in a large bowl. Add the quail and toss to coat. Cover the bowl with plastic wrap and refrigerate 1–3 hours.

2. Spray a grill or broiler rack with nonstick spray; prepare the grill or preheat the broiler. Wipe any excess marinade off the quail. Grill or broil, 5 inches from the heat, until cooked through, 3–4 minutes per side.

*Per serving  199 Calories, 12 g Total Fat, 3 g Saturated Fat, 73 mg Cholesterol, 327 mg Sodium, 0 g Total Carbohydrate, 0 g Dietary Fiber, 21 g Protein, 13 mg Calcium.*

*POINTS per serving: 5.*

★ *American Way* This simple recipe is complete with a classic green salad and crusty bread.

# Cornish Hens with Oyster Stuffing

## MAKES 8 SERVINGS

*Oyster stuffing, a popular dish in colonial times, was used to add both flavor and bulk to a meal. In this recipe, try Malpeque oysters, New England's indigenous breed. They have a pleasant, briny flavor.*

2 slices bacon, cut into 1-inch pieces

1 onion, chopped

1 celery stalk, chopped

3/4 teaspoon poultry seasoning

15 shucked oysters or 1 (8-ounce) can oysters, drained

4 cups baguette or French bread cubes

3/4 cup low-sodium chicken broth

1 egg white, lightly beaten

1/2 teaspoon salt

1/8 teaspoon freshly ground pepper

4 (1-pound) Cornish hens, skinned

2 teaspoons dried sage leaves

1 teaspoon dried thyme

1 teaspoon sweet paprika

1 teaspoon garlic powder

1 tablespoon reduced-fat margarine, melted

1. Preheat the oven to 425°F. To make the stuffing, cook the bacon in a nonstick skillet until almost crisp, about 4 minutes. Add the onion, celery, and poultry seasoning; cook until the onion and celery begin to soften, 3–4 minutes. Transfer to a bowl and add the oysters, bread cubes, broth, egg white, 1/4 teaspoon of the salt, and the pepper; stir to combine.

2. Stuff each hen with about 1/2 cup of the stuffing; truss the legs.

3. Combine the sage, thyme, paprika, garlic powder, and remaining 1/4 teaspoon salt in a small bowl. Brush the hens with the melted margarine and sprinkle with the sage mixture. Place the hens, breast-side up, on a rack in a large roasting pan. Spray with nonstick spray. Roast 15 minutes; reduce the heat to 375°F and continue roasting until an instant-read thermometer inserted in the thigh registers 180°F, 45–55 minutes. Let stand 10 minutes before carving.

*Per serving 302 Calories, 12 g Total Fat, 4 g Saturated Fat, 146 mg Cholesterol, 478 mg Sodium, 13 g Total Carbohydrate, 1 g Dietary Fiber, 33 g Protein, 54 mg Calcium.*

*POINTS per serving: 7.*

★ *American Way* If you have any leftover stuffing, simply place it in an oven-safe dish, cover it with foil, and bake it alongside the hens during the last 30 minutes of cooking. The stuffing is also tasty with chicken; use it to fill a 3 1/2- to 4-pound oven stuffer. For leftovers, remove stuffing from the game hens and store separately in the refrigerator.

# Maple-Glazed Turkey Breast with Mushroom Stuffing

MAKES 12 SERVINGS

*Maple syrup and turkey—two foods introduced to early New Englanders by Native Americans—make a delightful pairing in this easy entrée. Consider serving this dish, instead of a whole turkey, when just a few guests are coming for Thanksgiving.*

## TURKEY

1 (5-pound) bone-in skinless turkey breast

1/2 teaspoon salt

1/4 teaspoon freshly ground pepper

3/4 cup pure maple syrup

1/2 teaspoon vanilla extract

1/4 teaspoon ground nutmeg

1/4 teaspoon ground allspice

## STUFFING

1 tablespoon unsalted butter

2 onions, chopped

1 celery stalk, chopped

1 carrot, peeled and chopped

3 garlic cloves, minced

1 Granny Smith apple, cored and chopped

1 pound white mushrooms, chopped

1/2 pound shiitake mushrooms, chopped

3/4 teaspoon salt

1/4 cup sherry

2 tablespoons chopped fresh sage,
    or 2 teaspoons dried

1 tablespoon chopped fresh thyme,
    or 1 teaspoon dried

1 1/2 pounds firm white bread,
    cut into 1-inch cubes and dried

1 (14 1/2-ounce) can low-sodium chicken
    broth

1/2 teaspoon freshly ground pepper

1. To prepare the turkey, preheat the oven to 400°F. Place the turkey breast on a rack in a roasting pan and sprinkle with the salt and pepper. Roast 15 minutes, then reduce the heat to 350°F and roast another 30 minutes.

2. Meanwhile, combine the maple syrup, vanilla, nutmeg, and allspice in a saucepan and bring to a boil. Reduce the heat and simmer until the liquid is reduced by about one-fourth, 3–5 minutes. After the first 45 minutes of roasting, brush the turkey with the glaze. Roast 15 minutes more and brush with glaze. Roast 10 minutes more and glaze again. Roast 5 minutes, brush with the remaining glaze, and continue roasting until an instant-read thermometer inserted in the thickest part registers 180°F, 5–10 minutes more.

3. To make the stuffing, spray a 3-quart baking dish with nonstick spray. Melt the butter in a large skillet. Add the onions, celery, carrot, and garlic and sauté until the vegetables begin to soften, 7–8 minutes. Stir in the apple and cook 3 minutes. Add the white and shiitake mushrooms and 1/4 teaspoon of the salt; sauté until the mushrooms begin to give off their liquid and soften, about 6 minutes. Stir in the sherry, sage, and thyme; cook until the liquid has evaporated, 2–3 minutes. Remove from the heat.

4. Combine the vegetable mixture, bread cubes, broth, remaining 1/2 teaspoon salt, and the pepper in a large bowl. Toss well to combine and transfer to the baking dish. Cover the dish with foil. After the turkey has roasted 1 hour, place the stuffing in the oven and bake 15 minutes. Remove the foil and bake until the stuffing is heated through and crisp on top, 15–20 minutes more.

*Per serving  384 Calories, 5 g Total Fat, 2 g Saturated Fat, 98 mg Cholesterol, 583 mg Sodium, 43 g Total Carbohydrate, 3 g Dietary Fiber, 41 g Protein, 97 mg Calcium.*

*POINTS per serving: 7.*

*Maple-Glazed Turkey Breast with Mushroom Stuffing,
and Roasted Brussels Sprouts with Bacon (page 19)*

# New England Boiled Dinner

MAKES 6 SERVINGS

*The New England boiled dinner is a tribute to industrious and frugal pioneers. The hearty meal focused on inexpensive ingredients and was typically piled onto farmers' plates at their midday meal to refuel them for the long hours of labor to follow.*

1 pound flank steak, trimmed of all
    visible fat

1 pound skinless, boneless chicken thighs

1 tablespoon Worcestershire sauce

1 teaspoon mustard seeds

1 teaspoon allspice berries

5 sprigs fresh thyme, or 1 teaspoon dried

2 bay leaves

10 whole black peppercorns

1 pound baking potatoes, peeled and
    cut into eighths

3 medium carrots, peeled and cut into
    2-inch pieces

3 medium turnips, peeled and quartered

1 small green cabbage, cut into 8 wedges

2 cups pearl onions, peeled or thawed
    frozen

2 teaspoons salt

1/2 cup light sour cream

2 tablespoons prepared horseradish,
    squeezed dry

1. Combine the flank steak, chicken thighs, Worcestershire sauce, mustard seeds, allspice berries, thyme, bay leaves, and peppercorns in an 8-quart pot. Add enough water to cover and bring to a boil; skim any foam that rises to the surface. Reduce the heat to low and simmer, uncovered for 1 hour. Stir in the potatoes, carrots, turnips, cabbage, onions, and salt. Simmer until the meat and vegetables are tender, about 45 minutes. Drain, discarding the liquid. Discard the bay leaves.

2. Meanwhile, combine the sour cream and horseradish in a small bowl. Serve with the boiled dinner.

*Per serving 402 Calories, 14 g Total Fat, 5 g Saturated Fat, 90 mg Cholesterol, 255 mg Sodium, 31 g Total Carbohydrate, 8 g Dietary Fiber, 39 g Protein, 139 mg Calcium.*

*POINTS per serving: 8.*

★ *American Way* Horseradish sour cream is the traditional accompaniment— or give coarse-grain mustard a try—it's traditional as well.

FLASHBACK>>1621

The colonists who landed in Massachusetts on the *Mayflower* (a scant year earlier) celebrate their first Thanksgiving Day feast with some 90 Indian guests. The Pilgrims are believed to have feasted on roast duck and goose, venison, clams, eels, leeks, watercress, corn and wheat breads, plums, and homemade wine. While some sources contend no turkey was on the menu, others believe wild turkeys also were part of the meal—and they have now become the tradition.

# Yankee Pot Roast

MAKES 6 SERVINGS

*Pot roast was born in New England and is deemed "Yankee" when the vegetables are added to the pot at a later stage of the cooking process. This lengthy roasting method was developed to cook and soften the tougher cuts of meat that came from work animals—rather than from the livestock raised specifically for food, another testament to the frugality of New Englanders.*

1/3 cup all-purpose flour

3/4 teaspoon salt

1/4 teaspoon freshly ground pepper

1 (1 1/2-pound) beef eye round roast, trimmed of all visible fat

1 teaspoon vegetable oil

1 cup dry red wine

1 cup low-sodium beef broth

1 cup water

1 tablespoon Dijon mustard

1 tablespoon Worcestershire sauce

2 bay leaves

4 sprigs fresh thyme, or 1/4 teaspoon dried

6 medium red potatoes, cut into eighths

3 medium carrots, peeled and cut into 1 1/2-inch pieces

3 large parsnips, peeled, halved lengthwise, and cut into 1 1/2-inch pieces

2 cups pearl onions, peeled or thawed frozen

1. Combine the flour, 1/4 teaspoon of the salt, and 1/8 teaspoon of the pepper in a large bowl. Add the roast and turn to coat well. Heat a large Dutch oven over medium-high heat. Swirl in the oil, then add the roast and cook until browned, 2–3 minutes per side. Add the wine and cook, scraping up any browned bits, 2–3 minutes. Stir in the remaining 1/2 teaspoon salt and 1/8 teaspoon pepper, the broth, water, mustard, Worcestershire sauce, bay leaves, and thyme; bring the mixture to a boil. Reduce the heat, cover, and simmer 1 hour 45 minutes.

2. Stir in the potatoes, carrots, parsnips, and onions. Return to a simmer; cover and cook until the meat and vegetables are tender, 45–60 minutes more.

*Per serving* 375 Calories, 6 g Total Fat, 2 g Saturated Fat, 42 mg Cholesterol, 327 mg Sodium, 52 g Total Carbohydrate, 6 g Dietary Fiber, 27 g Protein, 65 mg Calcium.

*POINTS per serving:* 7.

# Molasses and Black Pepper–Crusted Pork Tenderloin

MAKES 6 SERVINGS

*Yankee traders discovered molasses on their frequent jaunts to the West Indies. Although molasses was not an item profitable enough to ship to Europe, barrels of the brownish-black syrup were brought back to New England, where some of it was used to make rum and the rest sold as an inexpensive sweetener. Molasses is a traditional flavoring for pork since its dark sweetness provides a pleasing contrast to the salty meat.*

3 tablespoons molasses

³/4 teaspoon balsamic vinegar

¹/2 teaspoon Worcestershire sauce

1 garlic clove, minced

1 (1¹/2-pound) pork tenderloin, trimmed of all visible fat

¹/2 teaspoon salt

2 teaspoons coarsely ground black pepper

1. Preheat the oven to 400°F. Combine the molasses, vinegar, Worcestershire sauce, and garlic in a large bowl. Pat the pork dry with paper towels and add it to the molasses mixture; turn to coat.

2. Transfer the meat to a rack in a roasting pan. Sprinkle all over with the salt and the pepper, and press the seasoning into the meat with your hands. Roast until the pork reaches an internal temperature of 160°F, 22–25 minutes. Let stand 5–10 minutes before slicing.

*Per serving  170 Calories, 4 g Total Fat, 1 g Saturated Fat, 67 mg Cholesterol, 250 mg Sodium, 8 g Total Carbohydrate, 0 g Dietary Fiber, 24 g Protein, 30 mg Calcium.*

*POINTS per serving: 4.*

# Vermont Veal Chop with Apples and Sage

## MAKES 4 SERVINGS

*The quality veal production that is rapidly growing throughout New England, especially in Vermont, is a 20th-century development that is well-suited for the rolling hills of the region.*

2 teaspoons light margarine

2 medium shallots, thinly sliced

1 tablespoon sugar

2 Granny Smith apples, peeled, cored, and sliced

1/2 cup dry white wine

2 teaspoons chopped fresh sage, or 1/2 teaspoon dried

3/4 teaspoon salt

1/4 teaspoon freshly ground pepper

4 (6-ounce) lean bone-in veal chops, about 1/2-inch thick and trimmed of all visible fat

1. Spray the grill or broiler rack with nonstick spray; prepare the grill or preheat the broiler.

2. Melt the margarine in a nonstick skillet, then add the shallots and sugar. Sauté, stirring occasionally, until the shallots soften, 2–3 minutes. Add the apples and sauté until they begin to soften, 3–5 minutes. Stir in the wine, sage, 1/2 teaspoon of the salt, and 1/8 teaspoon of the pepper. Cook until the mixture is thick and almost all of the liquid has evaporated, 3–4 minutes. Set aside.

3. Sprinkle the veal chops with the remaining 1/4 teaspoon salt and 1/8 teaspoon pepper. Grill or broil the chops, 5 inches from the heat, until medium-rare, 3–4 minutes per side. Spoon the apple mixture over the veal.

*Per serving 167 Calories, 5 g Total Fat, 2 g Saturated Fat, 70 mg Cholesterol, 365 mg Sodium, 11 g Total Carbohydrate, 1 g Dietary Fiber, 18 g Protein, 23 mg Calcium.*

*POINTS per serving: 4.*

★ *American Way* Be sure to use Granny Smith apples; their firmness and bite hold up well in cooking and provide a sweet-tart contrast to the mellow veal.

# New Hampshire Stuffed Leg of Lamb with Roasted Potatoes

MAKES 12 SERVINGS

*New Hampshire is one of the leading producers of lamb in the New England area, where the land and climate provide ideal conditions for raising them. This elegant dish is sure to impress guests at your next dinner party.*

1 cup plain dried bread crumbs

1/4 cup Dijon mustard

3 tablespoons chopped fresh mint

6 garlic cloves, minced

4 teaspoons chopped fresh rosemary

3 teaspoons olive oil

1 1/4 teaspoons salt

1/2 teaspoon freshly ground pepper

1 (3-pound) lean, rolled, butterflied leg of lamb, trimmed of all visible fat

1/4 cup tomato paste

4 pounds red potatoes, quartered lengthwise

1. Preheat the oven to 425°F. Combine the bread crumbs, mustard, and mint in a bowl. Add half the minced garlic, the rosemary, 2 teaspoons of the oil, 1/2 teaspoon of the salt, and 1/4 teaspoon of the pepper.

2. Unroll the lamb and spread on the tomato paste. Top with an even coating of the bread crumb mixture. Reroll the lamb and tie at 1-inch intervals with heavy string. Rub the outside of the lamb with the remaining 1 teaspoon oil, and sprinkle with 1/4 teaspoon of the salt and the remaining garlic. Transfer the lamb to a roasting pan.

3. Lightly spray the potatoes with nonstick spray. Sprinkle with the remaining 1/2 teaspoon salt and 1/4 teaspoon pepper; toss to coat. Arrange the potatoes around the lamb. Roast 15 minutes. Reduce the heat to 350°F and roast until the potatoes are browned and tender and the lamb has reached an internal temperature of 140°F for medium rare or 160°F for medium, 1 hour to 1 hour 15 minutes. If the potatoes start to become too browned, transfer them to a serving bowl and cover to keep warm. Let lamb stand 10 minutes before slicing.

*Per serving* (one 2-ounce slice lamb plus 4 potato quarters): 285 Calories, 7 g Total Fat, 2 g Saturated Fat, 52 mg Cholesterol, 297 mg Sodium, 36 g Total Carbohydrate, 3 g Dietary Fiber, 20 g Protein, 43 mg Calcium.

*POINTS per serving: 6.*

★ *American Way* Pay careful attention not to overcook the lamb; cooking the meat until just medium-rare provides the most succulent, mellow flavor. Leftover lamb is delicious layered in pita bread, with shredded lettuce and a tangy, mint-spiked yogurt dressing.

# Roasted Brussels Sprouts with Bacon

## MAKES 6 SERVINGS

*Brussels sprouts were eaten as long ago as 1554, when they are mentioned in a cookbook by a Dutch botanist. Although not indigenous to the Americas, some of the most popular varieties are now grown in the Northeastern United States. The small green sprouts look like mini cabbages and are, in fact, members of the cabbage family.*

1/4 pound turkey bacon

2 pounds Brussels sprouts, trimmed and halved

3/4 teaspoon salt

1/2 teaspoon caraway seeds

1/4 teaspoon freshly ground pepper

2 tablespoons plain dried bread crumbs

1. Preheat the oven to 400°F. Cook the bacon in a nonstick skillet until almost crisp, about 4 minutes per side. With a slotted spatula, transfer the bacon to a paper towel–lined plate to drain. Add the Brussels sprouts to the pan and toss to coat with the bacon fat. Stir in the salt, caraway seeds, and pepper. Cut the bacon into 1/2-inch pieces and add to the Brussels sprouts.

2. Spread the sprouts on a baking sheet and bake until lightly browned, 15–20 minutes. Transfer to an oval baking dish and sprinkle with the bread crumbs. Broil the sprouts, 4 inches from the heat, until the bread crumbs are browned, 1–2 minutes.

*Per serving  108 Calories, 4 g Total Fat, 1 g Saturated Fat, 14 mg Cholesterol, 601 mg Sodium, 14 g Total Carbohydrate, 6 g Dietary Fiber, 8 g Protein, 64 mg Calcium.*

*POINTS per serving: 1.*

# Glazed Onions and Root Vegetables

MAKES 4 SERVINGS

*The first recipe for turnips appeared in 1485, but they weren't introduced in England until 1558. These delicate-tasting root vegetables officially became a part of the American food repertoire in 1828, when the first recipe for preparing them appeared in the New World cookbook,* Directions for Cookery.

2 cups pearl onions, peeled or thawed frozen

3 carrots, peeled and cut diagonally into 1/2-inch slices

2 medium turnips, peeled and cut into 1/2-inch–thick wedges

1/2 cup low-sodium chicken broth

2 tablespoons sugar

1 1/2 tablespoons unsalted butter

1/2 teaspoon chopped fresh thyme, or 1/8 teaspoon dried

1/4 teaspoon ground nutmeg

3/4 teaspoon salt

Freshly ground pepper, to taste

Combine the onions, carrots, turnips, broth, sugar, butter, thyme, nutmeg, salt, and pepper in a large nonstick skillet; bring the broth to a boil. Reduce the heat and simmer, uncovered, shaking the skillet occasionally, until most of the liquid has evaporated, 20–25 minutes. Continue cooking, shaking the skillet more frequently, until the vegetables become golden and shiny, 4–6 minutes more.

*Per serving 120 Calories, 5 g Total Fat, 3 g Saturated Fat, 13 mg Cholesterol, 490 mg Sodium, 18 g Total Carbohydrate, 4 g Dietary Fiber, 2 g Protein, 112 mg Calcium.*

*POINTS per serving: 2.*

★ *American Way* Except for the effort you have to put in peeling the onions, this dish is surprisingly effortless. To peel pearl onions, slice off a small piece of the root end and make an "x" with a sharp knife; toss in a pot of boiling water for 1 minute, drain, and squeeze the onions to remove the skin. Want it even easier? Substitute thawed, frozen pearl onions.

# Tomatoes Stuffed with Salmon Salad

## MAKES 6 SERVINGS

*In colonial times, the Connecticut River was teeming with spawning Atlantic salmon. Indeed, salmon were so abundant that it had the same value as the humble cod. Salmon, like cod, was salted and used in dishes throughout the year. This elegant luncheon dish showcases salmon as the star it is today.*

2 cups water

2 tablespoons + 2 teaspoons fresh lemon juice

1/2 pound salmon fillet, skinned

1 cup thawed frozen peas

1/2 red onion, minced

1 celery stalk, diced

1/3 cup plain nonfat yogurt

2 tablespoons chopped fresh dill

2 teaspoons prepared horseradish, squeezed dry

1 teaspoon Worcestershire sauce

1/2 teaspoon salt

6 tomatoes

1. Combine the water and 2 tablespoons of the lemon juice in a saucepan; bring to a boil. Add the salmon, reduce the heat, and simmer, turning once, until the salmon is cooked through, 8–10 minutes. Transfer the salmon to a medium bowl and refrigerate 20 minutes. Meanwhile, add the peas to the saucepan; heat through and drain.

2. Flake the salmon and add the peas, onion, and celery; toss well. Combine the remaining 2 teaspoons lemon juice, the yogurt, dill, horseradish, Worcestershire sauce, and salt in a separate bowl; pour the mixture over the salmon and toss to coat.

3. Slice the top quarter from each tomato and reserve. With a spoon, scoop out the seeds and flesh; discard. Fill each tomato with about 1/2 cup of the salmon salad and replace the reserved lids.

*Per serving 108 Calories, 2 g Total Fat, 1 g Saturated Fat, 25 mg Cholesterol, 275 mg Sodium, 10 g Total Carbohydrate, 3 g Dietary Fiber, 12 g Protein, 60 mg Calcium.*

*POINTS per serving: 2.*

★ *American Way* To prevent these stuffed jewels from rolling, remove a small slice from the bottom of each tomato.

# Potato and Green Bean Salad

MAKES 8 SERVINGS

*The potato was discovered in the Andes Mountains in South America, traveled to Ireland, and arrived in Boston in 1718, thanks to Irish immigrants. Today, consumption of America's most beloved tuber is a staggering 142 pounds per person each year. Mixed with tangy buttermilk dressing and tossed with crispy, sweet green beans in this recipe, the lowly potato reaches new heights.*

1 pound new potatoes, quartered

1 pound green beans, trimmed and halved crosswise

1 red bell pepper, seeded and chopped

4 scallions, chopped

1/2 cup fat-free buttermilk

1/4 cup light sour cream

1/4 cup nonfat mayonnaise

1 teaspoon fresh lemon juice

1/4 teaspoon garlic powder

1/4 teaspoon salt

1/4 teaspoon freshly ground pepper

1. Combine the potatoes and enough water to cover in a large saucepan. Bring to a boil and cook 6 minutes. Add the green beans and cook until the beans are tender, about 3 minutes. Drain and rinse with cold water.

2. Combine the bell pepper, scallions, buttermilk, sour cream, mayonnaise, lemon juice, garlic powder, salt, and pepper in a large bowl. Add the potatoes and green beans and toss well to combine.

*Per serving 95 Calories, 1 g Total Fat, 0 g Saturated Fat, 3 mg Cholesterol, 160 mg Sodium, 19 g Total Carbohydrate, 3 g Dietary Fiber, 3 g Protein, 70 mg Calcium.*

*POINTS per serving: 1.*

# Mashed Parsnips with Roasted Garlic

MAKES 6 SERVINGS

*Although not native to New England, parsnips made it to the New World via early European settlers. The white root vegetable flourished in the region's climate and soon became a staple crop, helping the settlers survive long winters.*

1 garlic head

3 parsnips, peeled and cut into 1-inch pieces

1 large baking potato, peeled and cut into 1-inch pieces

1/2 cup evaporated fat-free milk

2 tablespoons unsalted butter

3/4 teaspoon salt

1/4 teaspoon freshly ground pepper

1. Preheat the oven to 425°F. Slice the top third from the head of garlic, wrap in foil, and bake until softened, about 35 minutes. Allow to cool 5 minutes, then squeeze the garlic pulp out of the skin and set aside.

2. Meanwhile, combine the parsnips, potato, and enough cold water to cover in a saucepan. Bring to a boil and cook until tender, 8–10 minutes. Drain, return to the pot, and cover to keep warm.

3. Combine the garlic pulp, evaporated milk, butter, salt, and pepper in a small saucepan and heat through, about 3 minutes. Add the milk mixture to the parsnips and potatoes. Mash until all the ingredients are thoroughly combined.

*Per serving 141 Calories, 4 g Total Fat, 3 g Saturated Fat, 12 mg Cholesterol, 325 mg Sodium, 23 g Total Carbohydrate, 3 g Dietary Fiber, 3 g Protein, 99 mg Calcium.*

*POINTS per serving: 3.*

★ *American Way* Peeling the parsnips is a breeze when you use a vegetable peeler.

# Red Flannel Hash

MAKES 4 SERVINGS

*Brilliant red beets combined with creamy white potatoes give this dish its quirky name. A perfect complement to any robust entrée, the hash is traditionally made from cooked beets and the leftovers from a New England Boiled Dinner (page 14) and bacon. Here is a lighter version of this New England specialty. It also can be served topped with an egg for a hearty breakfast.*

3$^1$/2 cups cooked chopped potatoes
1$^1$/2 cups cooked chopped beets
1 cup cooked chopped cabbage
3 scallions, chopped
$^3$/4 teaspoon salt
$^1$/4 teaspoon freshly ground pepper
$^2$/3 cup low-sodium chicken broth

Combine the potatoes, beets, cabbage, scallions, salt, and pepper in a bowl. Spray a large nonstick skillet with nonstick spray and set over low heat. Add the beet mixture and gently flatten into a disk shape with the back of a spoon. Add $^1$/3 cup of the broth. Cover and cook, shaking occasionally, about 20 minutes. Add the remaining $^1$/3 cup broth. Cover and cook until crisp on the bottom, 15–20 minutes. With a spatula, transfer the hash to a plate and cut into 4 wedges.

*Per serving  163 Calories, 1 g Total Fat, 0 g Saturated Fat, 1 mg Cholesterol, 520 mg Sodium, 36 g Total Carbohydrate, 5 g Dietary Fiber, 5 g Protein, 44 mg Calcium.*

*POINTS per serving: 2.*

★ *American Way*  To save on time, use canned beets, although be fore-warned, their flavor is no match for the fresh.

# Johnnycakes with Warm Apple-Quince Sauce

## MAKES 4 SERVINGS

*Johnnycakes, a Rhode Island institution, are thin, flat pancakes traditionally made from locally grown Indian corn (also called flint corn) that is ground in a water-powered grist mill. Purists contend only flint cornmeal will produce the authentic Rhode Island johnnycake, but white cornmeal is a suitable substitution. Serve them drizzled with maple syrup for breakfast or brunch, or with a pat of margarine at dinner.*

### APPLE-QUINCE SAUCE

2 Granny Smith apples, peeled, cored, and chopped

1 large quince, cored, peeled, and chopped

1/2 cup water

1/4 teaspoon vanilla extract

1/4 teaspoon cinnamon

1/8 teaspoon salt

### JOHNNYCAKES

3/4 cup flint cornmeal or white cornmeal

3/4 cup fat-free milk

1 large egg, lightly beaten

3/4 teaspoon salt

1/4 teaspoon freshly ground pepper

1. To make the sauce, combine the apples, quince, water, vanilla, cinnamon, and salt in a saucepan; bring to a boil. Cook over medium heat, stirring occasionally, 10 minutes. Reduce the heat, cover, and simmer, stirring occasionally, until some of the fruit loses its shape and breaks down, 15–18 minutes. Uncover and cook until the excess liquid has evaporated, 2–3 minutes more.

2. To make the johnnycakes, combine the cornmeal, milk, egg, salt, and pepper in a bowl. Allow the mixture to rest 15 minutes.

3. Spray a nonstick skillet with nonstick spray. Heat the skillet until a drop of water sizzles. Pour the batter—2 tablespoons for each johnnycake—into the skillet. Cook until bubbles appear on the top of the cakes, 1–2 minutes. Flip and cook 1–2 minutes longer. Repeat with the remaining batter, to make a total of 8 johnnycakes. Serve with the sauce.

*Per serving (2 johnnycakes and 2 tablespoons sauce): 171 Calories, 2 g Total Fat, 1 g Saturated Fat, 54 mg Cholesterol, 557 mg Sodium, 34 g Total Carbohydrate, 4 g Dietary Fiber, 5 g Protein, 72 mg Calcium.*

*POINTS per serving: 3.*

★ *American Way* Quince trees, once abundant in New England, are now rare. Quinces can be found in large supermarkets and green grocers in the fall months. If quinces are not available, Granny Smith apples can be used as a substitute. Flint cornmeal is available from Kenyon's Grist Mill in West Kingston, Rhode Island, 800-7-KENYON.

### FLASHBACK >> 1628

Puritan Governor John Endicott plants apple seeds in the Massachusetts Bay Colony. His seeds (originally from England) are believed to be the first step toward large-scale apple cultivation in North America.

# Boston Baked Beans

## MAKES 16 SERVINGS

*Some assert that the early colonists learned to cook dried beans from the Indians, while others believe they picked up the technique from sailors who discovered the drying method in North Africa. All are in agreement that baked beans quickly became a New England staple. They were usually prepared in large quantities and eaten for Saturday dinner and then again for Sunday breakfast and lunch, since the Sabbath was set aside as a day of rest and no cooking could be done.*

1 pound dried small white beans, rinsed, picked over, and drained

7 slices bacon

2 onions, chopped

1 cup maple syrup

1 cup ketchup

1/2 cup yellow mustard

1/4 cup packed dark brown sugar

2 teaspoons ground ginger

1 teaspoon vanilla extract

1 teaspoon salt

1/2 teaspoon freshly ground pepper

1/4 teaspoon ground allspice

1/8 teaspoon ground cloves

1. Soak the beans overnight in cold water to cover. (For a faster method, combine the beans with enough water to cover by 1 inch in a large saucepan. Bring the water to a boil and simmer 2 minutes. Remove the pan from the heat; cover and let stand 1 hour.)

2. Drain the beans and return them to the saucepan. Add enough cold water to cover by at least 3 inches and bring to a boil. Reduce the heat and simmer until the beans are just tender, 40–45 minutes. Drain the beans, reserving 3 cups of the cooking liquid.

3. Preheat the oven to 350°F. Chop 3 slices of the bacon into 1/2-inch pieces and combine with the beans and onions in a 12-cup ovenproof casserole. Combine the reserved cooking liquid, maple syrup, ketchup, mustard, brown sugar, ginger, vanilla, salt, pepper, allspice, and cloves in a medium bowl. Pour the mixture over the beans and arrange the remaining 4 slices of bacon on top. Bake until the sauce has thickened and the beans are tender, about 2 hours.

*Per serving (1/2 cup): 283 Calories, 10 g Total Fat, 4 g Saturated Fat, 11 mg Cholesterol, 567 mg Sodium, 39 g Total Carbohydrate, 5 g Dietary Fiber, 9 g Protein, 88 mg Calcium.*

*POINTS per serving: 5.*

★ *American Way* Be revolutionary and bury the hatchet with the Mother country and try serving these beans on toast with a cup of tea—as many English and Irish do for a light supper. It's a great hearty meal with a shot of fiber to keep you full and satisfied.

# American Classics from New England Kitchens

As America's new cooks grew more proficient and confident in the kitchen, it comes as no surprise that the list of New England-based culinary delicacies also grew. Several creations include Boston's beloved baked beans (colonial times), Sylvester Graham's graham crackers (1840), Gail Borden's sweetened condensed milk (1856), and even the hamburger (Louis Lunch in New Haven claims to have invented it in 1895).

But perhaps the most famous dish to come from New England's kitchens is the Toll House cookie. These gooey treats were invented by chance when innkeeper Ruth Wakefield was baking butter cookies to serve the guests at her Toll House Inn in Whitman, Massachusetts. Realizing she was short on nuts, she improvised by adding handfuls of chopped chocolate to the batter instead. Thus, the classic cookie was born. In 1930, the recipe, which included both chocolate and nuts, was printed in her *Toll House Cook Book* and sparked an immediate increase in sales of Nestle chocolate bars, which prompted the company to redesign the bars for easier chopping. In 1939, Nestle made baking with chocolate even simpler by introducing chocolate morsels to the market. Today, Americans bake more chocolate chip cookies than any other variety.

Founded in 1855, the Parker House Hotel in Boston, which continues to operate today, also has been the home for the development of several classic recipes, most notably the folded roll that bears the hotel's name. In addition to Parker House Rolls, the hotel's kitchen is credited with creating the chocolate-frosted version of the Boston Cream Pie and popularizing the menu term "scrod," to describe small cod, haddock, or related fish interchangeably.

# Blackberry Slump

MAKES 8 SERVINGS

*Slumps and their close cousins, grunts, are descendants of steamed fruit puddings, topped with dumplings and cooked over a fire. Slumps, like this one, are cooked in a covered pan with the dumplings on top.*

1 cup all-purpose flour

3 tablespoons + ²/3 cup sugar

1¼ teaspoons baking powder

½ teaspoon salt

¼ teaspoon baking soda

½ teaspoon cinnamon

½ cup fat-free buttermilk

2 tablespoons unsalted butter, melted

4 cups blackberries

1/3 cup water

1 tablespoon fresh lemon juice

1. Combine the flour with 3 tablespoons sugar in a medium bowl. Add the baking powder, salt, baking soda, and ¼ teaspoon of the cinnamon. Stir in the buttermilk and butter. Mix until a soft, sticky dough forms; set aside.

2. In a heavy 10-inch skillet (preferably cast iron), combine the blackberries, the remaining ²/3 cup sugar, the water, lemon juice, and the remaining ¼ teaspoon cinnamon; bring to a boil. Reduce the heat and simmer, uncovered, 2 minutes.

3. Spoon the dough, by tablespoons, onto the fruit. Cover and simmer until the dough is firm to the touch, 8–10 minutes.

*Per serving  208 Calories, 4 g Total Fat, 2 g Saturated Fat, 8 mg Cholesterol, 255 mg Sodium, 43 g Total Carbohydrate, 4 g Dietary Fiber, 3 g Protein, 58 mg Calcium.*

*POINTS per serving: 4.*

★ *American Way* Although blackberries are delicious and indigenous to New England, 4 cups of apples, pears, or berries of any kind will make a scrumptious substitution.

# Pear Pandowdy

*Originally enjoyed for breakfast, pandowdy was cooked, long and slow, overnight above the embers of a fire. The origin of the name* pandowdy *is unclear, but it may be derived from the traditional method of cutting baked topping into squares—"dowdying"—then pressing them down into the fruit and baking the dish again.*

7 medium Bartlett pears, peeled, cored, and thinly sliced

1/2 cup molasses

2 tablespoons + 1 1/2 cups all-purpose flour

1 tablespoon fresh lemon juice

2 teaspoons vanilla extract

1 teaspoon cinnamon

1/2 teaspoon ground nutmeg

1/8 teaspoon ground cloves

1 1/2 teaspoons baking powder

1/2 teaspoon salt

1 cup sugar

2 egg whites, lightly beaten

1/2 cup unsalted butter, melted

1/2 cup fat-free milk

1. Preheat the oven to 350°F. To make the filling, combine the pears and molasses in a large bowl. Add 2 tablespoons flour, the lemon juice, 1 teaspoon of the vanilla, the cinnamon, nutmeg, and cloves; mix well. Transfer to a shallow 8-cup baking dish.

2. To make the topping, combine the remaining 1 1/2 cups flour, the baking powder, and salt in a large bowl. Combine the sugar, egg whites, butter, milk, and the remaining 1 teaspoon vanilla in a separate bowl. Add the sugar mixture to the flour mixture and stir until just combined. Pour the batter over the pears, spreading as necessary. Bake until the filling is bubbling and the top is golden brown, 40–45 minutes.

*Per serving* 288 Calories, 9 g Total Fat, 5 g Saturated Fat, 22 mg Cholesterol, 168 mg Sodium, 51 g Total Carbohydrate, 2 g Dietary Fiber, 3 g Protein, 65 mg Calcium.

*POINTS per serving: 6.*

# Maine Blueberry-Crumb Pie

### MAKES 12 SERVINGS

*Wild blueberries thrive throughout the northern United States and Canada, but most commercially available berries come from Maine, where they are hand-picked with a blueberry rake that was invented in the state in 1822. If possible, use wild blueberries, which have a more intense berry flavor.*

1 (15-ounce) package refrigerated pie dough

6 cups fresh blueberries, picked over and rinsed

2/3 cup + 1/2 cup sugar

5 tablespoons + 1/4 cup all-purpose flour

1 teaspoon grated lemon zest

3 tablespoons fresh lemon juice

1/2 teaspoon vanilla extract

1/4 teaspoon ground nutmeg

2/3 cup rolled oats

1/4 teaspoon cinnamon

1/4 teaspoon salt

2 tablespoons reduced-fat margarine, melted

1 teaspoon water

1. Place 1 rack in the center of the oven and the other in the bottom third; preheat the oven to 425°F. Line a 9-inch pie pan with the pie dough, crimp the edges with your fingers, and refrigerate.

2. To make the filling, combine the blueberries, 2/3 cup sugar, 5 tablespoons flour, the lemon zest, 2 tablespoons lemon juice, the vanilla, and nutmeg in a large bowl.

3. To make the topping, combine the oats, the remaining 1/2 cup sugar, the remaining 1/4 cup flour, the cinnamon, and salt in another bowl. Add the margarine, the remaining 1 tablespoon lemon juice, and water; stir to combine. With your fingers, press the topping together to form clumps.

4. Spoon the berry filling into the pie crust. Break the topping into smaller pieces and cover the filling. Place a sheet of foil on the oven's bottom rack to catch any overflow. Place the pie on the rack above and bake 20 minutes. Cover the pie loosely with foil to prevent the topping from burning and bake until the filling is bubbling and the top golden brown, 45–55 minutes more. Let cool 20–30 minutes before serving. Serve warm or at room temperature.

*Per serving  246 Calories, 6 g Total Fat, 2 g Saturated Fat, 3 mg Cholesterol, 133 mg Sodium, 46 g Total Carbohydrate, 3 g Dietary Fiber, 2 g Protein, 9 mg Calcium.*

*POINTS per serving:* 5.

★ *American Way* To clean blueberries, rinse with water in a colander or strainer. Give the strainer several good shakes, then pour the blueberries onto a towel and pat dry.

*Maine Blueberry-Crumb Pie*

# Indian Pudding

MAKES 12 SERVINGS

*Corn and cornmeal, introduced to New England settlers by the natives, was so closely associated with Native Americans that the colonists called the new cereal* Indian *corn. In fact, they frequently used the term* Indian *to describe the numerous dishes that incorporated using the versatile grain, including this filling dessert.*

4 cups low-fat (2%) milk
3/4 cup yellow cornmeal
1/2 cup molasses
1/3 cup sugar
1 tablespoon unsalted butter
1 large egg, lightly beaten
1/2 teaspoon cinnamon
1/2 teaspoon ground ginger
1/2 teaspoon salt
1/4 teaspoon ground nutmeg

1. Place a large roasting pan in the oven and preheat the oven to 300°F. Spray a 2-quart square baking dish with nonstick spray.

2. Gently heat 3 cups of the milk in a medium saucepan until it begins to steam. Slowly stir in the cornmeal and cook, stirring constantly, until the mixture thickens, 4–5 minutes. Remove from the heat and stir in the molasses, sugar, butter, egg, cinnamon, ginger, salt, and nutmeg. Pour the mixture into the baking dish.

3. Place the baking dish inside the heated roasting pan. Fill the roasting pan with enough boiling water to come halfway up the sides of the baking dish. Bake 30 minutes. Carefully pour the remaining 1 cup milk on top of the pudding. Continue baking until the pudding is set and the top has formed a brown skin, about 1 hour 45 minutes. Cool slightly before serving.

*Per serving  144 Calories, 3 g Total Fat, 2 g Saturated Fat, 27 mg Cholesterol, 148 mg Sodium, 25 g Total Carbohydrate, 1 g Dietary Fiber, 4 g Protein, 130 mg Calcium.*

*POINTS per serving: 3.*

★ *American Way* Serve this hearty dessert warm with a dollop of nonfat yogurt, if you like.

# Portuguese Rolls

## MAKES 12 ROLLS

*In Portugal, vendors sell these delicious rolls in the morning; they are enjoyed on the way to work. The Portuguese settlers, who called this white bread* pão *(pronounced* poun*), brought this bread-making technique with them to New England. The simple crusty rolls are light and airy, with a slightly chewy texture.*

1¼ cups warm water (105–115°F)
1 (¼-ounce) packet active dry yeast
3½ cups all-purpose flour
1½ teaspoons salt
2 tablespoons cornmeal

1. Place the warm water in a small bowl, sprinkle in the yeast, and let stand until foamy, about 5 minutes. Combine the flour and salt in a large bowl. Stir the yeast mixture into the flour mixture until a dough forms and pulls away from the sides of the bowl. Turn out the dough on a lightly floured counter and knead, adding flour if the dough becomes sticky, until it becomes smooth and elastic, 7–9 minutes.

2. Spray a large bowl with nonstick spray; put the dough in the bowl. Cover tightly with plastic wrap and let the dough rise in a warm spot until it doubles in size, about 45 minutes.

3. Preheat the oven to 425°F. Sprinkle a baking sheet with the cornmeal.

4. Punch down the dough and turn out onto a lightly floured counter; knead 1 minute. Divide the dough in half, then divide each half in half. Divide each of the 4 pieces into thirds, forming 12 pieces in all. Place a piece of dough in a cupped palm and move your other hand in a circular motion, pressing the dough gently, to form a tight ball. Transfer the dough to the baking sheet. Repeat with the remaining dough. Cover the dough with a lightly oiled piece of plastic wrap and let rise until almost doubled in size, 15–25 minutes.

5. Uncover the dough and, with a serrated knife, make a 1½-inch–long, ½-inch–deep slash in the top of each roll. Bake until golden brown, 14–16 minutes. Cool the rolls on a rack before serving.

*Per serving (1 roll): 140 Calories, 0 g Total Fat, 0 g Saturated Fat, 0 mg Cholesterol, 292 mg Sodium, 29 g Total Carbohydrate, 1 g Dietary Fiber, 4 g Protein, 6 mg Calcium.*

*POINTS per serving: 3.*

# New England Cornbread

MAKES 12 SERVINGS

*Native Americans were making cornbread, also known as* pone, *long before the first settlers reached the Americas. The earliest breads were simply a mixture of cornmeal, water, and salt that was then baked. Cornbread recipes from around the country vary greatly, but Northern style cornbread tends to contain more flour and sugar than does Southern style cornbread.*

1½ cups yellow cornmeal

¾ cup all-purpose flour

2 tablespoons sugar

2 teaspoons baking powder

1½ teaspoons salt

1½ cups fat-free milk

2 eggs, lightly beaten

3 tablespoons unsalted butter, melted

1. Preheat the oven to 425°F. Spray a 9-inch cast-iron skillet or a 9-inch round cake pan with nonstick spray.

2. Combine the cornmeal, flour, sugar, baking powder, and salt in a medium bowl. Combine the milk, eggs, and butter in another bowl. Slowly stir the milk mixture into the cornmeal mixture until just combined. Pour the batter into the skillet and bake until the cornbread pulls away from the sides of the pan and the edges brown slightly, 20–25 minutes. Cool in the skillet 10 minutes before cutting into 12 wedges.

*Per serving  150 Calories, 4 g Total Fat, 2 g Saturated Fat, 44 mg Cholesterol, 384 mg Sodium, 23 g Total Carbohydrate, 1 g Dietary Fiber, 4 g Protein, 57 mg Calcium.*

*POINTS per serving: 3.*

*Boston Brown Bread (page 36), Portuguese Rolls (page 33), and New England Cornbread*

# Boston Brown Bread

MAKES 12 SERVINGS

*Brown bread, one of the early New Englanders' typically frugal dishes, uses inexpensive cornmeal mixed with just a touch of more expensive wheat flour. The flour provides gluten, the protein that traps air bubbles and helps the dough rise during steaming.*

1/2 cup rye flour

1/2 cup whole-wheat flour

1/2 cup cornmeal

1 teaspoon baking soda

1/2 teaspoon salt

1 cup fat-free buttermilk

1/3 cup molasses

1/2 cup packed raisins

1 tablespoon unsalted butter, at room temperature

1. Combine the rye flour, whole-wheat flour, cornmeal, baking soda, and salt in a large bowl. Stir in the buttermilk and molasses; mix until a thick batter forms. Stir in the raisins.

2. Grease a clean 1-pound coffee can or a pudding mold with the butter. Pour the batter into the can (the can should be about two-thirds full). Cover with foil and secure tightly with string. Place the can in a large pot and pour in enough boiling water to come about halfway up the side of the can. Cover the pot and bring to a boil. Steam 2 hours, adding water as necessary.

3. Remove the can from the pot, remove the foil from the can, and let cool 5 minutes. Invert the can over a rack and remove the bread. Slice and serve hot.

*Per serving   111 Calories, 1 g Total Fat, 1 g Saturated Fat, 3 mg Cholesterol, 217 mg Sodium, 23 g Total Carbohydrate, 2 g Dietary Fiber, 2 g Protein, 50 mg Calcium.*

*POINTS per serving: 2.*

FLASHBACK >> 1867

The city of Boston is the birthplace of canned red devil ham, a delicacy introduced to Bostonians by William Underwood & Co.

★

*chapter two*
# Mid-Atlantic

## APPETIZERS/SOUPS/SALADS

Roasted Red Pepper Crostini

Clams Casino

Buffalo Chicken Tenders

Chicken Matzo Ball Soup

Manhattan Clam Chowder

Jersey Tomato Salad with Fresh Herbs

Roasted Beet Salad with Goat Cheese

## ENTRÉES

Wild Mushroom Frittata

Maryland Crab Cakes

Rockfish Roulades

Shad and Spring Vegetable Pouches

Buttery Broiled Shad Roe

Brown-Butter Sea Scallops with Ginger Sweet Potatoes

Quick Seafood Stew

Perfect Herb Roasted Chicken and Potatoes

Pork and Apple Skillet Supper

Spaghetti and Meatballs

## SIDES

Stewed Tomatoes

Garden State Creamed Corn

Corn Pudding–Stuffed Tomatoes

## DESSERTS/BREADS/CONDIMENTS

White Peach Melba

Shoofly Pie

Whoopie Pies

New York Cheesecake

Chocolate Bar Ice Cream

New York Deli Rye

Amish Cinnamon Bread

Apple Butter

# Roasted Red Pepper Crostini

MAKES 16 SERVINGS

*The small state of Delaware is made up of only three counties, but it's big in produce, including bell peppers. These crostini (which means* little toasts *in Italian) highlight the intense, sweet flavor of roasted red peppers.*

2 red bell peppers
1 tablespoon olive oil
2 garlic cloves, thinly sliced
¹/₂ teaspoon paprika
¹/₄ teaspoon sugar
¹/₄ teaspoon salt
¹/₄ teaspoon freshly ground pepper
1 loaf Italian bread, cut into 32 slices, and toasted

1. Preheat the broiler. Broil the peppers 5 inches from the heat, turning often, until blackened on all sides. Place in a bowl, cover with plastic wrap, and cool completely. Remove the skin from the peppers. Remove the seeds, and cut the peppers into thin strips. Set aside.

2. Heat the oil in a nonstick skillet, then add the garlic. Sauté until fragrant, 30 seconds. Stir in the peppers, paprika, sugar, salt, and ground pepper; reduce the heat and simmer, covered, until the peppers are tender, about 10 minutes. Cool to room temperature.

3. Top the toast rounds with the pepper mixture. Serve immediately.

*Per serving (2 crostini): 89 Calories, 2 g Total Fat, 0 g Saturated Fat, 00 mg Cholesterol, 202 mg Sodium, 15 g Total Carbohydrate, 1 g Dietary Fiber, 3 g Protein, 24 mg Calcium.*

*POINTS per serving: 2.*

★ *American Way* Since the bread is toasted, this recipe is a great way to make use of day-old bread.

# Clams Casino

MAKES 4 SERVINGS

*Clams Casino—baked clams on the half shell with bacon, shallots, and seasonings—was created for a luncheon held by the socialite, Mrs. Paran Stevens, at the Casino restaurant on Narragansett Pier in New York City. It quickly became a popular appetizer at seafood restaurants all along the Jersey shore.*

3 tablespoons minced shallots

2 tablespoons minced green chile peppers, such as Anaheim or Poblano (wear gloves to prevent irritation)

1 tablespoon chopped fresh parsley

1 1/2 teaspoons unsalted butter, softened

1/8 teaspoon paprika

16 littleneck clams, on the half shell

1 slice turkey bacon, minced

Lemon wedges

1. Preheat the oven to 450°F.

2. Combine the shallots, chiles, parsley, butter, and paprika in a small bowl. Spoon about 1/4 teaspoon of the shallot mixture on top of each clam. Top each with a sprinkling of the bacon. Arrange the clams on a baking sheet.

3. Bake until the filling is hot and the bacon is golden and crisp, 6–8 minutes. Serve with lemon wedges.

*Per serving (4 clams): 66 Calories, 3 g Total Fat, 1 g Saturated Fat, 24 mg Cholesterol, 93 mg Sodium, 3 g Total Carbohydrate, 0 g Dietary Fiber, 7 g Protein, 28 mg Calcium.*

*POINTS per serving: 2.*

★ *American Way*  To open clams, use a towel to protect your hand and hold the clam with the hinge facing you. Slide a strong knife between the two shells, moving it around to separate them; lift up on the knife to pry open the shells.

FLASHBACK >> 1970

Knife acrobatics abound and Americans get a taste of "Japanese" cuisine when the first Benihana restaurant opens in New York City.

# Buffalo Chicken Tenders

MAKES 6 SERVINGS

*Buffalo wings were first created at the Anchor Bar in Buffalo, New York in the early 1960s. To make use of a surplus of chicken wings, the restaurant's chef fried the wings and tossed them with margarine and hot sauce. Our leaner version uses broiled chicken tenders.*

3/4 pound skinless boneless chicken breasts, cut into 1/2-inch–thick strips
1 tablespoon unsalted butter, melted
1 tablespoon hot pepper sauce
1/4 cup reduced-fat blue cheese dressing
2 tablespoons low-fat (1%) milk

1. Spray a broiler rack with nonstick spray. Preheat the broiler.

2. Toss the chicken with the butter and pepper sauce in a medium bowl. Arrange the chicken on a rack and place in a broiler pan. Drizzle any remaining butter mixture over the chicken. Broil, 5 inches from the heat, turning once, until browned on all sides, about 8 minutes.

3. Whisk the blue cheese dressing together with the milk in a small bowl. Serve the dressing with the chicken.

*Per serving (including 1 tablespoon sauce): 101 Calories, 4 g Total Fat, 2 g Saturated Fat, 42 mg Cholesterol, 198 mg Sodium, 1 g Total Carbohydrate, 0 g Dietary Fiber, 14 g Protein, 23 mg Calcium.*

*POINTS per serving: 2.*

★ *American Way* To give this appetizer an even healthier edge, serve the tenders alongside carrot and celery sticks.

# Chicken Matzo Ball Soup

## MAKES 8 SERVINGS

*This comforting soup can be found year round in Jewish delicatessens throughout New York City. Matzo meal—the base for the tasty matzo balls—is the result of grinding matzo, the unleavened crackers traditionally eaten during Passover. Matzo meal is frequently used as a breading and as a thickener for soups. Here, the matzo meal is rolled into matzo balls. The matzo balls are cooked and then added to the soup to prevent clouding the broth.*

### SOUP
3¹/2 quarts water
1 (3¹/2-pound) chicken, rinsed
4 carrots, peeled and chopped
4 celery stalks, chopped
3 onions, chopped
3 turnips, peeled and quartered
2 parsnips, peeled and chopped
¹/2 cup chopped fresh parsley
¹/2 teaspoon salt
¹/2 teaspoon freshly ground pepper

### MATZO BALLS
2 large eggs
2 egg whites
2 tablespoons canola oil
³/4 teaspoon salt
³/4 cup matzo meal
1–2 tablespoons seltzer

1. To make the soup, combine the water, chicken, carrots, celery, onions, turnips, parsnips, parsley, salt, and pepper in a large pot and bring to a boil. Simmer, partially covered, skimming off the foam occasionally, until the chicken is fork-tender, about 2 hours.

2. Meanwhile, to make the matzo balls, bring 4 quarts of water to a boil. Beat the eggs, egg whites, oil, and salt together in a bowl until frothy. Add the matzo meal and 1 tablespoon of the seltzer, adding up to a tablespoon more if the mixture is dry; stir until blended. Shape the matzo mixture into 8 balls; add the matzo balls to the boiling water. Simmer 35–40 minutes; drain. Add the matzo balls to the soup just before serving.

3. Transfer the chicken to a cutting board; cool slightly. Continue simmering the soup. Meanwhile, remove the meat from the bone and cut into bite-size pieces. Discard the bones. When the soup is reduced to about 6 cups, return the meat to the soup and keep warm.

*Per serving (about 1¹/4 cups + 1 matzo ball): 291 Calories, 10 g Total Fat, 2 g Saturated Fat, 112 mg Cholesterol, 550 mg Sodium, 24 g Total Carbohydrate, 5 g Dietary Fiber, 26 g Protein, 74 mg Calcium.*

*POINTS per serving: 6.*

## Melting-Pot Cuisine

Just after the Civil War, pioneering European immigrants in search of work made their way to the big cities of the Mid-Atlantic States, which had sprung up at the beginning of the Industrial Revolution. Workers from England, Ireland, Germany, Holland, and Scandinavia flocked to neighborhoods in New York City, Philadelphia, Wilmington, and Baltimore where earlier settlers from the workers' homelands had already established themselves. Since earlier immigrants already grew the necessary ingredients or had them imported, they continued to prepare the familiar, hearty fare of their homelands. Before long, these ethnic cuisines became the basis for the American menu, inspiring countless ways to prepare potatoes, cabbage dishes, pork specialties, a variety of sausages and beers, traditional breads, and even waffles.

After the turn of the century, southern and eastern Europeans, including Italians, Poles, and Russians, joined the earlier immigrants, bringing herbs, spices, garlic, tomato sauces, stews, and wines to the newly ethnic national diet. Since that time, pizza has become a true American standard, bagels and lox have taken a place at numerous breakfast tables, and frozen pirogi comprise a speedy dinner in many households.

This rich, and decidedly American, tradition of eagerly and effortlessly combining the flavors and foods of our pioneers continues to this day. Witness the modern-day trends of melding Asian, Middle Eastern, and Latin American cuisines in our everyday food repertoires.

# Manhattan Clam Chowder

MAKES 6 SERVINGS

*Chock-full of tomatoes and other vegetables, the rich red color easily distinguishes Manhattan clam chowder from its white, cream-based New England cousin. Although both varieties have their devotees, this tasty—and easy— recipe will likely win praise from both camps.*

1 1/2 teaspoons olive oil

2 slices turkey bacon, diced

2 celery stalks, sliced

1 onion, chopped

1 (28-ounce) can crushed tomatoes

2 1/2 cups water

2 large baking potatoes, scrubbed and cut into chunks

1/2 teaspoon dried thyme

1/2 teaspoon salt

1/4 teaspoon freshly ground pepper

1 bay leaf

1/2 pound green beans, cut into 1/2-inch pieces

24 hard-shell clams, shucked

1/4 cup chopped fresh parsley

1. Heat the oil in a large nonstick saucepan. Add the bacon and cook until browned; stir in the celery and onion and cook until the vegetables are tender, about 6 minutes.

2. Stir in the tomatoes, water, potatoes, thyme, salt, pepper, and bay leaf; bring to a boil. Simmer, uncovered, until the potatoes are tender, about 20 minutes. Add the beans and clams; cook until the beans are tender and the clams are cooked through, about 6 minutes. Stir in the parsley. Discard the bay leaf before serving.

*Per serving* (about 1 1/2 cups): 180 Calories, 3 g Total Fat, 0 g Saturated Fat, 26 mg Cholesterol, 728 mg Sodium, 27 g Total Carbohydrate, 5 g Dietary Fiber, 13 g Protein, 96 mg Calcium.

*POINTS per serving: 3.*

★ *American Way* Hard shell clams, also known as quahogs, come in three sizes. Select Cherrystone or chowder clams for this recipe. When fresh clams aren't available or you're short on time, use three 6 1/2-ounce cans of minced clams—but add them at the last minute so they stay tender.

# Jersey Tomato Salad with Fresh Herbs

MAKES 8 SERVINGS

*The Garden State—where the climate and duration of the season is ideal for growing tomatoes—ranks fourth in the U.S. for tomato production. There are approximately 25 varieties of tomatoes, including those used in this recipe, grown commercially in the state.*

2 medium tomatoes, cut into wedges

2 cups yellow pear tomatoes, halved

1 cup cherry tomatoes, halved

1 cup red currant tomatoes, left whole

2 1/2 tablespoons extra-virgin olive oil

1 teaspoon balsamic vinegar

1/4 teaspoon salt

2 bunches (about 1/4 pound each) arugula, cleaned and coarsely chopped

1 teaspoon fresh lemon juice

1 tablespoon chopped fresh mint

1 tablespoon chopped fresh chives

1/4 teaspoon freshly ground pepper

1. Combine all the tomatoes, 1 1/2 tablespoons of the olive oil, the vinegar, and 1/8 teaspoon salt in a large bowl. Let stand at room temperature for 1 hour.

2. Toss the arugula with the remaining 1 tablespoon olive oil, lemon juice, and the remaining 1/8 teaspoon salt in a medium bowl. Arrange the arugula in a ring on a large platter. Spoon the tomato mixture in the center. Sprinkle the tomatoes with the mint, chives, and pepper. Serve immediately.

*Per serving  71 Calories, 5 g Total Fat, 1 g Saturated Fat, 0 mg Cholesterol, 91 mg Sodium, 7 g Total Carbohydrate, 2 g Dietary Fiber, 2 g Protein, 53 mg Calcium.*

*POINTS per serving: 1.*

★ *American Way* Select vine-ripened tomatoes when possible. Tomatoes should be blemish-free and fragrant. Store them at room temperature—the cold temperature destroys the wonderful flavor.

FLASHBACK >> 1840

Scottish-American brewer Peter Ballantine produces ale at his brewery on the Passaic River in New Jersey. By 1914, he will be manufacturing approximately half a million barrels of beer and ale per year.

# Roasted Beet Salad with Goat Cheese

## MAKES 4 SERVINGS

*Goat cheese, also known as* chevre, *is pure white and tart in flavor—textures range from creamy to slightly dry and firm. Over the years, it has grown increasingly popular; in fact, the goat cheese produced in New York State is now distributed nationally in many supermarkets. Its flavor is the perfect partner to the sugary sweet flavor of beets.*

8 beets, trimmed and scrubbed

1 tablespoon olive oil

1 tablespoon orange juice

1 1/2 teaspoons balsamic vinegar

1/4 teaspoon salt

1/4 teaspoon freshly ground pepper

8 cups mixed salad greens

1/4 pound goat cheese, crumbled

2 tablespoons minced fresh chives

1 tablespoon sliced almonds, toasted (optional)

1 orange, peeled and cut into segments

1. Preheat the oven to 400°F. Wrap the beets in a large piece of foil and bake until they are tender, about 1 1/2 hours. Remove the foil and let the beets cool. Hold the beets under cold running water so the skins will slip off (you may have to rub gently). Cut the beets into wedges. Combine the beets with the olive oil, orange juice, vinegar, salt, and pepper in a bowl.

2. Arrange the greens on each of 4 salad plates; top with the beets. Sprinkle with the cheese, chives, and the almonds, if using. Serve with orange segments.

*Per serving  257 Calories, 11 g Total Fat, 5 g Saturated Fat, 13 mg Cholesterol, 468 mg Sodium, 32 g Total Carbohydrate, 10 g Dietary Fiber, 12 g Protein, 159 mg Calcium.*

*POINTS per serving: 4.*

# Wild Mushroom Frittata

### MAKES 4 SERVINGS

*In 1896, the commercial cultivation of mushrooms began outside Philadelphia in the Brandywine Valley, where the cool climate and rich soil is ideal for growing a variety of fungi. More recently, farmers have begun cultivating the more exotic wild varieties, such as portobello and shiitake. Use any assortment of mushrooms to add wonderful flavor to the frittata, a fast and tasty dinner when served with a mixed green salad.*

2 large eggs

6 egg whites

2 tablespoons water

1/4 teaspoon salt

1/4 teaspoon freshly ground pepper

1 tablespoon olive oil

3/4 pound assorted mushrooms (such as cremini, portobello, and shiitake), coarsely chopped

1 shallot, thinly sliced

1/2 teaspoon dried oregano

1/4 cup shredded light mozzarella cheese

1 tablespoon grated Parmesan cheese

1 tablespoon chopped fresh basil

1. Beat the eggs, egg whites, water, salt, and pepper together in a bowl until frothy.

2. Heat the oil in a medium nonstick skillet with an ovenproof handle. Add the mushrooms, shallot, and oregano and sauté until the mushrooms are golden, about 5 minutes. Add the egg mixture to the mushrooms, stirring gently to combine. Reduce the heat and cook, without stirring, until the eggs are set, 12–15 minutes. Sprinkle with the mozzarella. Preheat the broiler.

3. Broil the frittata 5 inches from the heat, until the top is lightly browned, about 2 minutes. Allow to stand 5 minutes before serving. Sprinkle with the Parmesan and basil and cut into 4 wedges.

*Per serving  156 Calories, 7 g Total Fat, 2 g Saturated Fat, 110 mg Cholesterol, 334 mg Sodium, 9 g Total Carbohydrate, 2 g Dietary Fiber, 14 g Protein, 103 mg Calcium.*

*POINTS per serving: 3.*

*Wild Mushroom Frittata*

# Maryland Crab Cakes

MAKES 6 SERVINGS

*Crab cakes and Maryland have a long history together. Lord Baltimore, founding father of the state of Maryland, is said to have dined on them on the 1630s, though the term* crab cake *was not seen in print until 300 years later.*

1 pound jumbo lump crabmeat, picked over

3 tablespoons light mayonnaise

4 teaspoons Dijon mustard

2 tablespoons minced fresh chives

1/2 teaspoon freshly ground pepper

1/8 teaspoon salt

1/3 cup plain dried bread crumbs

1 tablespoon canola oil

Lemon wedges

1. Gently combine the crabmeat, mayonnaise, mustard, chives, pepper, and salt in a medium bowl. Shape the mixture into 6 cakes. Place the bread crumbs on wax paper. Dredge each patty in the crumbs, evenly coating both sides; shake off any excess.

2. Heat the oil in a large nonstick skillet. Add the crab cakes in batches. Cook, turning once, until browned and heated through, about 5 minutes on each side. Serve with the lemon wedges.

*Per serving  225 Calories, 10 g Total Fat, 1 g Saturated Fat, 117 mg Cholesterol, 580 mg Sodium, 8 g Total Carbohydrate, 0 g Dietary Fiber, 24 g Protein, 146 mg Calcium.*

*POINTS per serving: 5.*

★ *American Way*  Although it's less costly, don't be tempted to use surimi, or imitation crab, in this dish—they just won't be the same.

# Rockfish Roulades

MAKES 4 SERVINGS

*In Maryland, striped bass is known as rockfish. According to fishermen's lore, the fish were once so abundant that they jumped into fishing boats on the waters of Rock Hall, Maryland. This recipe combines the sweet-fleshed bass with another of the Old Line State's beloved foods—crabs—to create an elegant, party-ready entrée.*

1/2 pound lump crab meat, picked over

2 tablespoons chopped fresh parsley

1/4 teaspoon freshly ground pepper

4 (6-ounce) striped bass or red snapper fillets

1 cup low-sodium chicken broth

4 teaspoons unsalted butter

Lemon wedges

1. Preheat the oven to 400°F. Combine the crab meat, $1^1/2$ tablespoons parsley, and the pepper in a small bowl.

2. Place the fish fillets, skin-side up, on a work surface. Spoon one-fourth of the crab mixture in the center of each fillet and spread evenly. Roll the fillets around the crab starting from the narrow end. Place the rolls, seam side down, in a shallow baking dish, and pour in the broth. Dot each fillet with butter and sprinkle with the remaining $1/2$ tablespoon parsley. Bake until the fish is opaque and filling is hot, 8–10 minutes. Serve with the lemon wedges.

*Per serving  257 Calories, 9 g Total Fat, 4 g Saturated Fat, 200 mg Cholesterol, 289 mg Sodium, 0 g Total Carbohydrate, 0 g Dietary Fiber, 41 g Protein, 89 mg Calcium.*

*POINTS per serving: 6.*

# Shad and Spring Vegetable Pouches

MAKES 4 SERVINGS

*Shad, the largest member of the herring family, begin their journey up the Delaware, Hudson, and Connecticut Rivers in the spring. The fillets are best prepared with little fuss to preserve their delicate flavor. Cooking in foil pouches, as we've done here, helps to further retain moisture without adding any fat.*

1 pound asparagus, cut into ³/4-inch pieces

1¹/3 cups sugar-snap peas

4 (¹/4-pound) shad fillets

2 teaspoons fresh thyme, or ¹/2 teaspoon dried

¹/2 teaspoon salt

¹/2 teaspoon freshly ground pepper

4 scallions, thinly sliced

4 teaspoons unsalted butter

¹/4 cup dry white wine or vermouth

2 radishes, cut into matchstick-thin strips

1. Preheat the oven to 400°F.

2. Cook the asparagus and peas in a large pot of boiling water until tender-crisp, 1–2 minutes. Drain and rinse with cold water until cool. Pat dry with paper towels.

3. Place four 12-inch squares of heavy-duty foil on a work surface. Place a shad fillet in the center of each square. Season with the thyme, salt, and pepper. Top with the asparagus and peas. Sprinkle with the scallions, then dot with the butter. Make pouches by bringing the sides of the foil up to meet in the center; carefully pour 1 tablespoon wine in each pouch. Fold the edges together, then secure and crimp the edges, allowing room for the pouches to expand.

4. Place the pouches on a cookie sheet and bake until the fish is opaque in the center, about 12 minutes; open the pouches carefully when testing for doneness, as steam will escape. Sprinkle with the radishes. Serve drizzled with any juices that collect in the pouches.

*Per serving  320 Calories, 20 g Total Fat, 6 g Saturated Fat, 96 mg Cholesterol, 453 mg Sodium, 11 g Total Carbohydrate, 4 g Dietary Fiber, 24 g Protein, 121 mg Calcium.*

*POINTS per serving: 7.*

★ *American Way*  Any firm-fleshed fish, such as red snapper, sole, or flounder may be prepared in pouches. Serve this dish with steamed new potatoes and a mixed green salad. If you don't have heavy-duty foil on hand, use a double-thickness of regular foil.

# Buttery Broiled Shad Roe

## MAKES 6 SERVINGS

*Female shad are considered more desirable than male for both the superior quality of their flesh and their eggs, known as shad roe, which they produce before spawning. Shad roe is a spring delicacy that is simple to prepare— and simply delicious. As with most fish, freshness is key to the best-tasting dish, so have your fishmonger take the roe directly from the shad, if possible.*

6 (3-ounce) shad roe
2 tablespoons unsalted butter, melted
1/4 teaspoon salt
1/4 teaspoon freshly ground pepper
Lemon wedges

Spray the broiler rack with nonstick spray. Preheat the broiler. Brush both sides of the shad roe with the butter. Sprinkle with salt and pepper. Broil until golden brown, about 2 minutes each side. Serve with the lemon wedges.

*Per serving  190 Calories, 10 g Total Fat, 4 g Saturated Fat, 373 mg Cholesterol, 227 mg Sodium, 1 g Total Carbohydrate, 0 g Dietary Fiber, 22 g Protein, 22 mg Calcium.*

*POINTS per serving: 5.*

# Brown-Butter Sea Scallops with Ginger Sweet Potatoes

## MAKES 4 SERVINGS

*On the East Coast, peak season for fresh sea scallops is mid-fall to mid-spring. Almost any farm-fresh produce, such as asparagus or sweet peas, goes well with these larger scallops, which average 1 1/2 inches in diameter. Paired with the subtle flavor of sweet potatoes, the delicate taste of the scallops really shines.*

4 medium sweet potatoes

1/2 cup fat-free milk

1 (1-inch) piece fresh ginger, peeled and grated

1/2 teaspoon salt

1/4 teaspoon freshly ground pepper

1 tablespoon unsalted butter

3/4 pound large sea scallops, sliced into 1/4-inch–thick rounds

2 scallions, thinly sliced

1. Preheat the oven to 400°F. Pierce the potatoes in several places. Bake until tender, about 45 minutes. Halve the potatoes lengthwise, and scoop the pulp into a medium bowl. Stir in the milk, ginger, salt, and pepper. Beat with an electric mixer at low speed until blended and smooth; keep warm.

2. Heat the butter in a large nonstick skillet over medium-high heat. Cook until the butter just begins to brown slightly. Add the scallops; cook, turning once, until browned on the outside, and just opaque in the center, about 1 minute on each side. Sprinkle with the scallions and serve with the potatoes.

*Per serving  233 Calories, 4 g Total Fat, 2 g Saturated Fat, 37 mg Cholesterol, 487 mg Sodium, 32 g Total Carbohydrate, 4 g Dietary Fiber, 17 g Protein, 97 mg Calcium.*

*POINTS per serving: 4.*

*Brown-Butter Sea Scallops with Ginger Sweet Potatoes*

## TIDEWATER TREASURES

According to early records, fresh fish and shellfish have always been plentiful for fishermen on all of America's coastlines—and the economic possibilities of the sea's bounty were not overlooked by early settlers. In fact, smoked cod quickly became one of America's first exports to Europe. On the East alone, tidal estuaries supplied cod, mackerel, haddock, sea bass, herring, even sturgeon; fresh salmon spawned in northern rivers, the annual shad run arrived in the spring, and shellfish like lobsters, crabs, clams, mussels, and oysters were large and plentiful.

With such an abundance of seafood, it's not surprising that coastal city oyster houses, which began in the basements of waterfront buildings as rowdy establishments that served alcohol and a variety of oysters and sometimes other seafood to men, grew into some of the country's earliest independent restaurants. The productive tidewater areas along the Pacific coast provided Pacific salmon, Dungeness crab, razor and geoduck clams, cod, rockfish, sablefish, and smelt. However, local residents were the only ones able to enjoy the fresh catch of the day because such foods could not be safely transported far from the waters in which they were harvested.

Thanks to countless advancements in transportation, packaging, and preserving, today seafood is regularly shipped around the world. Yet, the regional fish and shellfish of tidewater America remain an integral part of an area's economy, identity, and cuisine. Just as lobster represents the cuisine of New England, blue crab is tied to the Mid-Atlantic States, shrimp with the Gulf Coast, and Pacific salmon and Dungeness crab with the Pacific Northwest.

# Quick Seafood Stew

MAKES 4 SERVINGS

*Zuppa di pesce—found on restaurant menus throughout New York City's Little Italy—gives the fresh catch available along the Eastern seaboard a starring role. This variation can be served with nothing more than a salad of fresh greens and a loaf of Italian bread.*

1/2 pound spaghetti

1 tablespoon olive oil

1 (1/2-pound) sturgeon or sea bass fillet

1/2 pound large shrimp, peeled, deveined, and halved lengthwise

1 dozen mussels, scrubbed and debearded

1 dozen littleneck clams, scrubbed

2 large garlic cloves, chopped

1 cup water

1/2 cup bottled clam juice

1/4 cup dry white wine

2 plum tomatoes, chopped

1/4 cup chopped fresh parsley

1/4 teaspoon freshly ground pepper

1. Cook the spaghetti according to package instructions. Drain, set aside, and keep warm.

2. Heat the oil in a large nonstick skillet. Then, add the sturgeon and cook until browned, about 2 minutes on each side. Transfer to a plate. Add the shrimp to the skillet; cook, stirring occasionally, until the shrimp just turn pink, about 2 minutes. Transfer the shrimp to the plate with the sturgeon and keep warm.

3. Add the mussels, clams, and garlic to the same skillet. Cook, stirring and shaking the pan occasionally, until the garlic just begins to turn golden, about 2 minutes. Add the water, clam juice, wine, tomatoes, parsley, and pepper; bring to a boil. Cover and cook until the clams and mussels have opened, 6–7 minutes. Discard any clams or mussels that do not open. Stir in the sturgeon and shrimp; heat through.

4. Serve the seafood stew over the spaghetti.

*Per serving  422 Calories, 9 g Total Fat, 1 g Saturated Fat, 126 mg Cholesterol, 300 mg Sodium, 48 g Total Carbohydrate, 2 g Dietary Fiber, 35 g Protein, 81 mg Calcium.*

*POINTS per serving: 9.*

# Perfect Herb Roasted Chicken and Potatoes

MAKES 4 SERVINGS

*The poultry industry is a booming business in the region known as Delmarva, a 200-mile–long peninsula bordered by the Delaware and Chesapeake Bays; the area gets its name from the three states that comprise it, Delaware, Maryland, and Virginia. There are countless ways to cook chicken, but a classic roasting preparation is a surefire crowd-pleaser.*

1 (3$^1$/2-pound) chicken, rinsed and patted dry

1 lemon, halved

1 onion, quartered

8 garlic cloves, coarsely chopped

$^3$/4 teaspoon chopped fresh thyme

$^3$/4 teaspoon salt

$^1$/2 teaspoon freshly ground pepper

2 medium baking potatoes, cut into eighths

2 teaspoons olive oil

1 tablespoon chopped fresh rosemary or $^1$/2 teaspoon dried, crumbled

1. Preheat the oven to 400°F. Spray a roasting rack with nonstick spray and place it in a roasting pan. Rub the inside and outside of the chicken with the lemon halves. Stuff the cavity with the lemon halves, onion, and $^1$/4 of the garlic. In a small bowl, combine the thyme with $^1$/4 teaspoon salt, and $^1$/4 teaspoon pepper. Place the chicken, breast-side up, on the rack. Gently loosen the skin from the breast. Rub the thyme mixture under the skin and onto the breast.

2. Reduce the oven temperature to 350°F. Roast the chicken until an instant-read thermometer inserted in the thigh, not touching any bone, registers 180°F, about 1 hour 20 minutes. Transfer the chicken to a cutting board and let stand 10 minutes before carving and removing the skin. Discard the lemon halves, onion, and garlic from the cavity.

3. Meanwhile, spray a small baking pan with nonstick cooking spray. Combine the potatoes, olive oil, rosemary, and the remaining garlic in a medium bowl. Add the remaining $^1$/2 teaspoon salt and $^1$/4 teaspoon pepper; toss to coat. Arrange the potatoes in one layer in the pan. After the chicken has been roasting 40 minutes, put the potatoes in the oven and roast until tender, 40—50 minutes. Serve the chicken with the potatoes.

*Per serving 390 Calories, 12 g Total Fat, 3 g Saturated Fat, 118 mg Cholesterol, 559 mg Sodium, 27 g Total Carbohydrate, 2 g Dietary Fiber, 41 g Protein, 41 mg Calcium.*

*POINTS per serving: 8.*

★ *American Way* Rubbing the chicken skin with lemon juice boosts the flavor of the chicken.

# Pork and Apple Skillet Supper

## MAKES 4 SERVINGS

*The German-speaking settlers known as the Pennsylvania Dutch received their name because their native language, "Deutsche," sounded like "Dutch" to the English-speaking people of the colonies. Widely known for their home cooking, this robust German-style skillet supper is a perfect wintertime meal and can be made in less than 30 minutes.*

$1/2$ pound boneless pork loin, cut into $1/2$-inch cubes

1 tablespoon all-purpose flour

$1/4$ teaspoon salt

$1/4$ teaspoon freshly ground pepper

1 tablespoon unsalted butter

2 onions, cut into $1/2$-inch–thick wedges

$1/2$ cup water

1 Golden Delicious apple, peeled, cored, and chopped

1 (8-ounce) package extra-wide yolk-free noodles

1 (13$3/4$-ounce) can vegetable or chicken broth

$1/3$ cup chopped fresh parsley

1. Place the pork, flour, salt, and pepper in a large zip-close plastic bag; seal and shake to coat. Heat half the butter in a large nonstick skillet. Add the pork and sauté until browned all over, about 5 minutes; transfer to a plate.

2. Add the remaining butter to the skillet. Add the onions and sauté until softened, about 5 minutes. Stir in the water and bring to a boil. Reduce the heat, cover, and simmer until the onions are very tender and the liquid has reduced, about 8 minutes. Stir in the apple. Cook, stirring occasionally, until the apple is tender, about 5 minutes more.

3. Meanwhile, prepare the noodles according to package directions.

4. Return the pork to the skillet. Stir in the noodles, broth, and parsley. Simmer gently until the liquid is reduced slightly and the pork and noodles are heated through.

*Per serving  381 Calories, 8 g Total Fat, 3 g Saturated Fat, 42 mg Cholesterol, 627 mg Sodium, 56 g Total Carbohydrate, 3 g Dietary Fiber, 22 g Protein, 31 mg Calcium.*

*POINTS per serving: 8.*

# Spaghetti and Meatballs

MAKES 8 SERVINGS

*From 1892 to 1943, New York's Ellis Island was the main immigration station of the United States where count-less Italians and other immigrants in search of prosperity and a new life were ushered through its halls. Among the traditional recipes that Italians who settled in New York brought with them was this classic, which has since become an American family favorite.*

**TOMATO SAUCE**

1 tablespoon olive oil

1 onion, chopped

1 garlic clove, minced

1 (28-ounce) can crushed tomatoes

1/4 teaspoon salt

1/4 teaspoon freshly ground pepper

**MEATBALLS**

1 tablespoon olive oil

1/2 pound white mushrooms, finely
    chopped

1 onion, chopped

3/4 pound ground skinless turkey

2 tablespoons plain dried bread crumbs

2 tablespoons grated Parmesan cheese

2 tablespoons chopped fresh parsley

1 garlic clove, minced

1/4 teaspoon salt

1/4 teaspoon freshly ground pepper

1 pound spaghetti

1. To make the sauce, heat the oil in a nonstick skillet, then add the onion and garlic. Sauté until the onion is translucent, 3–5 minutes. Stir in the tomatoes, salt, and pepper; cook, stirring occasionally, until the sauce is slightly thickened, about 20 minutes. Remove from the heat, cover, and let stand 15 minutes.

2. Meanwhile, to make the meatballs, preheat the oven to 350°F. Spray a baking sheet with nonstick spray. Heat the oil in a large non-stick skillet, then add the mushrooms and onion. Sauté until the onion is lightly browned, about 6 minutes. Transfer to a large bowl and cool slightly. Add the turkey, bread crumbs, cheese, parsley, gar-lic, salt, and pepper. Form into 16 meatballs and place on baking sheet. Bake until browned, 15–20 minutes. Add the meatballs to the sauce; cook, stirring occasionally, until heated through, about 10 minutes.

3. Cook the spaghetti according to package directions; drain and place in a serving bowl. Top with the sauce and meatballs and toss gently.

*Per serving  345 Calories, 6 g Total Fat, 1 g Saturated Fat, 23 mg Cholesterol, 522 mg Sodium, 53 g Total Carbohydrate, 4 g Dietary Fiber, 20 g Protein, 68 mg Calcium.*

*POINTS per serving: 7.*

★ *American Way*  If you prefer a heftier pasta, try fettuccine instead of spaghetti. A hearty Italian bread (for sopping up any remaining sauce) is a welcome accompaniment.

# Stewed Tomatoes

MAKES 6 SERVINGS

*Stewed tomatoes—a Maryland favorite for decades—is a great way to use tomatoes that are a little less ripe, since the slow stewing intensifies flavor. With their sweet, complex taste, these tomatoes go best with simple entrées, like broiled steak or roasted chicken. If making ahead, cool, then cover and refrigerate the tomatoes until ready to use. Serve at room temperature or gently reheat and serve warm.*

2 pounds plum tomatoes, cored and peeled
1 tablespoon sugar
1 1/2 teaspoons unsalted butter
1/2 teaspoon freshly ground pepper
1/8 teaspoon salt
1/8 teaspoon ground nutmeg

Combine the tomatoes, sugar, butter, pepper, salt, and nutmeg in a nonreactive saucepan; bring to a boil. Cover and simmer, stirring occasionally to break up the tomatoes, until tomatoes are tender, and the flavors are well blended, about 2 hours.

*Per serving* (3/4 cup): *49 Calories, 2 g Total Fat, 1 g Saturated Fat, 3 mg Cholesterol, 72 mg Sodium, 9 g Total Carbohydrate, 1 g Dietary Fiber, 1 g Protein, 9 mg Calcium.*

POINTS *per serving: 1.*

# Garden State Creamed Corn

MAKES 6 SERVINGS

*For thousands of years, corn has been grown in the New World. Native Americans revered it, deeming it "Sacred Mother," and the colonists served it at the Plymouth Thanksgiving in place of wheat and barley crops that had failed. If possible, use fresh corn immediately after it's picked, as the natural sugars gradually turn to starch, lessening the corn's natural sweetness.*

1 1/2 teaspoons unsalted butter

1 1/2 teaspoons all-purpose flour

2 cups fresh corn kernels (from about 4 ears), or thawed frozen

1 1/2 teaspoons cornstarch

1/2 teaspoon salt

1/4 teaspoon freshly ground pepper

1/8 teaspoon sugar

2/3 cup low-fat (1%) milk

Melt the butter in a saucepan. Stir in the flour and cook, stirring constantly, for 1 minute. Add the corn, cornstarch, salt, pepper, and sugar. Gradually stir in the milk and bring to a boil. Reduce the heat and simmer until the mixture thickens, about 3 minutes more. Cool slightly before serving.

*Per serving 85 Calories, 2 g Total Fat, 1 g Saturated Fat, 4 mg Cholesterol, 227 mg Sodium, 16 g Total Carbohydrate, 2 g Dietary Fiber, 3 g Protein, 35 mg Calcium.*

*POINTS per serving: 1.*

★ *American Way* If you are short on time, substitute frozen corn for the fresh.

# Corn Pudding–Stuffed Tomatoes

## MAKES 6 SERVINGS

*This colorful combination of two New Jersey crops that are at their peak in late summer—corn and tomatoes— makes an attractive presentation. Either fresh or frozen corn works well in this recipe.*

6 tomatoes

1½ teaspoons unsalted butter

1 tablespoon all-purpose flour

½ cup fat-free milk

¼ cup minced fresh chives

½ teaspoon salt

¼ teaspoon freshly ground pepper

1 large egg, lightly beaten

1½ cups fresh corn kernels (from about 3 ears), or thawed frozen

2 teaspoons plain dried bread crumbs

1. Preheat the oven to 400°F. Cut a thin slice from the stem end of each tomato; scoop out and discard the pulp. Arrange the tomatoes in a shallow baking dish.

2. Heat the butter in a small saucepan. Stir in the flour and cook 1 minute. Whisk in the milk, chives, salt, and pepper and bring to a boil. Cook, stirring constantly, until the mixture thickens slightly, about 5 minutes. Remove from the heat and let stand 5 minutes. Whisk in the egg, then fold in the corn. Spoon the mixture evenly into the tomato shells and sprinkle with the bread crumbs. Bake until golden and bubbling, 35–40 minutes. Serve immediately.

*Per serving  98 Calories, 3 g Total Fat, 1 g Saturated Fat, 39 mg Cholesterol, 246 mg Sodium, 17 g Total Carbohydrate, 2 g Dietary Fiber, 4 g Protein, 38 mg Calcium.*

*POINTS per serving: 2.*

# White Peach Melba

*At the turn of the century the legendary chef, Auguste Escoffier, created peach melba for the famed opera singer Nellie Melba. Although the dessert was created in London by a Frenchman, for an Australian, it quickly became an American classic, appearing on restaurant menus across the country. In the traditional recipe, the peaches are poached in a high-calorie sugar syrup. Our version uses sweet, ripe, white peaches, which eliminates the need for poaching, and the extra sugar.*

2¹/2 cups fresh raspberries

¹/4 cup black currant preserves

2 tablespoons sugar

1 tablespoon orange juice

1¹/2 teaspoons cornstarch

4 ripe white peaches, peeled and sliced

4 scoops (about ¹/3 cup each) low-fat vanilla frozen yogurt

1. With the back of a spoon, press 2 cups of the raspberries through a medium-mesh sieve into a saucepan; discard the seeds. Stir in the preserves, sugar, orange juice, and cornstarch. Cook over medium-low heat, stirring frequently, until the sauce boils and thickens. Allow to cool to room temperature. Cover and refrigerate until chilled, about 45 minutes.

2. Arrange a few peach slices on each of 4 dessert plates. Drizzle each with 2 tablespoons of the sauce. Top with a scoop of frozen yogurt, then the remaining peaches, sauce, and raspberries. Serve immediately.

*Per serving 237 Calories, 2 g Total Fat, 1 g Saturated Fat, 7 mg Cholesterol, 58 mg Sodium, 55 g Total Carbohydrate, 5 g Dietary Fiber, 4 g Protein, 126 mg Calcium.*

*POINTS per serving: 4.*

# Shoofly Pie

MAKES 8 SERVINGS

*A dessert of Pennsylvania Dutch origin, this gooey pie—also known as Molasses Cake—may have received its name because of its intense sweetness, which created the need to shoo the flies away from the pie as it cooled on an open windowsill. This version uses lower-fat graham crackers and margarine to keep the fat and calories down.*

8 reduced-fat graham cracker sheets

5 1/2 tablespoons reduced-calorie margarine

2/3 cup all-purpose flour

1/3 cup sugar

3/4 teaspoon cinnamon

1/4 teaspoon ground nutmeg

3/4 cup molasses

3/4 cup water

1/2 teaspoon baking soda

1. Preheat the oven to 350°F. Spray a 9-inch pie pan with nonstick spray. Crush the graham crackers in a food processor; pulse in 2 1/2 tablespoons of the margarine. Transfer the crumbs to the pie pan and press firmly over the bottom and up the sides. Bake until lightly browned, about 10 minutes. Transfer to rack to cool. Increase the oven temperature to 450°F.

2. To make the topping, combine the remaining 3 tablespoons margarine, the flour, sugar, cinnamon, and nutmeg in a bowl. Mix until the mixture is crumbly.

3. Stir together the molasses, water, and baking soda in a bowl. Pour the molasses mixture into the prepared crust and sprinkle on the topping. Bake for 15 minutes. Then, reduce the oven temperature to 375°F and bake the pie until the filling is set, about 40 minutes more. Allow to cool on a rack.

*Per serving 241 Calories, 5 g Total Fat, 1 g Saturated Fat, 0 mg Cholesterol, 188 mg Sodium, 49 g Total Carbohydrate, 1 g Dietary Fiber, 2 g Protein, 66 mg Calcium.*

*POINTS per serving: 5.*

# Whoopie Pies

MAKES 18 PIES

*These Pennsylvania Dutch treats are a cross between a cookie and a cupcake. They may have evolved from a baking practice of Amish women, who sometimes used leftover cake batter to make mini cakes, then sandwiched the layers together with a marshmallow-like filling.*

1 cup all-purpose flour

1/4 cup unsweetened cocoa powder

1 teaspoon baking soda

1/4 teaspoon salt

1/2 cup sugar

1/4 cup solid vegetable shortening

1 egg white

1/2 cup low-fat (1%) milk

3/4 cup marshmallow spread

1. Preheat the oven to 425°F. Combine the flour, cocoa, baking soda, and salt in a small bowl. With an electric mixer on medium speed, beat the sugar, shortening, and egg white in a medium bowl until fluffy and well blended, about 2 minutes. Stir in the flour mixture, then the milk until just blended.

2. Drop the dough by spoonfuls onto large, ungreased baking sheets, making 36 cookies. Bake until top springs back when lightly touched, 5–7 minutes. Cool completely on the sheets on a rack. Spoon 2 teaspoons marshmallow spread on the bottoms of half the cookies. Top with remaining cookies. Store in an airtight container for up to 3 days.

*Per serving 119 Calories, 3 g Total Fat, 1 g Saturated Fat, 0 mg Cholesterol, 109 mg Sodium, 21 g Total Carbohydrate, 1 g Dietary Fiber, 1 g Protein, 11 mg Calcium.*

*POINTS per serving: 2.*

*Whoopie Pies*

# Religious Kitchens

Political turmoil in 18th- and early 19th-century Europe, along with the promise of religious freedom in America, attracted a variety of utopian groups to America. Primarily farmers, these groups settled into communities where they were free to worship in their own way, follow their own rules—and produce quality farm products.

Perhaps one of the most famous of these groups were the Shakers, an ingenious community of settlers who were involved in all areas of agriculture—seed production; medicinal and cooking herbs; raising livestock; making honey, maple syrup, and dairy products; canning fruits, vegetables, jams, and jellies; and, in their early years, making and selling alcoholic beverages. The Shakers are credited with producing one of the country's first commercial pancake mixes. An ever-enterprising group, the Shakers added value to their wares by supplying free recipes with their products. They're also credited with the invention of oyster pie, corn oysters, a lemon pie made from thinly sliced whole lemons, and other unique recipes.

The Amish and Moravians are two groups of settlers who are also acclaimed for their cooking. An austere branch of Mennonites, the Amish are lauded for fine organic farm products they create without the use of modern conveniences. Their cuisine includes an array of simple and robust soups, stews, sausages, pies, breads, cookies, and preserves. Moravian cooks, from areas now within the Czech Republic, are distinguished to this day for their baking, and particularly the paper-thin ginger cookies which are produced in the restored Moravian community of New Salem, North Carolina, and often given as a special holiday gift.

# New York Cheesecake

MAKES 12 SERVINGS

*In the 1940s, Lindy's restaurant in Manhattan became known for its rich and creamy cheesecake, and it soon became a New York classic. This recipe, made with Neufchâtel cheese, falls short on fat—it has one-third less than the original—but reaches delicious heights in texture and flavor.*

1 tablespoon unsalted butter, softened

1½ reduced-fat graham cracker sheets, finely crushed (about 3 tablespoons)

¾ pound Neufchâtel cheese

9 tablespoons sugar

3 egg whites

1½ tablespoons cornstarch

1 teaspoon vanilla extract

1 cup light sour cream

1. Preheat the oven to 400°F. Grease the bottom of a 9-inch spring-form pan with the butter. Add the crumbs, shaking and tilting the pan to coat the bottom. Refrigerate until chilled, about 15 minutes.

2. With an electric mixer on medium speed, beat the cheese and the sugar in a large bowl until light and fluffy, about 3 minutes. Beat in the egg whites, cornstarch, and vanilla. Stir in the sour cream.

3. Pour the batter into the pan. Bake until the cheesecake is almost set in the center, 35–40 minutes. Turn off the oven, prop open the oven door with a wooden spoon, and let the cheesecake cool in the oven 30 minutes, then remove the cake from the oven and cool completely on a rack. Chill 2–3 hours before serving.

*Per serving 159 Calories, 9 g Total Fat, 6 g Saturated Fat, 31 mg Cholesterol, 155 mg Sodium, 14 g Total Carbohydrate, 0 g Dietary Fiber, 5 g Protein, 62 mg Calcium.*

*POINTS per serving: 4.*

★ *American Way* To make a fruity sauce to serve alongside each slice, simply warm ¼ cup of your favorite preserves (try raspberry or strawberry) in a saucepan. Garnish with fresh berries.

# Chocolate Bar Ice Cream

MAKES 1 QUART

*Today, ice cream is an American institution and available in nearly any flavor you can imagine. This recipe conjures up the taste of still another American classic, the Hershey Bar. Since 1894, Hershey Park and the Hotel Hershey have been landmarks in Pennsylvania, where the heavenly aroma of chocolate fills the air in the streets of Hershey.*

1½ tablespoons all-purpose flour
½ cup sugar
⅛ teaspoon salt
2⅓ cups low-fat (1%) milk
3 ounces dark chocolate, chopped
2 egg whites
1 large egg
2 teaspoons vanilla extract

1. Combine the flour, sugar, and salt in a medium saucepan; stir in the milk and chocolate. Cook over medium heat, stirring frequently, until the mixture thickens slightly and boils.

2. Beat the egg whites and egg lightly in a small bowl; whisk in a small amount of the hot milk mixture. Slowly pour the egg mixture back into milk mixture, stirring constantly to prevent lumping. Cook the mixture over low heat, stirring constantly, until it thickens, about 5 minutes. Do not allow the mixture to come to a boil or it will curdle. Remove the saucepan from the heat. At once, stir in the vanilla, and transfer to a bowl. Lay plastic wrap directly on the surface of the mixture and refrigerate, stirring occasionally, until completely chilled, about 3 hours.

3. Pour the mixture into an ice cream maker and freeze according to the manufacturer's instructions. Pack the ice cream into an airtight container and freeze for at least 4 hours and up to 3 days. Allow the ice cream to soften slightly before serving.

*Per serving* (½ cup): 157 Calories, 5 g Total Fat, 3 g Saturated Fat, 30 mg Cholesterol, 94 mg Sodium, 23 g Total Carbohydrate, 1 g Dietary Fiber, 5 g Protein, 95 mg Calcium.

*POINTS per serving: 3.*

FLASHBACK >> 1904

Italo Marchiony patents the ice cream cone with little notice from the public. The cone is introduced at the St. Louis World's Fair and is wildly successful; about 5,000 gallons of ice cream are sold a day.

# New York Deli Rye

MAKES 2 LOAVES, 12 SLICES EACH LOAF

*This bread, also known as Jewish rye, is a fixture at delicatessens in New York, where it is the bread of choice for mile-high sandwiches. Deli rye is traditionally made from a mixture of ground rye and wheat flour, and is sometimes sprinkled with caraway seeds. In this version a sour dough starter is prepared and left for two days. It's a little time intensive but worth the effort.*

## SOURDOUGH STARTER

2 cups warm (105–115°F) water

2 teaspoons sugar

1 (1/4-ounce) packet active dry yeast

3 cups bread flour

## DOUGH

1 1/3 cups warm (105–115°F) water

2 teaspoons sugar

1 (1/4-ounce) packet active dry yeast

About 3 1/2 cups bread flour

2 cups rye flour

3 tablespoons caraway seeds

2 tablespoons molasses

1 tablespoon salt

1. To make the starter, combine the water and sugar in a medium bowl. Sprinkle in the yeast and let stand until foamy, about 5 minutes. Stir in the flour. Cover with plastic wrap and let stand at room temperature for 2 days.

2. To make the dough, combine the warm water and sugar in a small bowl. Sprinkle in the yeast and let stand until foamy, about 5 minutes.

3. Combine the starter (made 2 days ahead), 3 cups of the bread flour, the rye flour, caraway seeds, molasses, and salt in a food processor. With the machine running, scrape the yeast mixture through the feed tube. After the dough forms a ball, continue processing 5 minutes to knead. Turn out the dough on a lightly floured counter; knead briefly, adding more flour if necessary to prevent sticking, until the dough is smooth, elastic, and slightly sticky, about 5 minutes.

4. Spray a large bowl with nonstick spray; put the dough in the bowl. Cover tightly with plastic wrap and let the dough rise in a warm spot until it doubles in size, about 1 1/2 hours. Punch the dough down; let rest, covered, 15 minutes.

5. Spray a large baking sheet with nonstick spray. Divide the dough in half; shape each half into an oval. Place on the baking sheet at least 4 inches apart. Cover with a towel and let rise in a warm spot until it doubles in size, about 45 minutes.

6. Preheat the oven to 400°F. Place the loaves in the oven; spray lightly with water. Quickly shut the oven door for 2 minutes, then spray the loaves lightly with water again. Bake until the loaves are well browned and sound hollow when tapped, about 55 minutes. Transfer the bread to racks to cool.

*Per serving 175 Calories, 1 g Total Fat, 0 g Saturated Fat, 0 mg Cholesterol, 293 mg Sodium, 36 g Total Carbohydrate, 3 g Dietary Fiber, 6 g Protein, 17 mg Calcium.*

*POINTS per serving: 3.*

# Amish Cinnamon Bread

MAKES 2 LOAVES, 24 SLICES EACH LOAF

*Unlike many of the enterprising early American settlers, the Amish and Mennonites found their niches in the North and East and did not venture beyond the region. Known for their inspired gardening and cooking, the Amish community continues a tradition of self-sufficiency, embracing a simple lifestyle even in modern times. Their bonafide tender sweet cakes and breads can be sampled at flea markets across New Jersey, Pennsylvania, and some spots in the Midwest.*

2 cups low-fat (1%) warm (105–115°F) milk

3 tablespoons unsalted butter, softened

3 tablespoons sugar

1 (¼-ounce) packet active-dry yeast

About 5 cups bread flour

1 teaspoon salt

¼ cup packed light brown sugar

1 tablespoon cinnamon

1 egg white, lightly beaten

1. Combine the milk, butter, and sugar in a small bowl. Sprinkle in the yeast and let stand until foamy, about 5 minutes.

2. Combine 4 cups of the flour and the salt in a food processor. With the machine running, scrape the yeast mixture through the feed tube. After the dough forms a ball, continue processing 5 minutes to knead. Turn out the dough on a lightly floured counter; knead briefly, adding more flour if necessary to prevent sticking, until the dough is smooth and elastic, about 5 minutes.

3. Spray a large bowl with nonstick spray; place the dough in the bowl. Cover tightly with plastic wrap and let the dough rise in a warm spot until it doubles in size, about 1 hour.

4. Spray two 8 × 4-inch loaf pans with nonstick spray. Combine the brown sugar and cinnamon in a small bowl. On a lightly floured surface, roll the dough into a 12 × 16-inch rectangle. Cut the dough crosswise in half to make two 8 × 12-inch rectangles. Sprinkle each rectangle with the cinnamon mixture, leaving a 1-inch border around the edges. Roll up each rectangle from a long end, jelly-roll fashion. Place seam-side down in the pans. Cover loosely with plastic wrap and let the dough rise in warm spot until doubled in size, about 1 hour.

5. Preheat the oven to 350°F. Lightly brush the tops of each loaf with the egg white. Bake until the loaves are golden brown and sound hollow when tapped, about 35 minutes. Transfer the bread to racks to cool.

*Per serving  71 Calories, 1 g Total Fat, 1 g Saturated Fat, 2 mg Cholesterol, 63 mg Sodium, 13 g Total Carbohydrate, 0 g Dietary Fiber, 2 g Protein, 18 mg Calcium.*

*POINTS per serving: 2.*

# Apple Butter

MAKES 2 CUPS

*A Pennsylvania Dutch tradition, apple butter was made in large quantities by groups of women participating in a working "bee," an event that allowed the women of the community to socialize while they produced the tasty, spiced fruit butter. Then, the combination of apples, apple juice, sugar, and spices was slowly cooked over an open flame, but in this recipe we use a slow cooker.*

5–6 tart apples, cored, peeled, and quartered

1 (6-ounce) can frozen apple juice concentrate, thawed

2 tablespoons pure maple syrup

1/2 teaspoon cinnamon

1/4 teaspoon ground ginger

1. Puree the apples and the apple juice concentrate in a food processor. Transfer to a slow cooker. Cover and cook on medium until the mixture is very thick, about 8 hours. Stir in the maple syrup, cinnamon, and ginger.

2. Transfer the apple butter to jars. Cover and refrigerate for up to 2 weeks, or freeze in airtight containers for up to 6 months.

*Per serving  (2 tablespoons): 56 Calories, 0 g Total Fat, 0 g Saturated Fat, 0 mg Cholesterol, 4 mg Sodium, 14 g Total Carbohydrate, 1 g Dietary Fiber, 0 g Protein, 7 mg Calcium.*

*POINTS per serving: 1.*

★ *American Way* Use it as a spread on toast, along with cottage cheese as the Amish do, or serve it as a condiment with pork, turkey, or chicken.

*chapter three*
# Midwest

★

**APPETIZERS/SOUPS/SALADS**

Cream of Corn Soup

Smoked Fish Chowder

Acorn Squash and Pear Soup

Wild Mushroom Pierogi

Marinated Cucumber-Zucchini Salad

Blue Cheese–Cornmeal Crackers

**ENTRÉES**

Wild Rice Casserole with Asparagus and Morel Mushrooms

Oven-Braised Walleye with Succotash

Cornmeal-Crusted Smelts with Mustard Dipping Sauce

Steamed Cod with Cucumber-Beet Sauce

Poached Coho Salmon with Minted Sweet Pea Sauce

Wisconsin Fish-Boil Stew

Chicken-Noodle Casserole

Roasted Cornish Hens with Cornbread Stuffing

Slow-Roasted Duckling with Plum Glaze

Four-Way Cincinnati Turkey Chili

Cider-Braised Pot Roast

Pepper-Roasted Pork Tenderloin with Red Onion Jam

**SIDES**

Horseradish Mashed Potatoes

Savoy Cabbage in Caraway Cream

Wild Rice with Glazed Onions and Toasted Pecans

German Potato Salad

Three-Bean Salad with Roasted-Garlic Dressing

Corn Timbales with Vegetables and Cheese

**DESSERTS/BREADS/SNACKS**

Rhubarb-Oatmeal Bars

Dutch Apple Pie

Tapioca Pudding with Mixed Fruit Compote

Pumpkin Custard with Caramelized Pecans

Sour Cherry–Maple Topping

Cranberry–Black Walnut Breakfast Bread

Oatmeal Loaf with Raisins and Molasses

Onion-Dill Potato Rolls

# Cream of Corn Soup

MAKES 4 SERVINGS

*Cornfields are—understandably—a prominent part of the landscape in the Corn Belt states, especially in the principal corn-producing states of Iowa, Ohio, Indiana, and Illinois. Although sweet corn-on-the-cob is often cooked by a short dip in boiling water, the versatile grain may be enjoyed in a wide variety of preparations, including this sweet, creamy soup.*

1 tablespoon unsalted butter

2 cups fresh or thawed frozen corn kernels

1 small onion, chopped

1 carrot, peeled and chopped

1/3 cup dry white wine

2 cups low-sodium chicken broth

3/4 cup fat-free half-and-half

1/2 teaspoon salt

1/8 teaspoon ground white pepper

2 tablespoons chopped fresh chives

1. Melt the butter in a saucepan. Add the corn and sauté until it is lightly browned, about 8 minutes. Add the onion and carrot; cook until the onion is translucent, about 3 minutes. Stir in the wine and cook over medium-high heat until the liquid is almost evaporated, about 5 minutes. Stir in the broth and bring to a boil. Reduce the heat and simmer until the corn is tender, about 15 minutes.

2. Transfer the soup to a blender and puree, working in batches to prevent overflows and burns. Place a large sieve over the saucepan and strain the soup back into the saucepan. Stir in the half-and-half, salt, and pepper; heat through. Sprinkle with the chives and serve.

*Per serving* (3/4 cup): 181 Calories, 5 g Total Fat, 3 g Saturated Fat, 11 mg Cholesterol, 425 mg Sodium, 29 g Total Carbohydrate, 3 g Dietary Fiber, 6 g Protein, 50 mg Calcium.

*POINTS per serving: 3*

FLASHBACK>>1875

The commercial canning of corn gets a boost with the invention of a machine that strips the kernels from the cobs. Almost 30 years later, the Minnesota Valley Canning Company is created in Le Sueur to pack sweet corn.

# Smoked Fish Chowder

MAKES 8 SERVINGS

*Smoking was an important technique employed by early settlers to preserve foods. Today, fish is smoked for flavor, not necessity, so the amount of salt and smoking time have been greatly reduced. Smoked Lake Superior white-fish, used here, is extremely moist, with a delicate flavor and texture.*

1 tablespoon unsalted butter
2 onions, sliced
1 garlic clove, chopped
1 cup bottled clam juice
1 cup low-sodium chicken broth
1 cup dry white wine
1 cup water
1 3/4 pounds smoked whitefish, skinned and boned (3 1/2 cups)
3 tablespoons cornstarch
2 cups fat-free milk
1 red potato, chopped
1 carrot, peeled and chopped
1 onion, chopped
1/4 teaspoon salt
1/8 teaspoon freshly ground pepper
1/8 teaspoon cayenne
1/4 cup chopped fresh parsley
1 tablespoon chopped fresh thyme

1. To make the broth, melt the butter in a saucepan over medium-low heat, then add the sliced onions and the garlic. Sauté until the onion is transparent, about 5 minutes. Add the clam juice, broth, wine, water, and two cups of the whitefish; bring to a boil. Reduce the heat and simmer until the flavors are blended, about 45 minutes. Strain the broth and discard the solids. Return the broth to the saucepan.

2. To make the chowder, dissolve the cornstarch in 1/4 cup of the milk; stir it into the broth with the remaining milk. Add the potato, carrot, chopped onion, salt, pepper, and cayenne. Cook, stirring occasionally, until the vegetables are tender and the soup thickens slightly, about 20 minutes. Stir in the parsley, thyme, and the remaining fish; heat through. Serve immediately.

*Per serving  121 Calories, 2 g Total Fat, 1 g Saturated Fat, 17 mg Cholesterol, 665 mg Sodium, 13 g Total Carbohydrate, 1 g Dietary Fiber, 11 g Protein, 101 mg Calcium.*

*POINTS per serving: 2.*

★ *American Way*  The fish broth may be made up to 24 hours ahead; then chowder can be assembled and ready to serve in twenty minutes.

# Acorn Squash and Pear Soup

MAKES 4 SERVINGS

*Throughout the autumn months, the orchards and farmlands of the Midwest paint the landscape in yellow and orange—a color spectrum similar to the squash of the season. Acorn squash is a small, oval-shaped dark green squash with a ribbed skin and orange flesh. In this recipe, squash and juicy ripe pears come together to produce a sweet, nutty-tasting soup with a light, creamy texture.*

1 acorn squash

1 1/2 teaspoons unsalted butter

1 small onion, chopped

1 1/2 teaspoons chopped peeled fresh ginger

1 garlic clove, chopped

1 large ripe pear, cored, peeled, and cut into chunks

2 cups vegetable broth

1/8 teaspoon salt

1/8 teaspoon freshly ground pepper

2 tablespoons chopped fresh mint

1. Preheat the oven to 350°F. Line a baking sheet with foil. Cut the squash in half, remove the seeds, and place, cut-side down, on the baking sheet. Bake until the squash is tender, 35–45 minutes. Remove the squash from the oven; when it is cool enough to handle scoop out the flesh, discarding the skin, and place in a small bowl.

2. Melt the butter in a saucepan, then add the onion, ginger, and garlic. Sauté until the onion is softened, about 5 minutes. Add the squash, pear, broth, salt, and pepper; bring to a boil. Reduce the heat and simmer until the pear is tender, 5–10 minutes.

3. Transfer the soup to a blender and puree, working in batches to prevent overflows and burns. Return to the saucepan and heat through. Sprinkle with the mint and serve.

*Per serving (about 3/4 cup): 95 Calories, 2 g Total Fat, 1 g Saturated Fat, 4 mg Cholesterol, 577 mg Sodium, 19 g Total Carbohydrate, 4 g Dietary Fiber, 2 g Protein, 41 mg Calcium.*

*POINTS per serving: 1.*

# Wild Mushroom Pierogi

## MAKES 6 SERVINGS

*The Polish population is quite sizable in Chicago, Illinois, where the Polish culture has made a lasting impression along Milwaukee Avenue. In fact, many shopkeepers still converse with customers in Polish. These pierogi—luscious little pockets stuffed with wild mushrooms and dill—are the essence of Polish cuisine.*

1 cup all-purpose flour

1/2 teaspoon salt

1/4 cup fat-free milk

2 tablespoons plain nonfat yogurt

1 egg white

1 tablespoon unsalted butter

1 cup chopped wild mushrooms, such as shiitake, cremini, or portobellos

1 scallion, chopped

1 tablespoon chopped fresh dill

1/8 teaspoon freshly ground pepper

★ *American Way* Use one or more types of fresh mushrooms in the filling, such as shiitake, porcini, cremini, portobellos, oyster, or chanterelle. If using dried mushrooms, be sure to reconstitute them in very hot water for 20 minutes to soften before using.

1. Combine the flour and 1/4 teaspoon salt in a food processor. Whisk together the milk, yogurt, and egg white in a small bowl. With the machine running, pour the milk mixture through the feed tube. After the dough forms a ball, continue processing 5 minutes to knead. Turn out the dough on a lightly floured surface; knead until the dough is smooth and elastic, about 5 minutes. Cover the dough and let rest for 15 minutes.

2. Meanwhile, melt 1/2 tablespoon butter in a nonstick skillet. Add the mushrooms and scallion. Cook, stirring occasionally, until any liquid has evaporated and mushrooms are tender and golden brown, about 7 minutes. Stir in the dill, pepper, and the remaining 1/4 teaspoon salt. Remove the skillet from the heat and set aside.

3. On a floured surface, roll half the dough to an 1/8-inch thickness. Cut the dough into 18 rounds with a 2 1/2-inch biscuit cutter. Spoon 1 teaspoon of the filling on one side of each round. Fold the dough over to make a half moon. Crimp the edges to seal tightly. Repeat with remaining dough and filling to make 36 pierogi.

4. Bring a large pot of water to a boil. Add the pierogi, stirring gently to separate. Cook until tender but firm, about 5 minutes; drain.

5. Heat the remaining 1/2 tablespoon butter in a nonstick skillet. Add the pierogi and sauté until browned all over, about 4 minutes. Serve warm.

*Per serving* (6 pierogi): 109 Calories, 2 g Total Fat, 1 g Saturated Fat, 6 mg Cholesterol, 217 mg Sodium, 18 g Total Carbohydrate, 1 g Dietary Fiber, 4 g Protein, 33 mg Calcium.

*POINTS per serving: 2.*

### FLASHBACK >> 1921

Jelly candies are manufactured by Chicagoan Fred Amend, a candy-industry bigwig since 1875. His wife suggests the name, Chuckles. Two years later, Chicago's Schutter-Johnson Co. introduces Bit-O-Honey candy bars.

# Marinated Cucumber-Zucchini Salad

MAKES 4 SERVINGS

*Scandinavians immigrating to the northern Midwest brought along many of their old-world traditions. Smorgasbord, which is Swedish for bread and butter table, consists of a variety of sandwiches, salads, pickled vegetables, and meats. A fresh, crunchy cucumber salad is often part of this table. Here, we've added sliced zucchini for extra texture.*

1 cucumber, peeled, seeded, and sliced paper-thin

1 zucchini, sliced paper-thin

1/4 cup finely chopped onion

1/4 cup white vinegar

1 1/2 tablespoons chopped fresh dill

1 tablespoon aquavit or water

1 1/2 teaspoons sugar

1/4 teaspoon salt

1/8 teaspoon ground white pepper

Place the cucumber, zucchini, and onion in a shallow dish; set aside. Stir together the vinegar, dill, aquavit, sugar, salt, and pepper in a bowl. Pour the dressing over the cucumber mixture; Cover and refrigerate at least 2 hours before serving.

*Per serving* 32 Calories, 0 g Total Fat, 0 g Saturated Fat, 0 mg Cholesterol, 148 mg Sodium, 5 g Total Carbohydrate, 1 g Dietary Fiber, 1 g Protein, 19 mg Calcium.

*POINTS per serving: 0.*

★ *American Way* Aquavit is a potent Scandinavian liquor that tastes strongly of caraway seeds. If it's not in your cupboard, just use water.

# Sausage Glossary

The promise of a better life lured immigrants from all over the world to America and, it seems, no nation came without their own particular brand of sausage. As a result, many unique varieties of seasoned ground meats appear on today's supermarket shelves. A closer look can even reveal clues to the identity of the people who settled the area. The following is a list of some favorite American sausages:

**Banger:** A mild British or Scottish sausage made from meat and cereal.

**Bologna:** Cooked, smoked sausage made of finely ground cured beef; originally from Bologna, Italy.

**Bratwurst:** Highly seasoned, fresh, cooked or smoked German-style sausage made from pork or a pork and veal mixture; a favorite in Wisconsin.

**Cervelat:** General classification for mildly seasoned, smoked, semi-dry "Summer Sausages;" may be of Swedish, German and Swiss origin.

**Chorizo:** Smoked, highly spiced dry pork sausage links of Spanish origin. In the Southwest, fresh bulk Chorizo is available.

**Frankfurters:** Although it originated in Frankfurt, Germany, it's considered the all-American hot dog. It is fully cooked and seasoned with coriander, garlic, dry mustard, nutmeg, salt, sugar and white pepper. May also be called "wiener" (from Vienna.).

**Knockwurst:** Cooked, smoked sausage similar in ingredients to frankfurters and bologna with garlic added. Made in wide casings they are also known as Knoblouch or Garlic Sausage.

**Lebanon Bologna:** Originated in Lebanon, Pennsylvania; made of coarsely chopped beef; heavily smoked with a tart, tangy taste and dark appearance.

**Linguica:** An uncooked, smoked Portuguese sausage made from ground pork and seasoned with garlic, cumin seeds and cinnamon, cured in vinegar pickling liquid before stuffing.

**Kielbasa or Polish Sausage:** An uncooked, smoked sausage made from lean pork with beef added; highly seasoned with garlic.

**Italian Sausage:** An uncooked sausage made from fresh pork seasoned with fennel. Available "sweet" (mildly seasoned) or "hot" (with red pepper flakes).

# Blue Cheese–Cornmeal Crackers

## MAKES 5 DOZEN CRACKERS

*Some of the finest American blue cheese is made in Wisconsin and Iowa from pasteurized cow's milk. It has a sharp, peppery taste, so just a touch adds a lot of flavor to these crispy stone-ground crackers.*

1 cup stone-ground yellow cornmeal

1/2 cup whole-wheat flour

1/4 teaspoon baking soda

1/4 teaspoon salt

1/8 teaspoon cayenne

2 tablespoons crumbled blue cheese

1/2 cup low-fat buttermilk

2 tablespoons vegetable oil

1. Preheat the oven to 350°F. Spray nonstick baking sheets with nonstick spray. Combine the cornmeal, flour, baking soda, salt, and cayenne in a food processor. Add the cheese and pulse until finely crumbled. With the machine running, add the buttermilk and oil; run until the dough forms a ball.

2. Divide the dough in half. Keep unused dough covered until ready to use. On a lightly floured counter, roll out half the dough to an 1/8-inch thickness. Cut the dough into rounds with a 1 1/2-inch biscuit cutter; transfer the rounds onto the baking sheets. Prick the rounds in two or three places with a fork. Repeat with remaining dough.

3. Bake until the crackers are crisp and golden brown, 8–10 minutes. Cool completely on a rack; store in an airtight container for up to 7 days.

*Per serving (5 crackers): 83 Calories, 3 g Total Fat, 1 g Saturated Fat, 1 mg Cholesterol, 109 mg Sodium, 12 g Total Carbohydrate, 1 g Dietary Fiber, 2 g Protein, 22 mg Calcium.*

*POINTS per serving: 2.*

# Wild Rice Casserole with Asparagus and Morel Mushrooms

## MAKES 6 SERVINGS

*Wild rice, the state grain of Minnesota, is not rice at all, but rather an aquatic grass native to the central and upper Great Lakes region of the United States. Hand-harvesting wild rice, a Native American tradition, involves gathering the natural strands from lakes and rivers using canoes. Morels provide a complementary earthy flavor to the rice.*

1 ounce dried morel mushrooms, about 3/4 cup

1 cup hot water

1 cup wild rice, rinsed

1 1/2 teaspoons salt

1 tablespoon unsalted butter

1/3 cup grated Parmesan cheese

2 tablespoons plain dried bread crumbs

1 tablespoon olive oil

1 onion, chopped

2 garlic cloves, chopped

1 pound asparagus, trimmed and sliced

1/4 teaspoon freshly ground pepper

2 teaspoons chopped fresh oregano

1. Soak the mushrooms in the hot water until softened, about 20 minutes. Strain the mushrooms, reserving 3/4 the liquid. Slice the mushrooms and set aside.

2. Combine the wild rice with 1 teaspoon of the salt and 4 cups water in a medium saucepan; bring to a boil. Reduce the heat, cover, and simmer until the rice is just tender and the grains are beginning to split, 35–45 minutes, depending on the rice. Drain the rice and stir in the butter and cheese.

3. Preheat the oven to 400°F. Spray a 1 1/2-quart baking dish with nonstick spray. Coat the bottom and sides of the dish with the bread crumbs; set aside.

4. Heat the oil in a large nonstick skillet, then add the onions and garlic. Sauté until the onions are softened, about 5 minutes. Add the reserved mushroom liquid and bring to a boil. Add the mushrooms, asparagus, pepper, and the remaining 1/2 teaspoon salt. Reduce the heat, cover, and simmer until the vegetables are tender and liquid is almost evaporated, about 8 minutes. Remove the skillet from the heat; stir in the oregano and wild rice mixture.

5. Spoon the rice mixture into the baking dish. Bake until the top is browned and the casserole is hot, about 20 minutes. Serve immediately.

*Per serving 202 Calories, 7 g Total fat, 3 g Saturated Fat, 10 mg Cholesterol, 616 mg Sodium, 28 g Total Carbohydrate, 3 g Dietary Fiber, 9 g Protein, 100 mg Calcium.*

*POINTS per serving: 4.*

★ *American Way* Hand-harvested wild rice is available from Christmas Point Wild Rice Company, 800-726-0613.

## FRESHWATER BOUNTY

In the 17th century, French explorers discovered that America's central region was dominated by a surprising number of rivers and immense freshwater lakes. The explorers also discovered that tribes in the surrounding area, like the Sioux and Chippewa (or Ojibwe), relied on the resources of these bodies of water, living on the abundant lake trout and whitefish. The Indians also discovered a nutty grain (*Zizania aquatica*) that grew in the marshy areas and on the banks of the streams. Today, this grain, known as wild rice, is still collected by Native Americans in a labor-intensive process that involves poling a small boat through the shallow water and shaking the seeds from the plants into a collecting tray. To meet the demand for wild rice, a large portion of the grain is now raised commercially in California, but a taste of the real thing can still be found in packages with labels that indicate it was harvested by hand.

As settlers pushed westward into what is now Michigan, Minnesota, and Wisconsin, they were delighted to find that the crystalline Great Lakes were as full of fish as the coastal waters they had left behind. Fish again became an important part of their diet and this region's cuisine. Today, Midwesterners are so fond of their local fish that "fish fries" have become a traditional way of raising money for community organizations, while many local restaurants offer an all-you-can-eat fish fry on Friday evenings.

# Oven-Braised Walleye with Succotash

## MAKES 4 SERVINGS

*Many consider the freshwater walleye, prized for firm white flesh and delicate flavor, to be one of the finest fish in the Great Lakes region. Often called* walleye pike, *walleye is not truly a pike, but a member of the pike perch species. We've paired this light fish with succotash, the classic American combination of corn, lima beans, and tomatoes.*

1 cup thawed frozen corn kernels
1 cup thawed frozen lima beans
1 onion, chopped
1 tomato, seeded and chopped
1 tablespoon vegetable oil
1 garlic clove, chopped
1 teaspoon chopped fresh thyme
1/2 teaspoon salt
1/4 teaspoon freshly ground pepper
1/2 cup vegetable broth or water
11/2 pounds walleye pike fillets, skinned

Preheat the oven to 400°F. Spray a 9 × 13-inch baking pan with nonstick spray. Combine the corn, lima beans, onion, tomato, oil, garlic, thyme, salt, and pepper in the pan. Pour the broth over the vegetables. Arrange the pike in a single layer on top of the vegetables. Cover and bake until the vegetables are tender and the fish is opaque in the center, about 20 minutes.

*Per serving  272 Calories, 6 g Total Fat, 1 g Saturated Fat, 134 mg Cholesterol, 524 mg Sodium, 21 g Total Carbohydrate, 4 g Dietary Fiber, 34 g Protein, 192 mg Calcium.*

*POINTS per serving: 5.*

# Cornmeal-Crusted Smelts with Mustard Dipping Sauce

## MAKES 4 SERVINGS

*From late February through April, an evening ritual is played out along the Midwestern river banks and off the Great Lakes' piers known as smelt fishing. Sportsmen line up along the piers with net, knife, and cooking skillet, waiting for smelt, who feed only at night. The best smelt-eating is done on the spot, as soon as the slippery little fish are caught. Freshwater smelts are small, only two to four inches long, with silvery skin. They are quickly cleaned for cooking, then coated with seasoned cornmeal and pan-fried.*

1 pound fresh or thawed frozen smelts, cleaned

$1/3$ cup all-purpose flour

$1/2$ teaspoon salt

$1/4$ teaspoon freshly ground pepper

$1/4$ teaspoon cayenne

$2/3$ cup yellow cornmeal

2 egg whites

$1/3$ cup light mayonnaise

2 tablespoons horseradish mustard

1 tablespoon fresh lemon juice

$1/8$ teaspoon hot pepper sauce

1. Preheat the oven to 475°F. Spray a baking sheet with nonstick spray. Wash the smelts under cool water; drain and pat dry.

2. Combine the flour, salt, pepper, and cayenne in a shallow dish or pie pan. Place the cornmeal in another dish. In a shallow bowl, lightly beat the egg whites until frothy. Dredge the smelts in the flour, shaking off any excess, dip them in the egg whites, and then dredge in the cornmeal, shaking off the excess. Place the smelts on the baking sheet and spray with nonstick spray. Bake, turning once, until crisp and golden brown, about 10 minutes.

3. Meanwhile, combine the mayonnaise, mustard, lemon juice, and pepper sauce in a small bowl. Serve with the smelts.

*Per serving (including 2 tablespoons sauce): 310 Calories, 10 g Total Fat, 2 g Saturated Fat, 83 mg Cholesterol, 639 mg Sodium, 28 g Total Carbohydrate, 2 g Dietary Fiber, 24 g Protein, 79 mg Calcium.*

*POINTS per serving: 7.*

# Steamed Cod with Cucumber-Beet Sauce

## MAKES 4 SERVINGS

*Cod is just one of the many saltwater species shipped to the Midwest. In this colorful entrée, fresh Atlantic cod is steamed and served over wilted greens with a refreshing cucumber-beet sauce.*

1 cucumber, peeled, seeded, and coarsely chopped

1½ teaspoons vegetable oil

About ½ teaspoon salt

About ¼ teaspoon freshly ground pepper

1 (¼-pound) beet, peeled and cut into chunks

1 cup low-sodium vegetable broth

1 tablespoon aquavit (optional)

1 tablespoon fresh lemon juice

4 (6-ounce) cod fillets

1 bunch beet greens, or spinach, trimmed and cleaned

1. Place the cucumber and oil in a food processor; add a pinch of salt and a pinch of pepper, and puree. Transfer the puree to a sieve set over a bowl and allow to drain.

2. Combine the beet and broth in a small saucepan; bring to a boil. Reduce the heat and simmer until the beet is tender, about 20 minutes. Transfer the beet to food processor, reserving the broth. Add 1 tablespoon of the broth and the aquavit, if using, to the food processor and puree. Transfer the pureed beet to a saucepan and stir in the drained cucumber puree. Add 2 tablespoons of the reserved broth, the lemon juice, a pinch of salt, and a pinch of pepper. Keep the sauce warm.

3. Season the cod with ¼ teaspoon salt and ⅛ teaspoon pepper. Place the fillets in a steamer basket; set in a large saucepan over 1 inch of boiling water. Cover the pan tightly and steam until the fish is just opaque in the center, about 10 minutes.

4. Meanwhile, place the greens in a skillet with the remaining reserved broth and cook over high heat until wilted, about 2 minutes. Serve the fish on a bed of wilted greens, drizzled with the sauce.

*Per serving* 180 Calories, 3 g Total fat, 0 g Saturated Fat, 73 mg Cholesterol, 696 mg Sodium, 6 g Total Carbohydrate, 2 g Dietary Fiber, 32 g Protein, 68 mg Calcium.

*POINTS per serving: 3.*

★ *American Way* If you'd like to save time, you can use a canned beet—no vinegar added.

# Poached Coho Salmon with Minted Sweet Pea Sauce

### MAKES 4 SERVINGS

*The Great Lakes' coho, or silver, salmon was transplanted from the Northwest and is in season during late spring through early summer. In this recipe, the salmon is poached in a flavorful broth. A light, delicate sauce of fresh sweet peas and mint is a perfect accompaniment to this lovely summer dish.*

1 cup low-sodium chicken broth
1 cup fresh or thawed frozen sweet peas
1 teaspoon chopped fresh mint
4 cups water
1 teaspoon salt
4 (6-ounce) coho salmon fillets
1/4 cup plain nonfat yogurt
1/4 teaspoon freshly ground pepper

1. Combine the broth, peas, and mint in a saucepan; bring to boil. Reduce the heat, cover, and simmer until the peas are tender, 5–10 minutes. Transfer the mixture to a blender and puree. Place a large sieve over the saucepan and strain the mixture back into the saucepan.

2. Combine the water and 1/2 teaspoon salt in a large skillet. Add the fillets and bring to a boil. Reduce the heat, cover, and simmer until the fish is just opaque in the center, about 8 minutes; transfer the fillets to 4 warm plates; discard the cooking liquid.

3. Gently heat the pea puree but do not boil. Remove the saucepan from the heat and stir in the yogurt, a tablespoon at a time. Add the remaining 1/2 teaspoon salt and the pepper. Spoon the sauce over the fillets and serve immediately.

*Per serving   220 Calories, 5 g Total fat, 1 g Saturated Fat, 95 mg Cholesterol, 497 mg Sodium, 6 g Total Carbohydrate, 2 g Dietary Fiber, 37 g Protein, 99 mg Calcium.*

*POINTS per serving: 4.*

★ *American Way*  If coho salmon is not available, any other salmon will do nicely.

*Poached Coho Salmon with Minted Sweet Pea Sauce, and Corn Timbales with Vegetables and Cheese (page 101)*

# Wisconsin Fish-Boil Stew

MAKES 4 SERVINGS

*This simple summer stew is prepared in the style of the famous Wisconsin fish boils—outdoor parties starring a large kettle of boiling salted water, filled with all manner of fish and vegetables. We feature Lake Superior white-fish, as well as fresh dill, a favorite herb of the large Scandinavian population in Wisconsin.*

4 small potatoes, scrubbed and quartered

4 celery stalks, sliced

1 onion, sliced

1/2 cup fresh or thawed frozen corn kernels

2 cups bottled clam juice

2 cups water

1 cup low-fat (2%) milk

1 tablespoon unsalted butter

1/4 teaspoon salt

1/8 teaspoon freshly ground pepper

4 (6-ounce) whitefish fillets

2 tablespoons chopped fresh dill

1. Combine the potatoes, celery, onion, corn, clam juice, and water in a large saucepan and bring to a boil. Reduce the heat, cover, and simmer until the vegetables are tender, about 20 minutes. Stir in the milk, butter, salt, and pepper; heat the stew briefly but do not boil.

2. Combine the fillets with enough water to cover them in a skillet; bring the water to a boil. Reduce the heat, cover, and simmer until the fish is just opaque in the center, about 5 minutes.

3. Ladle the stew over the fillets and sprinkle with the dill. Serve immediately.

*Per serving  425 Calories, 15 g Total fat, 4 g Saturated Fat, 118 mg Cholesterol, 566 mg Sodium, 35 g Total Carbohydrate, 4 g Dietary Fiber, 39 g Protein, 168 mg Calcium.*

*POINTS per serving: 9.*

★ *American Way*  To keep the whitefish fillets intact, they are cooked separately from the vegetables.

# Chicken-Noodle Casserole

MAKES 6 SERVINGS

*The one-dish meal cooked in an oven casserole became popular during the early 20th century for several reasons. In response to shortages caused by World War I, American homemakers became more frugal with food, and leftovers were often recycled. About the same time, earthenware was being manufactured at an affordable price. Finally, women's magazines were singing the praises of using canned soups in place of scratch sauces. Casserole cooking remained popular through the Depression, World War II, and well into the 1950s. Today, casserole dishes are enjoying a healthy comeback, with this recipe setting a good, low-fat example of a revitalized classic.*

1/4 pound wide nonfat egg noodles

2 cups low-sodium chicken broth

2 cups cremini mushrooms, thickly sliced

1 small onion, chopped

1 green bell pepper, seeded and chopped

2 cups cooked cubed chicken breasts

1/4 cup chopped roasted red peppers

1 tablespoon unsalted butter

2 tablespoons all-purpose flour

2 tablespoons dry sherry

3–5 drops hot pepper sauce

1/2 teaspoon salt

1/4 teaspoon freshly ground pepper

1/2 cup plain dried bread crumbs

1/4 cup grated Parmesan cheese

1. Preheat the oven to 350°F. Spray a shallow 2-quart casserole with nonstick spray. Cook the noodles according to package directions. Drain, rinse with cold water, and transfer the noodles to a large bowl.

2. Combine the broth, mushrooms, onion, and bell pepper in a saucepan and bring to a boil. Reduce the heat and simmer until the vegetables are tender, about 5 minutes. Drain the vegetables, reserving the broth. Add the vegetables, chicken, and roasted pepper to the noodles.

3. Melt the butter in a saucepan. Stir in the flour and cook 1 minute. Whisk in the reserved broth, the sherry, pepper sauce, salt, and pepper. Cook, stirring constantly, until the sauce boils and thickens, about 5 minutes. Add the sauce to the noodle mixture and toss to combine. Spoon the mixture into the casserole. Sprinkle with the bread crumbs and cheese and spray with nonstick spray. Bake until golden brown, about 40 minutes.

*Per serving   261 Calories, 6 g Total Fat, 3 g Saturated Fat, 49 mg Cholesterol, 444 mg Sodium, 27 g Total Carbohydrate, 2 g Dietary Fiber, 23 g Protein, 84 mg Calcium.*

*POINTS per serving: 5.*

FLASHBACK > > 1955

Entrepreneur Ray Kroc opens the first McDonald's hamburger stand in Des Plaines, Illinois. A burger sells for 15 cents, French fries for 10 cents, and a creamy milkshake for 20.

# Roasted Cornish Hens with Cornbread Stuffing

## MAKES 8 SERVINGS

*Since local corn is plentiful throughout the Midwest, it's hardly surprising that cornbread stuffing is popular at many Midwestern Thanksgiving dinner tables.*

1 tablespoon unsalted butter

1 medium fennel bulb, chopped

2 celery stalks, chopped

3 cups crumbled cornbread

1/2 cup low-sodium chicken broth

1 egg white, lightly beaten

1 tablespoon chopped fresh sage,
    or 1 teaspoon dried sage

1/4 teaspoon salt

1/8 teaspoon freshly ground pepper

4 (11/2-pound) Cornish hens

1. To make the stuffing, melt the butter in a large skillet, then add the fennel and the celery. Sauté until the vegetables are tender, about 5 minutes. Remove from the heat. Stir in the cornbread, broth, egg white, sage, salt, and pepper.

2. Preheat the oven to 400°F. Stuff each hen with about 1/2 cup of the stuffing; truss the legs. Place the hens, breast-side up, on a rack in a large roasting pan. Spray with nonstick spray. Roast until an instant–read thermometer inserted in the thigh registers 180°F, about 45 minutes.

3. Let stand 10 minutes before carving. Split the hens in half using a sharp knife to cut along the backbone, spread the hen open, then cut along the breast bone. Remove the skin before eating.

*Per serving* 313 Calories, 10 g Total Fat, 3 g Saturated Fat, 126 mg Cholesterol, 536 mg Sodium, 24 g Total Carbohydrate, 3 g Dietary Fiber, 30 g Protein, 67 mg Calcium.

*POINTS per serving:* 6.

★ *American Way* Prepare the cornbread one day ahead from a box mix, substituting egg white for whole egg, and low-fat buttermilk for milk.

*Roasted Cornish Hens with Cornbread Stuffing*

# Slow-Roasted Duckling with Plum Glaze

MAKES 4 SERVINGS

*Indiana farm-raised ducklings, a close relative to the Long Island duck, are fed a diet of two local crops—corn and soybeans. A duckling, less than 50 days old, is tender and lower in fat than the older roasters. In fact, a skinless breast has only 2 grams of fat. Plum preserves and dark molasses pair up for a fruity and intensely flavored barbecue-style sauce. You may want to try it on pork, too.*

1 (4$^1$/$_2$-pound) duckling

$^1$/$_2$ teaspoon salt

$^3$/$_4$ teaspoon coarsely ground black pepper

1 lemon, cut in half

1 small onion, quartered

1 (1-inch) piece fresh ginger, peeled and coarsely chopped

2 cups water

$^1$/$_4$ cup plum preserves

2 tablespoons molasses

★ *American Way* Drying the duck in the refrigerator produces crispier skin; if you don't care to eat the skin, the step can be omitted.

1. Remove the giblets and the neck from the duckling. Rinse the duckling, giblets, and neck with cold running water; drain well. Pat the duckling dry with paper towels and trim any excess fat. Place the duckling, breast side up, on a rack in a roasting pan. Refrigerate, uncovered, for at least 8 and up to 24 hours to allow the duck to dry thoroughly.

2. Preheat the oven to 325°F. Sprinkle the duckling with the salt and $^1$/$_2$ teaspoon pepper. Coarsely chop one lemon half and place it, with the onion, in the duckling's cavity. Roast 45 minutes. Remove the pan from the oven and carefully pour off the fat. Turn the duckling breast-side down and return to the oven to roast another 45 minutes.

3. Meanwhile, chop the neck into 4 pieces. Combine it with the giblets, ginger, and water in a saucepan. Bring the water to a boil, reduce the heat, cover, and simmer until the giblets are tender, about 1 hour. Strain and reserve the broth, discarding the solids.

4. Heat the plum preserves, molasses, $^1$/$_2$ cup of the duck broth, and remaining $^1$/$_4$ teaspoon pepper in a saucepan. Squeeze the juice from the remaining lemon half through a strainer into the pan. Bring the sauce to a boil. Reduce the heat and cook until the sauce thickens slightly and is smooth, about 5 minutes.

5. Pour off the fat from the roasting pan again and turn the duck breast-side up. Add the remaining duck broth into the pan and return the pan to the oven. Roast until instant-read thermometer inserted in the thigh registers 180°F, 45–60 minutes more.

6. Discard the onion and lemon from the cavity. Let stand 15 minutes before carving. If you don't care to eat the skin, remove it. Serve with the plum glaze.

*Per serving   385 Calories, 17 g Total fat, 6 g Saturated Fat, 135 mg Cholesterol, 418 mg Sodium, 20 g Total Carbohydrate, 0 g Dietary Fiber, 36 g Protein, 45 mg Calcium.*

*POINTS per serving: 9.*

# Four-Way Cincinnati Turkey Chili

## MAKES 4 SERVINGS

*The raging chili debate, arguing whether the cubed meat should be cooked with beans or without, is moot in the state of Ohio. In Cincinnati, what is subject to debate is how many ingredients are necessary for a premier chili— and, of course, who cooks the best. Three separate restaurateurs in that city claim parenthood to what is known as Cincinnati Chili, a layered concoction centered around all-meat chili. Diners can choose from a stepladder of garnishes: Three-Way chili is the chili served over cooked spaghetti and topped with cheese; Four-Way adds onions; and Five-Way chili is topped off with beans*

1 pound lean ground turkey

1 large onion, chopped

2 garlic cloves, chopped

1 tablespoon chili powder

1 1/2 teaspoons packed brown sugar

1/2 teaspoon salt

1/2 teaspoon ground cumin

1/4 teaspoon ground allspice

1/4 teaspoon ground cardamom

1/4 teaspoon freshly ground pepper

1 (13 3/4-ounce) can low-sodium beef broth

1 (10-ounce) can diced tomatoes and green chiles

1 tablespoon cider vinegar

4 cups cooked elbow macaroni

1 (15 1/2-ounce) can chili beans in sauce, heated

8 scallions, chopped

1. Combine the turkey, onion, and garlic in a nonstick saucepan. Cook, stirring constantly, until the turkey is browned and the onion is tender, about 5 minutes.

2. Add the chili powder, brown sugar, salt, cumin, allspice, cardamom, and pepper; stir until the spices coat the turkey and the onions.

3. Stir in the broth, tomatoes and chiles, and the vinegar; bring to a boil. Reduce the heat, partially cover, and simmer until the broth is thickened and the flavors are blended, 30–40 minutes.

4. Serve the chili over the macaroni and top with the beans and scallions.

*Per serving  442 Calories, 4 g Total fat, 1 g Saturated Fat, 70 mg Cholesterol, 1,396 mg Sodium, 63 g Total Carbohydrate, 10 g Dietary Fiber, 42 g Protein, 91 mg Calcium.*

*POINTS per serving: 7.*

# Cider-Braised Pot Roast

MAKES 6 SERVINGS

*German immigrants from Pennsylvania who settled in the Midwest can claim ownership of sauerbraten, German for sour roast. It's traditionally made by marinating meat in a sweet-sour sauce for a few days; then the meat is simmered in the sauce, for several hours.*

1 (2–2¼-pound) boneless tip beef roast

½ teaspoon salt

¼ teaspoon freshly ground pepper

1 cup hard cider, apple cider, or dry Riesling wine

1 onion, sliced

1 bay leaf

4 carrots, peeled and cut into 3-inch– long diagonal slices

4 parsnips, peeled and cut into 3-inch– long diagonal slices

12 red or white pearl onions, peeled

1 tablespoon cider vinegar

1 tablespoon packed brown sugar

1. Preheat the oven to 350°F. Pat the beef dry with paper towels and sprinkle with the salt and pepper. Place the meat in a small roasting pan. Add the cider, sliced onion, and bay leaf. Cover and cook until the meat is fork-tender, about 2 hours.

2. Meanwhile, combine the carrots and parsnips with enough water to cover them in a saucepan. Bring the water to a boil, reduce the heat, and simmer until the vegetables are tender, about 10 minutes. Transfer the vegetables to a bowl, reserving the cooking liquid in the pan. Add the pearl onions to the liquid in the pan and bring the liquid to a boil. Reduce the heat and simmer until the onions are tender, about 7 minutes. Drain the onions, toss with the carrots and parsnips, and keep warm.

3. Transfer the meat to a cutting board; let stand 10 minutes before slicing. Strain the pan juices into a saucepan, discarding the solids. Stir in the vinegar and brown sugar; bring to a boil and cook 1 minute to blend flavors. Serve the pot roast, sliced with the vegetables and the sauce.

*Per serving  376 Calories, 18 g Total Fat, 7 g Saturated Fat, 98 mg Cholesterol, 302 mg Sodium, 18 g Total Carbohydrate, 4 g Dietary Fiber, 31 g Protein, 46 mg Calcium.*

*POINTS per serving: 8.*

★ *American Way* The most common beef cuts for braising are rump, round, and chuck. Our pot roast combines the sweet-sour flavors of sauerbraten with tip roast, a very lean cut that can be purchased in one compact piece, so it does not need to be rolled and tied.

# Pepper-Roasted Pork Tenderloin
# with Red Onion Jam

MAKES 6 SERVINGS

*A western migration of German immigrants from Pennsylvania increased pork consumption, as well as production. The German immigrants found a way to use all the parts of the pig. These meals often included sauerkraut, onions, and sweet-sour sauces.*

## RED ONION JAM

1 tablespoon unsalted butter

3 red onions, sliced

²/₃ cup dry red wine

2 tablespoons sherry vinegar

1 tablespoon grenadine (optional)

1 ¹/₂ teaspoons sugar

¹/₄ teaspoon salt

¹/₈ teaspoon freshly ground pepper

## PORK TENDERLOINS

2 tablespoons coarsely ground mixed
    pepper or ground black pepper

¹/₂ teaspoon coarse salt

2 (³/₄-pound) pork tenderloins

1. To make the onion jam, melt the butter in a large nonstick skillet over low heat, then add the onions. Sauté until the onions are softened, about 5 minutes. Stir in the wine, vinegar, grenadine, if using, sugar, salt, and pepper. Cook until the onion jam thickens and the liquid is syrupy, about 45 minutes. Set aside.

2. Meanwhile, preheat the oven to 500°F. Rub the mixed pepper and coarse salt all over the tenderloins; place the tenderloins in a shallow roasting pan. Roast until the pork reaches an internal temperature of 160°F, about 25 minutes. Let stand 10 minutes before slicing and serve with the jam.

*Per serving*   *203 Calories, 6 g Total Fat, 3 g Saturated Fat, 73 mg Cholesterol, 345 mg Sodium, 10 g Total Carbohydrate, 2 g Dietary Fiber, 25 g Protein, 29 mg Calcium.*

*POINTS per serving: 4.*

★ *American Way*   Tenderloin is the most tender cut, as well as the leanest. This pepper-coated roast is accompanied by a mellow, sweet and sour onion condiment. Grenadine is a sweet syrup made from pomegranates. Mixed peppercorns—a mixture of black, white, and pink peppercorns—can be found in some gourmet specialty shops.

# Horseradish Mashed Potatoes

### MAKES 4 SERVINGS

*Mashed potatoes are the epitome of American comfort food. Yukon Gold potatoes, grown extensively in Michigan, are ideally suited for mashing because of their smooth, yellow flesh and subtle buttery taste. We've paired these golden treasures with horseradish root—which is grown in Illinois—its sharp and spicy flavor makes it an ideal condiment.*

1¼ pounds Yukon Gold potatoes, peeled and quartered

2 large garlic cloves

1 teaspoon salt

2 tablespoons fresh grated horseradish root (or prepared horseradish packed in vinegar)

2 tablespoons light mayonnaise

1 tablespoon unsalted butter

¼ teaspoon freshly ground pepper

1. Combine the potatoes and garlic with ¹/2 teaspoon salt and enough water to cover the potatoes in a saucepan. Bring to a boil, cover, and simmer until the potatoes are tender, about 25 minutes. Drain the potatoes, reserving ³/4 cup of the cooking liquid.

2. Transfer the potatoes and garlic to a large mixing bowl; beat with an electric mixer, on medium speed, until blended. Beat in the horseradish, mayonnaise, butter, the remaining ¹/2 teaspoon salt, the pepper, and the reserved cooking liquid until well mixed. Serve immediately.

*Per serving* *178 Calories, 6 g Total Fat, 2 g Saturated Fat, 11 mg Cholesterol, 356 mg Sodium, 30 g Total Carbohydrate, 3 g Dietary Fiber, 3 g Protein, 25 mg Calcium.*

*POINTS per serving: 3.*

★ *American Way* Buy fresh horseradish root or prepared horseradish packed in vinegar. Fresh grated is superb in these potatoes, in salad dressing, or mixed with low-fat yogurt. The fumes from freshly grated horseradish are pungent and can burn eyes, so work in a well-ventilated area.

# Savoy Cabbage in Caraway Cream

### MAKES 4 SERVINGS

*Cabbage was brought to America by European settlers and it soon became a staple crop, probably because it has always been plentiful and easy to store. Such characteristics were a blessing for those early immigrants who endured harsh Midwest winters.*

2 teaspoons unsalted butter
1 head savoy cabbage, shredded
1 garlic clove, minced
1/2 teaspoon salt
1 tablespoon caraway seeds
1 1/2 teaspoons white vinegar
1 teaspoon sugar
1/3 cup light sour cream

Melt the butter in a large nonstick skillet over medium heat. Stir in the cabbage, garlic, and salt. Cover and cook until the cabbage is just wilted, about 10 minutes. Add the caraway seeds, vinegar, and sugar and blend well. Remove the pan from the heat. Stir in the sour cream and toss to coat.

*Per serving* 85 Calories, 5 g Total Fat, 3 g Saturated Fat, 13 mg Cholesterol, 331 mg Sodium, 10 g Total Carbohydrate, 4 g Dietary Fiber, 3 g Protein, 73 mg Calcium.

*POINTS per serving: 1.*

# Wild Rice with Glazed Onions and Toasted Pecans

MAKES 4 SERVINGS

*Hand-harvested wild rice, a delicacy from northern Minnesota, is still processed in the traditional method by some small companies: It involves parching the rice over a wood fire, threshing the hulls from the rice kernels, and fanning to remove the chaff. This technique produces a rich tasting, all-natural product.*

2 cups water

1/2 cup wild rice, rinsed

2 teaspoons olive oil

1 teaspoon unsalted butter

1 cup pearl onions, peeled and halved lengthwise

1 1/2 tablespoons sugar

2 tablespoons raspberry vinegar

1/2 teaspoon salt

1/4 teaspoon freshly ground pepper

1/4 cup pecans, toasted

1. Combine the water and rice in a medium saucepan and bring to a boil. Reduce the heat, cover, and simmer until the rice is just tender and the grains are beginning to split open, 35–45 minutes, depending on the rice.

2. Meanwhile, heat the oil and butter in a large skillet, then add the onions and sugar. Sauté until the onions are tender and golden, about 10 minutes. Stir in the vinegar, salt, and pepper; cook until the mixture begins to thicken and glaze the onions. Stir in the rice and pecans, heat through, and serve.

*Per serving   179 Calories, 8 g Total Fat, 1 g Saturated Fat, 3 mg Cholesterol, 294 mg Sodium, 25 g Total Carbohydrate, 2 g Dietary Fiber, 4 g Protein, 16 mg Calcium.*

*POINTS per serving: 4.*

★ *American Way*  Store wild rice in a cool, dry place. Once cooked, it will freeze well or may be refrigerated up to 1 week, tightly covered. Hand-harvested wild rice is available from Christmas Point Wild Rice Company, 800-726-0613.

# German Potato Salad

MAKES 6 SERVINGS

*In the late 19th century, Germans emigrating to the Midwest helped shape the region's culinary history. Traditional German potato salad, a Midwest staple, does not contain mayonnaise, but it still can be high in calories when loaded with bacon bits and a dressing prepared with rendered bacon fat. Our lighter version omits the bacon completely, but we've included turkey ham to maintain the smoky flavor.*

1½ pounds small red potatoes, cut into quarters

1 small onion, chopped

¼ cup chopped celery

⅓ cup chopped turkey ham

2 tablespoons chopped fresh parsley

¼ cup cider vinegar

2 tablespoons olive oil

½ teaspoon dry mustard

½ teaspoon sugar

½ teaspoon salt

⅛ teaspoon freshly ground pepper

1. Combine the potatoes with enough water to cover them in a saucepan. Bring the water to a boil and cook until the potatoes are tender, about 25 minutes. Drain and transfer to a large bowl.

2. Meanwhile, spray a small nonstick skillet with nonstick spray and set over medium heat. Add the onion and celery and sauté until slightly softened, about 3 minutes. Combine the onion mixture, potatoes, ham, and parsley; mix gently.

3. Whisk together the vinegar, oil, mustard, sugar, salt, and pepper in a bowl. Pour the dressing over the potatoes, toss to combine, and serve warm.

*Per serving   156 Calories, 5 g Total Fat, 1 g Saturated Fat, 5 mg Cholesterol, 288 mg Sodium, 25 g Total Carbohydrate, 2 g Dietary Fiber, 4 g Protein, 17 mg Calcium.*

*POINTS per serving: 3.*

FLASHBACK>>1850

German-American brewer Bernard Stroh founds the Lion Brewery in Detroit, which will later become Stroh's Brewery, the largest in Michigan.

# Three-Bean Salad with Roasted-Garlic Dressing

### MAKES 8 SERVINGS

*Michigan is bean country: a huge variety of field beans, such as cranberry, kidney, navy, black, and pinto, are grown in the state. Bean dishes are so popular; in fact, it would not be at all surprising if that 1940s classic, the three-bean salad, originated there.*

1/3 cup roasted-garlic vinegar

3 tablespoons olive oil

2 tablespoons chopped fresh parsley

1/2 teaspoon salt

1/4 teaspoon freshly ground pepper

1 (15-ounce) can dark red kidney beans, rinsed and drained

1 (15-ounce) can black-eyed peas, rinsed and drained

1 (15-ounce) can chickpeas, rinsed and drained

1 yellow bell pepper, chopped

1/2 cup chopped red onion

Combine the vinegar, oil, parsley, salt, and pepper in a large bowl. Add the kidney beans, black-eyed peas, chickpeas, bell pepper, and onion; toss to coat. Cover and refrigerate until chilled, about 2 hours.

*Per serving* 187 Calories, 6 g Total Fat, 1 g Saturated Fat, 0 mg Cholesterol, 423 mg Sodium, 25 g Total Carbohydrate, 7 g Dietary Fiber, 9 g Protein, 58 mg Calcium.

*POINTS per serving: 3.*

★ *American Way* Most bean salads can—and should—be prepared ahead of time; the marinating boosts the flavor. Roasted garlic vinegar can be found in large supermarkets or specialty food stores. To make your own, mix one large clove of roasted garlic into 1/3 cup vinegar.

# Corn Timbales with Vegetables and Cheese

## MAKES 6 SERVINGS

*Wisconsin—where cheese making has a long, rich history—provides some of the finest milk in the world for its many cheese makers. German immigrants, who owned the majority of farmland during the mid-19th century, made a precursor to cottage cheese—pot cheese—which has a slightly drier texture.*

1 tablespoon unsalted butter

4 cups packed, cleaned and coarsely chopped kale

1 red bell pepper, seeded and chopped

1 small onion, chopped

1 (8$\frac{1}{2}$-ounce) can cream-style corn

1 cup egg whites (about 8 large) or egg substitute

1 cup fat-free cottage cheese

1 cup shredded low-fat mozzarella cheese

$\frac{1}{3}$ cup grated Parmesan cheese

$\frac{1}{3}$ cup all-purpose flour

$\frac{1}{4}$ teaspoon salt

$\frac{1}{4}$ teaspoon cayenne

1. Preheat the oven to 350°F. Spray a 6-cup muffin pan with non-stick spray. Melt the butter in a large nonstick skillet. Stir in the kale, bell pepper, and onion. Cover and cook until the kale is just wilted, about 5 minutes. Transfer the mixture to a large bowl and cool 10 minutes.

2. Combine the corn, egg whites, cottage cheese, mozzarella, Parmesan, flour, salt, and cayenne in a food processor and blend, stopping once to scrape down the sides. Stir the corn mixture into the kale mixture until well blended.

3. Spoon the mixture into the cups, filling each about $\frac{2}{3}$ full. Bake until puffed and a toothpick inserted in the timbale comes out clean, 30–35 minutes. Turn the timbales out of the pan, using a small knife to loosen sides if necessary. Cool timbales on wire rack 5 minutes.

*Per serving   212 Calories, 5 g Total Fat, 3 g Saturated Fat, 11 mg Cholesterol, 673 mg Sodium, 22 g Total Carbohydrate, 2 g Dietary Fiber, 20 g Protein, 237 mg Calcium.*

*POINTS per serving: 4.*

★ *American Way* To make these timbales really colorful combine chopped red and orange bell peppers; spinach can be substituted for the kale.

### FLASHBACK ›› 1973

The Chicago National Housewares Exposition is the site for the unveiling of the Cusinart food processor. Despite its hefty price tag ($140), food guru James Beard claims "it has changed my life."

# AMERICA'S DAIRY INDUSTRY

Any settler with enough land and resources owned at least one cow to provide milk for the family. Larger dairy farms were typically located at the outskirts of town to provide milk for city-dwellers. Through most of the 1800s, New York was the nation's leading dairy state, but by the turn of the century, Wisconsin became "America's Dairyland." By the late 19th century, home delivery made a consistent supply of milk possible and the "milk man" an icon of American culture. Today, Wisconsin dairies produce many of the European-style cheeses that were once unavailable in this country.

Although the technique of pasteurization had been available since approximately 1860, it was not introduced in the U.S. until 1895, and before that time, fresh milk safety was a serious problem. The health issues were of particular concern in large cities where milk was transported from smaller towns, and then ladled out of open cans from milk trucks, allowing more possibilities for contamination. In fact, it was milk's perishable nature and importance in the diet which prompted Gail Borden's invention of sweetened condensed milk. Patented in 1856, the product became an overnight success when it was used by the Union army during the Civil War.

# Rhubarb-Oatmeal Bars

## MAKES 9 SERVINGS

*The appearance of fresh ruby-red rhubarb in May signals Midwestern cooks that the season of locally grown fresh fruit is beginning. Celery-like rhubarb needs plenty of cooking time—and sugar—to become edible. It's eaten primarily stewed or in pies (an alternate name for rhubarb is pieplant).*

$1^1/2$ pounds rhubarb, cut into $^1/4$-inch–thick pieces

1 tablespoon grated orange zest

1 teaspoon minced peeled fresh ginger

$^2/3$ cup packed brown sugar

$^3/4$ cup all-purpose flour

$^3/4$ cup old-fashioned rolled oats

3 tablespoons unsalted butter, cut into small pieces

1 egg white, lightly beaten

$^1/4$ teaspoon salt

1. Preheat the oven to 350°F. Spray an 8-inch square baking pan with nonstick spray; set aside. Combine the rhubarb, orange zest, and ginger with $^1/3$ cup brown sugar in a $1^1/2$-quart baking dish. Bake, uncovered, until the rhubarb is very tender, about 35 minutes. Set aside to cool.

2. Combine the remaining $^1/3$ cup brown sugar with the flour, oats, butter, egg white, and salt in a bowl. Stir until the mixture resembles coarse crumbs. Pat half of the oat mixture evenly into the bottom of the pan. Spoon the rhubarb mixture evenly over the top. Sprinkle with the remaining oat mixture. Bake until the topping is firm and the filling is hot, about 45 minutes. Cool in the pan on a rack 10 minutes. Cut into nine $2^1/2$-inch bar cookies; store in an airtight container for up to 3 days.

*Per serving  185 Calories, 5 g Total Fat, 3 g Saturated Fat, 11 mg Cholesterol, 81 mg Sodium, 33 g Total Carbohydrate, 3 g Dietary Fiber, 3 g Protein, 87 mg Calcium.*

*POINTS per serving: 4.*

★ *American Way*  Although you may be tempted to add more sugar to this recipe, don't. Cooked rhubarb should have a slightly acidic and pleasantly bitter edge. Too much sugar will mask the fruit's complex flavor.

# Dutch Apple Pie

### MAKES 10 SERVINGS

*Dutch settlements once dotted the Midwest. One of the largest is now a city appropriately named Holland, Michigan. A community best known for its annual tulip festival and Dutch apple pie—we've created our own version of this sweet pie using puff pastry and nonfat sour cream, which gives it just enough rich flavor.*

1 sheet thawed frozen puff pastry

7 firm tart apples, peeled, cored, and thinly sliced (about 6 cups)

1 cup packed light brown sugar

3 tablespoons all-purpose flour

3/4 teaspoon cinnamon

1/4 cup nonfat sour cream

1. Preheat the oven to 400°F. On a lightly floured counter, roll out the puff pastry to $1/8$-inch thickness. Trim the dough to 2 inches larger than an inverted 9-inch round pie plate; reserve the scraps for another use. Line the pie plate with the pastry. Flute the edge, and refrigerate 15 minutes.

2. Combine the apples, brown sugar, flour, and cinnamon in a saucepan. Cook, stirring occasionally, until the apples are just tender and the sauce thickens slightly, about 7 minutes. Remove the saucepan from the heat. Stir in the sour cream and allow to cool.

3. Pour the apple mixture into the pie shell. Bake until the crust browns and the filling is set, about 30 minutes. Cool completely on a rack.

*Per serving  240 Calories, 7 g Total Fat, 2 g Saturated Fat, 0 mg Cholesterol, 54 mg Sodium, 45 g Total Carbohydrate, 2 g Dietary Fiber, 2 g Protein, 34 mg Calcium.*

*POINTS per serving: 5.*

★ *American Way*  Firm, tart apples such as Jonathan, or Braeburn make a good choice for the pie.

FLASHBACK >> 1850

The number one apple variety, the Red Delicious, is discovered in Iowa.

# Tapioca Pudding with Mixed Fruit Compote

MAKES 6 SERVINGS

*Tapioca is a starch extracted from the root of the cassava plant. Homemakers traditionally made milk puddings with pearl tapioca, but it required long soaking and cooking, a time-consuming process for such a simple dish. Today, quick-cooking tapioca is used as a thickener for puddings and pies. This refreshing pudding is enhanced with dried fruit cooked in a vanilla bean syrup.*

1/2 cup + 51/2 tablespoons sugar

11/2 cups water

1 vanilla bean, split

1 (3 × 1-inch) strip lemon peel

1/2 cup dried apricots

1/2 cup pitted dried prunes

21/2 cups fat-free milk

1/4 cup quick-cooking tapioca

2 large egg whites, or 1/4 cup egg substitute

1. Combine 1/2 cup sugar, the water, vanilla bean, and lemon peel in a saucepan. Bring to a boil; boil 1 minute. Reduce the heat to low and stir in the apricots and prunes. Cover and simmer until the fruit is softened and the mixture thickens to a syrup, about 10 minutes. Remove the saucepan from the heat and set aside to cool completely. Discard the vanilla bean and lemon peel.

2. Combine 51/2 tablespoons sugar, the milk, tapioca, and egg whites in a saucepan. Let stand 5 minutes, then heat to a boil over medium heat. Cook, stirring constantly, 5–7 minutes. Remove the saucepan from the heat and stir in 1 teaspoon of the dried fruit syrup. Set aside to cool, about 30 minutes. The pudding will thicken as it cools.

3. Drain the fruit, reserving the syrup. Coarsely chop the fruit. Spoon half of the pudding into a small serving bowl. Layer half of the fruit mixture over the top. Repeat layering with the remaining pudding and fruit. Cover and refrigerate until ready to serve. Refrigerate the syrup in a separate container. Drizzle the pudding with the syrup and serve.

*Per serving (about 3/4 cup): 228 Calories, 0 g Total Fat, 0 g Saturated Fat, 2 mg Cholesterol, 71 mg Sodium, 53 g Total Carbohydrate, 2 g Dietary Fiber, 5 g Protein, 140 mg Calcium.*

*POINTS per serving: 4.*

★ *American Way* Don't be concerned if the tapioca doesn't appear more pudding-like. It will thicken as it cools. Try the syrup as a topping for other fruit desserts or stirred into plain yogurt.

# Pumpkin Custard with Caramelized Pecans

## MAKES 8 SERVINGS

*Pumpkins were just one of the many foods Native Americans introduced to European settlers in the early 1600s. Although available fresh from early fall through late winter, most American home cooks prefer the convenience of canned pumpkin, reserving the fresh variety mostly for carving Halloween jack-o'-lanterns and toasting their seeds. We've added rich-tasting pecans to the custard because pecan trees, though long associated with the South, were also cultivated by pioneers who settled Ohio in the 18th century.*

1/3 cup sugar

2 tablespoons water

1 cup pecan halves, coarsely chopped

2 cups low-fat (1%) milk

1/2 teaspoon cinnamon

1/4 teaspoon ground cardamom

1/4 teaspoon ground cloves

1/2 cup packed light brown sugar

4 large eggs

2 egg whites

2/3 cup canned solid-pack pumpkin

1 teaspoon vanilla extract

1. Preheat the oven to 350°F. Arrange eight 6-ounce custard cups in a large roasting pan.

2. Combine the sugar and water in a saucepan; bring to a boil. Cook, without stirring, until the sugar turns a light caramel color, about 5 minutes. Stir in the pecans and toss to coat. Cook until the mixture is a dark caramel color, about 3 minutes more. Quickly pour the pecan mixture onto a large nonstick baking sheet and cool completely on a rack. Break nut mixture into small pieces and sprinkle into the custard cups. Set aside.

3. Combine the milk, cinnamon, cardamom, and cloves in a saucepan and bring to a boil. Cook, stirring occasionally, 2 minutes. Whisk the brown sugar, eggs, and egg whites in a large bowl. Whisk the hot milk mixture into the egg mixture. Stir in the pumpkin and vanilla. Ladle the mixture into the custard cups.

4. Place the roasting pan in the oven, then pour enough hot water into the pan to come halfway up the sides of the custard cups. Bake until a toothpick inserted in the center of the custards comes out clean, about 30 minutes. Remove the cups from the roasting pan and cool on a rack. Cover and refrigerate at least 4 hours before serving.

*Per serving   249 Calories, 12 g Total Fat, 2 g Saturated Fat, 109 mg Cholesterol, 83 mg Sodium, 29 g Total Carbohydrate, 2 g Dietary Fiber, 7 g Protein, 112 mg Calcium.*

*POINTS per serving: 6.*

*Pumpkin Custard with Caramelized Pecans*

# Sour Cherry–Maple Topping

MAKES 2 CUPS

*In 1852, a missionary planted the first cherry orchard in Michigan on a narrow strip of land that juts out into Grand Traverse Bay just north of Traverse City. It proved to be an ideal growing area, due to Lake Michigan's help in tempering the climate. Today, 75 percent of America's cherries are harvested in Michigan each year. Tart cherries are traditionally used in pies and other desserts, but this versatile fruit topping has many uses. Try it warm or at room temperature, as a topping for cakes, frozen yogurt, shortcake biscuits, even roast turkey or ham.*

1/3 cup berry flavored fruit juice blend
    (100% fruit)

2 tablespoons cornstarch

1 cup pitted fresh or thawed frozen tart
    cherries

3/4 cup pure maple syrup

1/4 teaspoon ground nutmeg

1/3 cup slivered almonds

Whisk together the juice and cornstarch in a small saucepan until smooth. Stir in the cherries, maple syrup, and nutmeg; bring to a boil and cook, stirring occasionally, until the mixture thickens slightly, about 5 minutes. Stir in the almonds. Refrigerate, in an airtight container for up to 2 weeks.

*Per serving* (2 tablespoons): 66 Calories, 1 g Total Fat, 0 g Saturated Fat, 0 mg Cholesterol, 2 mg Sodium, 13 g Total Carbohydrate, 0 g Dietary Fiber, 1 g Protein, 18 mg Calcium.

*POINTS per serving: 1.*

# Cranberry–Black Walnut Breakfast Bread

## MAKES 12 SERVINGS

*The southwest portion of Missouri is home to "black gold," more commonly known as black walnuts. These walnuts have a pronounced earthy flavor and pair well with Wisconsin cranberries. Try this savory-but-still-sweet bread for breakfast, or as an afternoon snack with a cup of tea or coffee. The bread keeps very well—up to three days, tightly wrapped.*

2 cups all-purpose flour

3/4 cup sugar

1 1/2 teaspoons baking powder

1/2 teaspoon baking soda

1/2 teaspoon salt

1/4 teaspoon ground allspice

1/4 teaspoon ground ginger

2 egg whites, lightly beaten

1/4 cup vegetable oil

2 teaspoons grated orange zest

3/4 cup orange juice

1 cup coarsely chopped fresh or thawed
frozen cranberries

1/3 cup coarsely chopped black walnuts,
or regular walnuts

1. Preheat the oven to 375°F. Spray a nonstick 8 1/2-inch loaf pan with nonstick spray.

2. Sift the flour, sugar, baking powder, baking soda, salt, allspice, and ginger into a large bowl. Whisk the egg whites, oil, orange zest, and juice together in another bowl. Add the egg white mixture to the flour mixture; stir just until blended. Fold in the cranberries and walnuts. Scrape the batter into the loaf pan. Bake until the loaf begins to pull away from the edges of the pan and a toothpick inserted in the center comes out clean, 50–55 minutes. Cool on a rack.

*Per serving   199 Calories, 7 g Total Fat, 1 g Saturated Fat, 0 mg Cholesterol, 209 mg Sodium, 31 g Total Carbohydrate, 1 g Dietary Fiber, 4 g Protein, 18 mg Calcium.*

*POINTS per serving: 4.*

★ *American Way*  Black walnuts are available from Hammons Pantry, 800-872-6879.

# Oatmeal Loaf with Raisins and Molasses

## MAKES 12 SERVINGS

*The United States is the world's leading producer of oats, which are grown principally in Iowa, Minnesota, Illinois, and Wisconsin. Most of the oat crop is used to feed animals, the remainder goes to make breakfast cereals. Molasses, the sweetener of choice in the 19th century, was routinely used in cakes, cookies, and candies. At the end of World War I, however, sugar prices dropped and so did the popularity of molasses. Today, it is used more as a flavor-enhancer rather than a sweetener. We've included these two American products in a home-style loaf.*

2 cups all-purpose flour

1/2 cup whole-wheat flour

1 1/2 cups old-fashioned rolled oats

1 cup raisins

1 teaspoon baking soda

1 teaspoon salt

1 1/2 cups low-fat buttermilk

1/4 cup molasses

1 egg white

1. Preheat the oven to 375°F. Spray a 9-inch loaf pan with nonstick spray.

2. Combine the all-purpose and whole-wheat flours, the oats, raisins, baking soda, and salt a bowl. Whisk together the buttermilk, molasses, and egg white in another bowl. Stir the buttermilk mixture into the flour mixture just until blended. Pour the batter into the loaf pan.

3. Bake until golden and a toothpick inserted in center comes out clean, about 45 minutes. Cool in the pan on a rack 10 minutes; remove from the pan and cool completely on the rack.

*Per serving   236 Calories, 2 g Total Fat, 0 g Saturated Fat, 1 mg Cholesterol, 340 mg Sodium, 48 g Total Carbohydrate, 4 g Dietary Fiber, 8 g Protein, 71 mg Calcium.*

*POINTS per serving: 4.*

★ *American Way*  This bread is great toasted for breakfast (try it with melted butter or fresh fruit spread) or as a midday pick-me-up.

### FLASHBACK >> 1897

Farmer Jerome Smucker creates an apple butter that his wife sells from the back of her wagon in Orrville, Ohio. J.M. Smucker Co., one of the country's largest makers of jellies, jams, and preserves, is born.

# Onion-Dill Potato Rolls

MAKES 10 SERVINGS

*Potato bread and rolls have been popular in the Midwest ever since northern Europeans settled in the region. The pace of farm life dictated that the largest meal was eaten at midday. It was a family-style dinner that almost always included mashed potatoes. Frugal farm wives learned to make new dishes, such as these rolls, out of leftover potatoes. It was flavorful, as well as thrifty, because mashed potatoes lend a moist texture to the rolls, while buttermilk produces a rich, tender crumb.*

1 red potato, cubed
1 small onion, chopped
1 cup water
1 cup low-fat buttermilk
1/4 cup chopped fresh dill
1 tablespoon vegetable oil
1 egg white
1 tablespoon sugar
1 teaspoon salt
1 (1/4-ounce) packet active dry yeast
4 3/4 cups all-purpose flour

1. Combine the potato, onion, and water in a small saucepan; bring the water to a boil. Reduce the heat, cover, and simmer until potato is very soft, about 10 minutes. Drain, reserving 1/4 cup of the water. Return the potato to the saucepan and mash until smooth. Stir in the buttermilk, dill, oil, egg white, sugar, and salt.

2. Put the reserved potato water in a small bowl, let cool (105°–115°), and sprinkle in the yeast and let stand until foamy, about 5 minutes. Whisk the yeast mixture into the potato mixture.

3. Place 4 1/2 cups of the flour into a food processor. With the machine running, scrape the potato mixture through the feed tube. After the dough forms a ball, continue processing 5 minutes to knead. Turn out the dough on a lightly floured surface; knead until the dough is smooth and elastic, about 5 minutes.

4. Spray a large bowl with nonstick spray; put the dough in the bowl. Cover tightly with plastic wrap and let the dough rise at room temperature until it doubles in size, about 1 hour.

5. Preheat the oven to 375°F. Spray two 9-inch round cake pans with nonstick spray.

6. Punch the dough down and divide it into twenty 2-inch balls. Arrange 10 balls in each pan. Cover the pans and let the dough rise until nearly doubled, 30–40 minutes. Bake until the rolls are golden brown, about 25 minutes. Cool the rolls in the pans on racks 10 minutes. Pull apart to separate the rolls. Serve warm.

*Per serving (2 rolls): 262 Calories, 2 g Total Fat, 0 g Saturated Fat, 1 mg Cholesterol, 266 mg Sodium, 52 g Total Carbohydrate, 2 g Dietary Fiber, 8 g Protein, 42 mg Calcium.*

*POINTS per serving: 5.*

## FLASHBACK >> 1904

It's a popular year for food at the St. Louis exposition: German immigrants based in Missouri have a hit on their hands with the fried, chopped beef sandwich, or hamburger, while a new health food, peanut butter, is marketed as a food for the elderly. The St. Louis Exposition is the first time hamburger steak appears in print, according to James Villas in *American Taste* (1982). But the earliest spotting of the hamburger may be Delmonico's restaurant in New York. Chef Louis Szathmáry contends an 1836 menu carried this item.

*chapter four*
# Plains

**SALADS**

Cucumber Salad

Warm Spinach Salad

**ENTRÉES**

Smoked Fish Hash

Herbed Chicken and Dumplings

Braised Pheasant

Kansas City Steak Salad

Barbecued Beef

Cowboy Steak

Bison Steaks à la Russe

Bison Diane

Venison and Cabbage

**SIDES**

Roasted Corn with Chive Butter

Bread and Butter Pickles

Steakhouse Fries

Amaranth and Spinach Soufflé

Stagecoach Beans

Russian Cheese Pockets

Chili Sauce

**DESSERTS/SNACKS/BREADS**

Apricot Roll-Ups

Sunflower Seed–Plum Upside-Down Cake

Turkey Jerky

Multi-Grain Bread

Cherokee Bread

Country Loaf

# Cucumber Salad

MAKES 4 SERVINGS

*The zesty dill–caraway seed vinaigrette in this crunchy salad reflects the influence of Danish settlers in South Dakota. Short, crisp Kirby cucumbers, the type commonly used for making pickles, are abundant in the Plains states. For a more traditional Danish dish, substitute boiled or roasted beets for the cucumbers.*

1 pound Kirby cucumbers, peeled and thinly sliced

1 small red onion, minced

1 teaspoon caraway seeds

2 tablespoons light sour cream

2 tablespoons light mayonnaise

1 tablespoon rice vinegar

2 garlic cloves, minced

2 tablespoons chopped fresh dill

1/4 teaspoon coarse salt

1/4 teaspoon freshly ground pepper

Combine the cucumbers, onion, and caraway seeds in a mixing bowl. Stir in the sour cream, mayonnaise, and vinegar, then stir in the garlic, dill, salt, and pepper. Cover and refrigerate 45–60 minutes before serving.

*Per serving* 60 Calories, 3 g Total Fat, 1 g Saturated Fat, 3 mg Cholesterol, 203 mg Sodium, 7 g Total Carbohydrate, 1 g Dietary Fiber, 1 g Protein, 35 mg Calcium.

*POINTS per serving: 1.*

★ *American Way* Kirbies can have a somewhat tougher skin than other varieties and are usually peeled if used uncooked; however, they are seedless and retain their crisp texture even after cooking.

# Warm Spinach Salad

MAKES 8 SERVINGS

*This classic salad, studded with bacon and blue cheese, is a staple in steakhouses throughout the Plains, but try it alongside grilled or broiled chicken.*

1 (10-ounce) bag triple-washed spinach, rinsed and torn

1 small red onion, thinly sliced

4 radishes, thinly sliced

4 slices turkey bacon, cooked and crumbled

1/4 cup + 2 tablespoons honey

2 teaspoons Dijon mustard

1/4 cup + 2 tablespoons red-wine vinegar

2 tablespoons crumbled blue cheese

1. Combine the spinach, onion, radishes, and bacon in a salad bowl.

2. Warm the honey and mustard in a small nonstick skillet until liquefied, about 2 minutes. Stir in the vinegar and cook until steaming, about 1 minute. Pour the dressing over the salad, toss to coat, and sprinkle with the blue cheese.

*Per serving* 98 Calories, 3 g Total Fat, 1 g Saturated Fat, 9 mg Cholesterol, 231 mg Sodium, 16 g Total Carbohydrate, 1 g Dietary Fiber, 4 g Protein, 63 mg Calcium.

*POINTS per serving: 2.*

★ *American Way* For perfectly crisp and crumbly turkey bacon, cut each strip in half lengthwise, place on a baking sheet, and bake for 10 minutes in a 425°F oven. If you like, red or green leaf lettuce makes a tasty stand-in for the spinach.

# Smoked Fish Hash

MAKES 4 SERVINGS

*Smoking whitefish (the fish are abundant in the lakes and streams of North Dakota) is an easy and delicious way to prepare this mild-flavored member of the salmon family. A drive through the northern Plains, a large producer of commercially smoked fish, reveals a landscape dotted with smokehouses from Lake Superior on up. Serve this hash the traditional way: paired with poached eggs and chili sauce.*

1½ teaspoons vegetable oil

1 white onion, finely chopped

2 parsnips, peeled and finely chopped

2 carrots, peeled and finely chopped

⅓ cup chopped green bell pepper

2 (6-ounce) smoked whitefish, skinned and boned (or ½ pound smoked whitefish fillets, flaked)

¾ cup low-fat buttermilk

¼ cup water

2 tablespoons chopped cilantro

¼ teaspoon green hot pepper sauce

¼ teaspoon freshly ground pepper

⅛ teaspoon salt

Heat a large skillet. Swirl in the oil, then add the onion. Sauté until the onion is just beginning to brown, about 7 minutes. Add the parsnips, carrots, and bell pepper and sauté until the parsnips are tender, 9–10 minutes. Stir in the fish, buttermilk, water, cilantro, pepper sauce, pepper, and salt. Cover and cook until thickened and heated through, 5–6 minutes.

*Per serving  237 Calories, 9 g Total Fat, 2 g Saturated Fat, 60 mg Cholesterol, 386 mg Sodium, 15 g Total Carbohydrate, 3 g Dietary Fiber, 24 g Protein, 126 mg Calcium.*

*POINTS per serving: 5.*

★ *American Way*  We use whitefish, but almost any smoked seafood, including trout, tuna, and scallops, can be used.

# Herbed Chicken and Dumplings

## MAKES 6 SERVINGS

*Chicken and dumplings are farmhouse cooking at its best. A legacy of the German population that settled the Plains, variations on the dish are served in diners throughout the area. In this rendition, the chicken is seasoned with sprigs of thyme and the dumplings get a dash of rosemary.*

1 tablespoon vegetable oil

1 large white onion, cut into chunks

4 garlic cloves, minced

2–3 celery stalks, cut into chunks

4 carrots, peeled and cut into chunks

4 cups low-sodium chicken broth

2 sprigs fresh thyme

1 1/2 teaspoons chopped fresh parsley

1/4 teaspoon freshly ground pepper

6 (1/2-pound) bone-in skinned chicken breasts

1 large egg

1/3 cup fat-free milk

1 1/2 teaspoons baking powder

3/4 teaspoon chopped fresh rosemary

2 cups all-purpose flour

1 teaspoon cornstarch dissolved in 1 tablespoon water

1. Heat the oil in a nonstick Dutch oven, then add the onion and garlic. Sauté until the onion begins to turn translucent, about 3 minutes. Stir in the celery, carrots, broth, thyme, parsley, and pepper. Add the chicken and bring to a boil. Reduce the heat, cover, and simmer until the chicken is cooked through, about 30 minutes. Transfer the chicken to a plate and cover to keep warm.

2. Whisk the egg and milk in a mixing bowl until frothy. Whisk in the baking powder, rosemary, and 1 cup of the flour. Stir in the remaining 1 cup flour to create a thick batter.

3. Bring the broth to a simmer over high heat. Drop about 1/3 cup of the batter for each dumpling into the broth, and cook 7 minutes, then carefully turn the dumplings over. Cover and cook until the dumplings are light and fluffy, about 7 minutes more. Remove the dumplings and keep warm. Stir the dissolved cornstarch into the broth and vegetables and cook, stirring constantly, until thickened, about 2 minutes. Serve the chicken breast with the dumplings and vegetable sauce.

*Per serving  402 Calories, 7 g Total Fat, 2 g Saturated Fat, 120 mg Cholesterol, 340 mg Sodium, 42 g Total Carbohydrate, 3 g Dietary Fiber, 42 g Protein, 152 mg Calcium.*

*POINTS per serving: 8.*

★ *American Way*  This recipe can be made in advance. To do so, prepare the recipe to the end of step 1. Cover and refrigerate for up to 2 days; reheat before continuing.

## Pot Luck

With all the hardship the settlers faced, it's understandable that when pioneer families arrived to claim land in the Plains states with their possessions in a covered wagon, they welcomed any assistance they could get. Neighbors often gathered to help raise a cabin or barn, which created an occasion for a shared meal and an evening of celebration. In the course of a year, a variety of jobs—wells were dug, corn was harvested and husked, wheat was threshed—were completed more quickly with the help of many hands. These events were made festive, as cooks vied to bring the tastiest dishes, often earning their reputations based on the fried chicken, pies, breads, and preserves they brought along.

In addition, the churches in these pioneer communities rarely had a full-time minister, necessitating that pastors ride from town to town to care for many churches. This practice, too, created a fine excuse for a social occasion, since the church congregation was responsible for housing and feeding the visiting clergyman. Typically, each family donated some of the food and paid a small price to attend. While everyone enjoyed the food and revelry, the money raised became the minister's salary.

Weddings that took place in these communities were shared affairs, too. Each guest was expected to bring food and a cake layer, which would be used to create the wedding cake. At the location of the feast, the cake was assembled by frosting each guest's layer together with applesauce, resulting in a "stack cake."

Today, the spirit of cooperation that began with the pioneers, can still be seen in the "pot luck" or "covered dish" suppers enjoyed by community organizations and church congregations from coast to coast.

# Braised Pheasant

*Wild pheasant, abundant in the Upper Plains, is one of the more popular game birds. Wild or farm-raised pheasant is lean and braises nicely. You could also make the casserole using meatier birds, like chicken or Cornish game hens.*

2 tablespoons all-purpose flour

1/4 teaspoon hot paprika

1/4 teaspoon garlic powder

1/4 teaspoon salt

2-pounds pheasant, quartered and skinned

1 1/2 teaspoons olive oil

1/4 pound boiling onions, peeled

1/4 pound white mushrooms, quartered

3 garlic cloves, minced

1/4 cup dry white wine

1 (10-ounce) can tomatoes and green chiles

1 (15-ounce) can great Northern beans, rinsed and drained

1/2 cup low-sodium chicken broth

1/2 teaspoon grated lemon zest

3 sprigs fresh thyme

1 sprig fresh rosemary

1. Combine the flour, paprika, garlic powder, and salt in a shallow dish or pie pan. Dredge the pheasant quarters in the mixture, coating them evenly; shake off the excess.

2. Heat a nonstick Dutch oven over medium-high heat. Swirl in the olive oil, then add the pheasant, and cook until browned, 4–5 minutes each side. Transfer to a plate and keep warm.

3. Add the onions, mushrooms, and garlic to the Dutch oven and sauté until they just begin to brown, 1–2 minutes. Add the wine and boil 1 minute, scraping up the browned bits from the pan. Stir in the tomatoes and chiles, the beans, broth, lemon zest, thyme, and rosemary. Return the pheasant to the pan and bring to a boil. Reduce the heat, cover, and simmer until the pheasant is cooked through, about 1 hour.

*Per serving  439 Calories, 10 g Total Fat, 3 g Saturated Fat, 150 mg Cholesterol, 761 mg Sodium, 25 g Total Carbohydrate, 7 g Dietary Fiber, 61 g Protein, 100 mg Calcium.*

*POINTS per serving: 8.*

★ *American Way*  Look for canned tomatoes and green chiles in your market's Latin or Mexican foods section. If using smaller, wild birds simply weigh the birds for a total of two pounds, then split them, rather than cutting them into quarters.

# Kansas City Steak Salad

MAKES 4 SERVINGS

*Variously called New York strip, Delmonico, or shell steak in different regions, Kansas City strip steak is a very flavorful, tender cut of beef. For the authentic Kansas City preparation, choose a steak at least 1 1/2 inches thick.*

1 teaspoon lemon pepper

1/4 teaspoon freshly ground pepper

1 (1-pound) Kansas City strip steak

1 (8-ounce) package mixed greens, rinsed

1/4 pound steamed green beans, halved

4 radishes, thinly sliced

1 (10-ounce) can artichoke hearts, rinsed and drained

1/4 cup light mayonnaise

1 tablespoon red-wine vinegar

1 teaspoon Worcestershire sauce

1 teaspoon Dijon mustard

1 teaspoon anchovy paste

2 teaspoons snipped fresh chives

1. Mix together the lemon pepper and ground pepper in a small bowl, Rub the mixture all over the steak and let stand 15 minutes.

2. Heat a heavy skillet over medium heat. Add the steak and sear until done to taste, about 6 minutes on each side for medium-rare. Transfer to a cutting board and let stand 5 minutes before slicing thinly.

3. Meanwhile, combine the greens, beans, radishes, and artichoke hearts in a large mixing bowl. Combine the mayonnaise, vinegar, Worcestershire sauce, mustard, anchovy paste, and chives in a small bowl. Pour all but 2 tablespoons of the dressing over the salad and toss to coat.

4. Divide the salad among 4 dinner plates, evenly divide the steak slices on top, and spoon about 1/2 tablespoon of the reserved dressing over each.

*Per serving  326 Calories, 19 g Total Fat, 7 g Saturated Fat, 51 mg Cholesterol, 320 mg Sodium, 13 g Total Carbohydrate, 5 g Dietary Fiber, 27 g Protein, 72 mg Calcium.*

*POINTS per serving: 7.*

★ *American Way*  The steak is tastiest when crusty on the outside and still a bit pink inside—best achieved at home by searing in a heavy skillet.

*Kansas City Steak Salad*

# Barbecued Beef

## MAKES 8 SERVINGS

*In diners across the Southern Plains, barbecued beef is slow-smoked for hours, sliced, and then cooked for hours longer in a pungent sauce. Oven-baking a brisket reduces the preparation time and yields meat which is so tender that it need only be warmed in the sauce. Serve the slices whole, or shred the beef for sandwiches.*

1 tablespoon chili powder

1 teaspoon dried oregano

1 teaspoon garlic powder

1/2 teaspoon salt

1/8 teaspoon freshly ground pepper

1/8 teaspoon cayenne

1 (2-pound) beef brisket, trimmed of all visible fat

1/2 cup water

1 (8-ounce) can tomato sauce

1/4 cup blackberry preserves

2 tablespoons triple-sec or other orange liqueur, or orange juice

2 tablespoons cider vinegar

2 teaspoons mesquite-flavored liquid smoke

1. Preheat the oven to 325°F. Line a 10 × 15-inch baking dish with a very large piece of foil, leaving a 9-inch overhang on each short end.

2. Combine the chili powder, oregano, garlic powder, salt, pepper, and cayenne in a small bowl. Rub the mixture all over the brisket. Place in the baking dish, add the water, and fold the foil over the brisket securely to enclose. Bake until tender, about 2 hours. Transfer the brisket to a cutting board and thinly slice.

3. Skim the fat from the cooking liquid and discard. Pour the cooking liquid into a large skillet. Add the tomato sauce, preserves, triple-sec, vinegar, and liquid smoke. Cook, stirring constantly, until the preserves melt, and the sauce is steaming, 3–4 minutes. Add the sliced brisket, turn to coat the slices all over, and heat through.

*Per serving* 218 Calories, 9 g Total Fat, 3 g Saturated Fat, 70 mg Cholesterol, 453 mg Sodium, 11 g Total Carbohydrate, 1 g Dietary Fiber, 24 g Protein, 19 mg Calcium.

*POINTS per serving:* 5.

---

FLASHBACK >> 1921

Sleepy Wichita, Kansas is the site of the first White Castle hamburger stand.

# Cowboy Steak

## MAKES 4 SERVINGS

*A chuckwagon staple on long cattle drives, cowboy steak—also known as chicken-fried steak or country-fried steak—is a classic recipe found throughout the South, Southwest, and Midwest. The centerpiece of the traditional dish is a thin slice of beef that is heavily breaded, deep-fried, and then smothered with a thick gravy. We've lightened it up by baking instead of frying the meat and making a fat-free gravy. Feel free to substitute thin pieces of pork or chicken for the sirloin.*

2/3 cup + 2 tablespoons all-purpose flour

1 tablespoon garlic salt

1/2 teaspoon freshly ground pepper

1 large egg

1 1/2 teaspoons Worcestershire sauce

4 (1/4-pound) thin-cut beef round sirloin steaks

1/2 cup low-sodium beef broth

1/2 cup fat-free milk

1/4 teaspoon chopped fresh rosemary

1/4 teaspoon salt

1. Place a heavy nonstick baking sheet in the oven and preheat the oven to 475°F.

2. Combine 2/3 cup flour, the garlic salt, and pepper in a shallow plate or pie pan. Lightly beat the egg with the Worcestershire sauce in a large shallow bowl. Dredge each steak into the flour mixture, shaking off excess, then dip into the egg mixture, and finally dredge in the flour mixture again.

3. Spray the heated baking sheet with nonstick spray. Set the steaks on the sheet, then spray the steaks. Bake 5 minutes. Turn the steaks over and bake until very well browned, about 5 minutes more.

4. Meanwhile, make the gravy by combining the broth and milk with 2 tablespoons flour in a medium saucepan. Add the rosemary and salt. Cook, stirring frequently, until thick and bubbling, 7–8 minutes. Season to taste with additional pepper, if you like. Serve the steaks topped with the gravy.

*Per serving (1 steak and about 2 tablespoons gravy): 284 Calories, 7 g Total Fat, 3 g Saturated Fat, 97 mg Cholesterol, 394 mg Sodium, 23 g Total Carbohydrate, 1 g Dietary Fiber, 30 g Protein, 60 mg Calcium.*

*POINTS per serving: 6.*

# Bison Steaks à la Russe

### MAKES 4 SERVINGS

*North Dakota is home to the descendants of Russian immigrants who were among the state's first European settlers. Commercial bison, now farm-raised in North Dakota and other Plains states, is low in fat and has a beefy flavor that makes it a favorite of many beef lovers. These bison steaks are quickly seared, then topped with onions and mushrooms in a stroganoff-style sauce.*

1/2 teaspoon ground thyme

1/4 teaspoon salt

1/4 teaspoon freshly ground pepper

2 (1/2-pound) bison strip steaks, cut in half

1/2 pound boiling onions, peeled and quartered

1/2 pound white mushrooms, quartered

3/4 cup low-sodium beef broth

1 teaspoon cornstarch

1 teaspoon Dijon mustard

1/8 teaspoon thyme leaves

1/4 cup light sour cream

1. Heat a large skillet. Combine the ground thyme, salt, and pepper in a small bowl and rub the mixture all over the steaks. Place the steaks in the hot skillet and sear until done to taste, about 2 minutes on each side for medium-rare. Transfer the steaks to a plate and keep warm.

2. Remove the skillet from the heat and add the onions and mushrooms. Spray the vegetables with nonstick spray. Return the skillet to the heat and sauté the vegetables until lightly browned. Combine the broth, cornstarch, mustard, and thyme in a small bowl, then add to the skillet. Simmer, stirring, until the sauce thickens and reduces slightly, about 3 minutes. Remove the skillet from the heat and whisk in the sour cream.

3. Serve the steaks with the vegetables and gravy on top.

*Per serving 199 Calories, 5 g Total Fat, 2 g Saturated Fat, 77 mg Cholesterol, 384 mg Sodium, 12 g Total Carbohydrate, 2 g Dietary Fiber, 28 g Protein, 45 mg Calcium.*

*POINTS per serving: 4.*

### FLASHBACK >> 1875

Buffalo herds—a longtime fixture of the western Plains and the major source of food, fuel, and clothing for Plains Indians—are dramatically reduced when hunters begin killing the animals for their hides. This year, President Grant vetoes a bill that would protect bison from extinction.

# Bison Diane

MAKES 4 SERVINGS

*You can substitute beef rib-eye steaks for the bison steaks, but cook the beef twice as long as the leaner, quicker-cooking buffalo. Bison is also higher in iron and lower in fat and cholesterol than beef.*

2 (9-ounce) rib-eye bison steaks, halved

1/4 teaspoon salt

1/4 teaspoon freshly ground pepper

2 tablespoons cognac

1/4 cup low-sodium beef broth

1 teaspoon all-purpose flour

1 teaspoon olive oil

1 scallion, white part only, thinly sliced

2 tablespoons dry red wine

1 garlic clove, minced

1/2 teaspoon Worcestershire sauce

1/2 teaspoon Dijon mustard

1/4 teaspoon grated lemon zest

1/4 cup low-fat buttermilk

2 teaspoons unsalted butter

1. Heat a large nonstick skillet. Rub the steaks all over with the salt and pepper. Place the steaks in the hot skillet and sear until done to taste, about 2 minutes on each side for medium-rare. Remove the pan from the heat, pour the cognac over the steaks and let stand until evaporated, 1–2 minutes. Transfer the steaks to a plate and keep warm.

2. Combine the broth and flour in a small bowl and whisk to blend. Swirl the oil into the skillet, then add the scallion. Sauté over high heat until the scallion just begins to brown, 20–30 seconds. Add the wine and stir, scraping up the browned bits from the bottom of the pan. Add the broth mixture, garlic, Worcestershire sauce, mustard, and lemon zest. Cook, stirring, until the sauce is thickened and clear, 1–2 minutes. Remove from the heat, stir in the buttermilk and butter, and continue to stir until the butter melts to form a creamy sauce, about 1 minute. Pour the sauce over the steaks and serve.

*Per serving 203 Calories, 6 g Total Fat, 2 g Saturated Fat, 85 mg Cholesterol, 300 mg Sodium, 3 g Total Carbohydrate, 0 g Dietary Fiber, 29 g Protein, 32 mg Calcium.*

*POINTS per serving: 5.*

★ *American Way* Because bison is so lean, take care to cook it just to medium-rare. If cooked to medium or beyond, it will toughen.

# Venison and Cabbage

MAKES 6 SERVINGS

*Venison was the chosen fare of the early Native Americans, who dried it by grilling it over a fire, then stored it to eat during the winter. Here, we combine venison with cabbage—a reflection of the Danish heritage of many of today's Plains inhabitants.*

1 small red onion, sliced

1 small red cabbage, shredded

1/4 cup water

1/4 cup balsamic vinegar

1/2 teaspoon caraway seeds

1 1/2 teaspoons freshly ground pepper

1 teaspoon salt

1 Granny Smith apple, cored and chopped

1/2 cup dried sour cherries or dried cranberries

1 tablespoon honey

2 teaspoons unsalted butter

1 1/2 pounds venison tenderloin, cut into 6 medallions

1. Spray a large nonstick skillet with nonstick spray and set over medium-high heat. Add the onion and sauté until translucent, about 4 minutes. Add the cabbage, water, vinegar, and caraway seeds, with 1/2 teaspoon of the pepper, and 1/2 teaspoon of the salt. Cover and cook 5 minutes. Stir in the apple, cherries, honey, and butter. Cover and set aside.

2. Heat another nonstick skillet. Rub the medallions all over with the remaining 1 teaspoon pepper and 1/2 teaspoon salt. Place the medallions in the skillet and sear until done to taste, 2–3 minutes on each side for medium-rare. Serve the venison with the cabbage.

*Per serving 209 Calories, 4 g Total Fat, 2 g Saturated Fat, 100 mg Cholesterol, 457 mg Sodium, 15 g Total Carbohydrate, 3 g Dietary Fiber, 28 g Protein, 63 mg Calcium.*

*POINTS per serving: 4.*

★ *American Way Venison* is a term used for the meat of elk, moose, and caribou, as well as of deer. If you can't find venison, try pork medallions.

FLASHBACK>>1946

Lincoln, Nebraska is the site of the first Runza restaurant. Owner Sally Everett trademarks the name and sells it namesake sandwich bun filled with ground meat, cabbage, and onion. In the 1960s, her son Don will create a chain of Runza drive-ins.

# Roasted Corn with Chive Butter

## MAKES 6 SERVINGS

*A favorite snack at state fairs across the Plains in the summertime, "roasted" corn is typically grilled on huge outdoor grills. Our indoor baking method eliminates the need to pre-soak the ears to prevent the husks from burning.*

6 ears fresh corn
2 tablespoons unsalted butter
1 teaspoon chopped fresh chives
1/8 teaspoon salt
1/8 teaspoon freshly ground pepper

1. Preheat the oven to 400°F. Pull the corn husks down but leave them intact. Remove the silk from the ears of corn. Lightly spray the kernels with nonstick spray, fold the husks back over the ears, and place the ears directly on the oven rack in the oven. Roast, turning the ears after 15 minutes, until tender, 30 minutes.

2. Combine the butter, chives, salt, and pepper in a small bowl. Remove the husks from the corn, spread 1 teaspoon of the butter over each ear, and serve.

*Per serving  117 Calories, 5 g Total Fat, 3 g Saturated Fat, 10 mg Cholesterol, 242 mg Sodium, 19 g Total Carbohydrate, 3 g Dietary Fiber, 3 g Protein, 3 mg Calcium.*

*POINTS per serving: 2.*

★ *American Way*  For easier serving, or if you prefer a subtler flavor, the butter can be rubbed over the ears before roasting.

## MAIZE

Maize may be the most important—and mystical—of the agricultural treasures discovered by Europeans upon arriving in this hemisphere. For example, explorer Christopher Columbus, the first European to taste corn, became so fascinated with the sweet kernels that when he returned home, he entertained listeners with his tales of the multi-colored grain.

Renamed "Indian corn" by European explorers ("corn" was a generic term for all grains), maize supported large populations of Native Americans and helped to insure survival for the arriving explorers and colonists. Although they approached many New World products with skepticism, the colonists welcomed corn into their diet, first out of necessity and, later, for the many delicious ways it could be prepared.

Over centuries of cultivation, Native American farmers established various techniques to improve the quality of the grain—such as fertilizing their corn crops by planting a fish along with the seeds. In addition, they supplemented corn's nutritional inadequacies by cooking it with a pinch of ash (to release the niacin) and eating it with beans and squash (to provide missing essential amino acids.) For the Native Americans who farmed it, corn was not just something to eat: it was revered for its role in their survival. In fact, the meaning ascribed to the word maize was "our life."

# Bread and Butter Pickles

## MAKES 4 SERVINGS

*Zucchini, popular and plentiful in the Plains from late summer into the fall, replaces the more typical pickling cucumber (the Kirby) in this sweet-sour pickle. Bread and butter pickles are usually hot-sealed, a time-consuming method of preserving. This simplified version, which will keep for weeks in the refrigerator, saves time and preserves extra crunch.*

1 cup white vinegar

1 cup sugar

1/4 cup water

1 1/2 teaspoons salt

1/2 teaspoon mustard seeds

1/4 teaspoon celery seeds

1/8 teaspoon crushed red pepper

2 (quarter-size) slices fresh ginger, peeled

1/2 pound zucchini, cut into 1/4-inch rounds

1 small white onion, thinly sliced

Bring the vinegar, sugar, water, salt, mustard seeds, celery seeds, crushed red pepper, and ginger to a boil in a medium nonreactive saucepan. Boil the mixture for 2 minutes, remove the pan from the heat, and stir in the zucchini and onion. Let cool slightly, then pour the mixture into a tight-sealing container, and cover. Cool to room temperature, then refrigerate at least 2 hours before serving.

*Per serving  211 Calories, 0 g Total Fat, 0 g Saturated Fat, 0 mg Cholesterol, 895 mg Sodium, 55 g Total Carbohydrate, 1 g Dietary Fiber, 1 g Protein, 63 mg Calcium.*

*POINTS per serving: 4.*

# Steakhouse Fries

## MAKES 4 SERVINGS

*Often called* steak fries *or* Texas fries, *big, thick fries are popular in steakhouses all over cattle country. Ours are healthier because they are oven-baked, rather than deep-fried in oil. The potatoes emerge from the oven, crisp on the outside, soft and fluffy inside. They make a perfect accompaniment to Kansas City Steak Salad (page 120).*

2 teaspoons chili powder
1 teaspoon garlic powder
1 teaspoon onion powder
1/2 teaspoon salt
2 large baking potatoes

1. Preheat the oven to 425°F.

2. Combine the chili powder, garlic powder, onion powder, and salt in a zip-close plastic bag. Cut each potato into 8 spears. Spray the spears with nonstick spray and add them to the bag. Seal the bag and shake to coat the potatoes.

3. Place the potatoes, skin-side down, on a baking sheet. Spray with nonstick spray and bake until fork-tender and well browned, about 25 minutes.

*Per serving* *81 Calories, 0 g Total Fat, 0 g Saturated Fat, 0 mg Cholesterol, 310 mg Sodium, 18 g Total Carbohydrate, 2 g Dietary Fiber, 2 g Protein, 13 mg Calcium.*

*POINTS per serving: 1.*

# Amaranth and Spinach Soufflé

## MAKES 8 SERVINGS

*Amaranth (pronounced AM-ah-ranth), a grain native to the northern Plains states, was long discarded as a weed. In recent years it has come to be valued for its slightly sweet flavor, versatility, and exceptionally high nutritional content. In fact, it is now cultivated and has become a significant component of the regional agricultural economy of the Plains.*

½ cup amaranth

1 cup low-sodium chicken broth

1 (10-ounce) box frozen chopped
    spinach, thawed and squeezed dry

2 large eggs, lightly beaten

½ cup low-fat buttermilk

½ cup fat-free milk

1 small yellow onion, minced

2 teaspoons Dijon mustard

1 teaspoon prepared horseradish

½ teaspoon salt

1. Bring the amaranth and broth to a boil in a small saucepan. Cover, reduce the heat, and simmer for 25 minutes.

2. Meanwhile, preheat the oven to 375°F. Spray a 1-quart casserole with nonstick spray. Combine the spinach, eggs, buttermilk, milk, onion, mustard, horseradish, and salt in a large bowl.

3. Uncover the saucepan and continue to cook, stirring constantly, until the amaranth is very thick. Stir the amaranth into the spinach mixture, then pour into the casserole. Bake until lightly browned and a toothpick inserted in the center comes out clean, 55–60 minutes. Remove the soufflé from the oven and let stand 5 minutes before serving.

*Per serving  94 Calories, 3 g Total Fat, 1 g Saturated Fat, 54 mg Cholesterol, 327 mg Sodium, 12 g Total Carbohydrate, 3 g Dietary Fiber, 6 g Protein, 106 mg Calcium.*

*POINTS per serving: 2.*

# Stagecoach Beans

MAKES 6 SERVINGS

*This is a quick and easy version of a baked bean dish, historically long-cooked in a cast-iron pot. The carbonated cola breaks down the beans to thicken as well as flavor the sauce—cherry-cola adds a particularly interesting accent, but any cola or caramel-colored soda can be used.*

2 (15-ounce) cans pinto beans,
    rinsed and drained

4 slices Canadian bacon, chopped

1/4 cup chopped white onion

1/2 cup ketchup

1/4 cup cherry-flavored cola

2 tablespoons jalapeño mustard

2 tablespoons Worcestershire sauce

2 tablespoons molasses

2 teaspoons balsamic vinegar

1 teaspoon hickory-flavored liquid smoke

1 teaspoon green hot pepper sauce

1 teaspoon celery salt

1/2 teaspoon ground cumin

1/4 teaspoon freshly ground pepper

Preheat the oven to 350°F. Combine all the ingredients in a 2-quart casserole. Cover and bake 30 minutes. Uncover and bake until the sauce is thick and the beans are browned on top, about 10 minutes longer.

*Per serving* 205 Calories, 3 g Total Fat, 1 g Saturated Fat, 10 mg Cholesterol, 1,100 mg Sodium, 35 g Total Carbohydrate, 7 g Dietary Fiber, 12 g Protein, 144 mg Calcium.

*POINTS per serving: 3.*

★ *American Way* If you can't find jalapeño mustard, use Dijon and add 1/4 teaspoon chopped jalapeño pepper.

# Russian Cheese Pockets

## MAKES 8 SERVINGS

*This traditional Slavic recipe reflects the large Ukrainian influence in Kansas. The pockets, called* beroggi, *are similar to Polish pierogis, and taste best when served with nonfat sour cream or applesauce on the side. This recipe uses Wonton wrappers, a convenient and readily available stand-in for homemade dough; prepared pie crust, thinly rolled out, can also be used.*

½ pound dry skim-milk farmer's cheese, grated

1 egg white

2 teaspoons chopped fresh chives

2 teaspoons chopped fresh dill

¼ teaspoon garlic powder

¼ teaspoon freshly ground pepper

32 round wonton wrappers

1. Preheat the oven to 425°F.

2. Combine the cheese, egg white, chives, dill, garlic powder, and pepper in a bowl. Mound about ½ tablespoon of the mixture in the center of a wonton wrapper. Moisten the rim of the wrapper with water, fold one side over the filling to enclose, and pinch the edges together to seal. Repeat to fill the remaining wrappers.

3. Place the pockets on a baking sheet, spray with nonstick spray, and bake for 3 minutes. Turn the pockets over, spray again, and bake until golden brown and crisp, about 3 minutes more.

*Per serving (4 pockets): 120 Calories, 1 g Total Fat, 0 g Saturated Fat, 5 mg Cholesterol, 194 mg Sodium, 19 g Total Carbohydrate, 1 g Dietary Fiber, 9 g Protein, 25 mg Calcium.*

*POINTS per serving: 2.*

# Chili Sauce

MAKES 8 SERVINGS

*A farmhouse condiment that preceded ketchup, chili sauce is chunkier and zestier but can be used in much the same way. Try it on everything from hash to hamburgers to oven fries. It contains sufficient vinegar to give it a refrigerator shelf life of one week.*

1 green bell pepper, seeded and cut into chunks

1 red bell pepper, seeded and cut into chunks

1 large celery stalk, cut into chunks

1 small white onion, cut into chunks

2 garlic cloves, peeled

1 (14¹/2-ounce) can diced tomatoes

1 (6-ounce) can tomato paste

1 (4-ounce) can diced green chiles

¹/4 cup packed dark brown sugar

3 tablespoons white vinegar

1 tablespoon yellow mustard

1 teaspoon salt

¹/2 teaspoon ground allspice

¹/2 teaspoon ground ginger

¹/2 teaspoon ground nutmeg

¹/2 teaspoon cinnamon

Finely chop the bell peppers, celery, onion, and garlic in a food processor. Transfer the vegetables to a large nonreactive saucepan. Add the tomatoes, tomato paste, chiles, brown sugar, vinegar, mustard, salt, allspice, ginger, nutmeg, and cinnamon. Bring the mixture to a boil and cook, stirring occasionally, until very thick, about 20 minutes. Let cool slightly, then pour the chili sauce into an airtight container. Refrigerate any leftovers for up to one week.

*Per serving (2 tablespoons): 78 Calories, 0 g Total Fat, 0 g Saturated Fat, 0 mg Cholesterol, 492 mg Sodium, 19 g Total Carbohydrate, 3 g Dietary Fiber, 2 g Protein, 48 mg Calcium.*

*POINTS per serving: 1.*

# Apricot Roll-Ups

MAKES 4 SERVINGS

*Also called fruit leathers, dried fruit roll-ups were an outdoor staple throughout the Plains long before they became popular lunch-box treats. For strawberry roll-ups, substitute 1 pint hulled strawberries for the apricots. Store in a zip-close plastic storage bag for up to 3 months.*

1½ teaspoons vegetable oil
1 pound apricots, pitted and chopped
1 tablespoon fresh lemon juice
1 tablespoon boiling water
1 tablespoon sugar
2 teaspoons cornstarch

1. Preheat the oven to 170°F (or between 150°F and 200°F on the oven dial). Coat an 11 × 15-inch nonstick jelly-roll pan with the oil.

2. Puree the apricots, lemon juice, water, and sugar in a food processor or blender. Pour the puree into the pan and spread evenly with a spatula, leaving a 1-inch border all around. Bake until dry and solid to the touch, 4–5 hours.

3. Line a wire rack with baker's parchment or wax paper and sprinkle with 1 teaspoon of the cornstarch. Peel the dried fruit from the pan, place on the parchment, and allow to cool completely. Sprinkle the remaining 1 teaspoon of cornstarch over the fruit and roll up. Rip off pieces as desired.

*Per serving (approximately 2 × 12-inch piece): 87 Calories, 2 g Total Fat, 0 g Saturated Fat, 0 mg Cholesterol, 3 mg Sodium, 17 g Total Carbohydrate, 3 g Dietary Fiber, 2 g Protein, 19 mg Calcium.*

*POINTS per serving: 1.*

# Sunflower Seed–Plum Upside-Down Cake

## MAKES 12 SERVINGS

*Fields of large, bright yellow sunflowers with dark, seed-filled centers cover the landscape of the Plains, where they were first grown by Indians. Although the sunflower is the state flower of Kansas, North Dakota is now the nation's largest producer. Pale yellow, delicately flavored sunflower seeds are sold either in or out of their shells; look for shelled seeds in health food stores.*

1/4 cup unsalted shelled sunflower seeds
4 tablespoons unsalted butter
1/3 cup packed dark brown sugar
3 purple plums, thinly sliced
1 1/2 cups cake flour
1 teaspoon baking powder
1/2 teaspoon baking soda
1/4 teaspoon salt
1 cup granulated sugar
3/4 cup low-fat buttermilk
1 large egg
1 egg white
1 1/2 teaspoons vanilla extract

1. Preheat the oven to 350°F. Lightly toast the sunflower seeds in a dry skillet over high heat, 2–3 minutes.

2. Melt 3 tablespoons butter in a medium skillet with an ovenproof handle. Stir in the brown sugar and cook, stirring, until the sugar melts. Remove the skillet from the heat and sprinkle with the toasted sunflower seeds. Arrange the plums on top in a circular pattern.

3. Combine the flour, baking powder, baking soda, and salt in a bowl. With an electric mixer on medium speed, cream the remaining 1 tablespoon butter and the granulated sugar in another bowl. Slowly pour in the buttermilk, then add the egg, egg white, and vanilla. Reduce the speed to low and mix in the flour mixture.

4. Pour the batter over the fruit, then put the skillet in the oven. Bake until the cake is firm to the touch and a toothpick inserted into the center comes out clean, 35–40 minutes. Run a small knife around the sides. Transfer the skillet to a rack and cool until the bottom of the pan is cool enough to touch. Carefully invert the cake onto a plate and cool completely.

*Per serving  206 Calories, 5 g Total Fat, 3 g Saturated Fat, 27 mg Cholesterol, 137 mg Sodium, 37 g Total Carbohydrate, 1 g Dietary Fiber, 3 g Protein, 45 mg Calcium.*

*POINTS per serving: 4.*

# Turkey Jerky

MAKES 8 SERVINGS

*Jerky keeps for months and is a convenient take-along snack, which makes it as popular with today's campers and backpackers as it was with early Plains trappers. Then, jerky was made by drying beef in the sun; our updated version features teriyaki-flavored turkey, slow-cooked in the oven.*

½ pound skinless turkey breast slices, sliced crosswise into strips

¼ cup low-sodium teriyaki sauce

½ teaspoon hickory-flavored liquid smoke

1. Preheat the oven to 170°F (or between 150°F and 200°F on the oven dial). Combine the turkey slices, teriyaki sauce, and liquid smoke in a mixing bowl and let stand 10 minutes.

2. Transfer the strips to a nonstick baking sheet in a single layer and bake for 4 hours, then turn the strips over and bake until leathery but not brittle, 2°4 hours longer. Store in zip-close plastic bags up to 6 months.

*Per serving  52 Calories, 0 g Total Fat, 0 g Saturated Fat, 18 mg Cholesterol, 754 mg Sodium, 4 g Total Carbohydrate, 1 g Dietary Fiber, 8 g Protein, 20 mg Calcium.*

*POINTS per serving: 1.*

# Multi-Grain Bread

## MAKES 12 SERVINGS

*This is a robust, dark loaf that reflects the Middle European heritage of many Nebraskans. Use it to make hearty meat sandwiches, like roast beef and turkey—perfect for lazy night suppers. Amaranth, one of the principal grains used in the bread, is very low in fat and a rich source of calcium, vitamins, and minerals. It is sold in bulk and has an extremely long shelf life.*

3 tablespoons amaranth

2/3 cup rye flour

2/3 cup whole-wheat flour

2/3 cup bread flour

1 teaspoon salt

1 (1/4-ounce) packet quick-rise yeast

2/3 cup hot (about 120°F) water

2 tablespoons molasses

1 tablespoon vegetable oil

1 tablespoon cornmeal

1 egg white, lightly beaten

1 1/2 tablespoons old-fashioned rolled oats

1. Heat a skillet until a drop of water sizzles. Sprinkle in 1 table-spoon of the amaranth and cook until the kernels puff, about 20 seconds; transfer to a food processor. Repeat 2 times with the remaining amaranth. Combine the rye, whole-wheat, and bread flours in a food processor. Add the salt and yeast.

2. Combine the water, molasses, and oil in a measuring cup. With the machine running, drizzle the mixture through the feed tube. After the dough forms a ball, continue processing until the ball has made 20 rotations.

3. Spray a large bowl with nonstick spray; place the dough into the bowl. Cover tightly with plastic wrap and let the dough rise in a warm place until it doubles in size, 45–55 minutes.

4. Punch down the dough and roll it into a 1 × 8-inch loaf. Dust a baking sheet with the cornmeal and place the loaf on top. Cover with a towel, and let the dough rise, a second time, in a warm spot until it doubles in size, about 45 minutes.

5. Preheat the oven to 350°F. Brush the loaf with the egg white and sprinkle with the oats. Bake until the loaf sounds hollow when tapped, 45–50 minutes. Remove the loaf from the baking sheet and cool on a rack.

*Per serving 111 Calories, 2 g Total Fat, 0 g Saturated Fat, 0 mg Cholesterol, 209 mg Sodium, 21 g Total Carbohydrate, 3 g Dietary Fiber, 4 g Protein, 48 mg Calcium.*

*POINTS per serving: 2.*

★ *American Way* Amaranth must be pre-cooked before it can be used in a recipe; here we simply "pop" it as you would popcorn. Despite its nutty flavor and pop-ability, stick with popcorn as a snack.

## AMERICA'S BREAD BASKET

Wheat had long been the staple grain for most settlers of Northern and Central European ancestry. But when planted on new soils, it proved unreceptive to life in the New World. First, New England farmers experienced years of meager wheat production due to the Hessian fly and, again, when settlers moved into the prairie—an area that at first seemed ideal for wheat fields—it performed poorly.

In 1870, however, German Mennonites who had been living in Russia arrived in Kansas with the seeds of a hard winter wheat known as Turkey Red, and finally helped to turn around wheat production's dismal performance in this country. Now, wheat thrived on the plains and within 20 years the area became America's "Wheat Bowl" or "Bread Basket."

Although the wheat problem was remedied, making a decent loaf of bread was still a trying task for a home cook: It was often difficult to get quality flour, the yeast had to be kept alive from the previous day's baking, the oven temperature was judged by the length of time you could keep your hand in its heat, and the resulting bread didn't stay fresh for very long. Yet, American cooks were expected to have an exceptional loaf of bread on the table at each meal—as well as be inventive conjuring up countless ways to use the stale loaves. It's no "wonder" homemakers gave up bread baking for several decades when big, soft, fluffy loaves of prepackaged sliced white bread appeared on the market just after World War I.

# Cherokee Bread

MAKES 4 SERVINGS

*The nomadic Cherokee Indians of Oklahoma prepared this bread over campfires. Traditionally deep-fried to make it puff, our version uses baking powder to make the bread rise up like a pita. Serve the bread plain or drizzled with honey as a dessert.*

1 cup all-purpose flour
1 1/2 teaspoons baking powder
1/2 teaspoon salt
1/2 cup minus 1 tablespoon water

1. Combine the flour, baking powder, and salt in a mixing bowl. Stir in the water to form a smooth dough. Gather the dough and cut it into 4 equal pieces. Cut each piece into 4 pieces and form each into a ball. Let rest for 20 minutes, turning the balls over after 10 minutes.

2. With lightly floured hands, flatten and work each ball into a thin 5-inch round.

3. Heat a large skillet or griddle pan until smoking. One at a time, cook each round in the skillet until well-browned, about 1 minute each side. Serve immediately.

*Per serving  123 Calories, 0 g Total Fat, 0 g Saturated Fat, 0 mg Cholesterol, 295 mg Sodium, 25 g Total Carbohydrate, 2 g Dietary Fiber, 4 g Protein, 11 mg Calcium.*

*POINTS per serving: 2.*

# Country Loaf

## MAKES 8 SERVINGS

*This classic farmhouse white bread is a good example of simple, yet versatile, Plains baking. Try the bread for toast, sandwiches, or to accompany dinner. The loaf has a crusty exterior and a soft, airy center. It's simply delicious— and bakes in just 30 minutes.*

3 cups bread flour
1 (¼-ounce) packet quick-rise yeast
2 tablespoons sugar
½ teaspoon salt
1 cup hot (about 120°F) water
2 tablespoons unsalted butter, melted

1. Combine the flour, yeast, sugar, and salt in a food processor. Turn the machine on and run for 1 minute to mix. With the machine running, drizzle the water through the feed tube. After the dough forms a ball, continue processing 45 seconds to knead.

2. Spray a large bowl with nonstick spray; place the dough in the bowl. Cover tightly with plastic wrap and let the dough rise in a warm place until it doubles in size, 35–40 minutes.

3. Spray an 8-inch loaf pan with nonstick spray. Punch down the dough, knead it a few times, and shape it into a loaf. Place it in the pan. Cover with a towel, and set aside for the dough to double again, 40–45 minutes.

4. Preheat the oven to 400°F. Bake the bread 10 minutes. With a sharp knife, make a slit down the center of the bread and drizzle with the butter. Return to the oven and bake until the loaf is well browned and sounds hollow when tapped, about 20 minutes longer. Remove the loaf from the pan and cool on a rack.

*Per serving (2 slices): 210 Calories, 3 g Total Fat, 2 g Saturated Fat, 8 mg Cholesterol, 148 mg Sodium, 39 g Total Carbohydrate, 1 g Dietary Fiber, 5 g Protein, 11 mg Calcium.*

*POINTS per serving: 4.*

★ *American Way* For a loaf with an herb or garlic flavor, add ½ tablespoon of any chopped fresh herb or 2 minced garlic cloves and ½ tablespoon grated Parmesan cheese to the melted butter.

## FLASHBACK >> 1896

Turkey Red wheat—a hearty, drought-resistant, and high yielding wheat first introduced in 1874 by German speaking Mennonites on their way to Kansas—becomes the predominate winter wheat crop of farmers throughout Kansas, Nebraska, Oklahoma, and Texas. Montana, Minnesota, and the Dakotas will plant Turkey Red in the spring for fall harvesting.

★

*chapter five*
# The South

## APPETIZERS/SOUPS/SALADS

Oysters Rockefeller

Pickled Shrimp

Peanut Soup

White Bean Soup

Warm Dandelion Salad

She-Crab Soup

## ENTRÉES

Hoppin' John

Ozark Barbecued Beans

Cornmeal-Fried Catfish

Fish Muddle

Kentucky Hot Brown

Oven-Fried Chicken

Country Ham and Red-Eye Gravy

Pork Barbecue

Frogmore Stew

Kentucky Burgoo

Brunswick Stew

## SIDES

Ramps and Grits

Yellow Squash Casserole

Fresh Peach Chutney

Low-Country Pilau

Spoonbread Soufflé

Hush Puppies

Peppery Cornsticks

## DESSERTS/SNACKS/BREADS

Moravian Spice Cookies

Pecan Lace Cookies

Pecan Bourbon Cake

Strawberry Shortcake

Lady Baltimore Cake

Lemon Chess Pie

Apple Stack Cake

Baked Apples in Phyllo Crust

Apple Cobbler

Sally Lunn

Benne Seed Wafers

Beaten Biscuits

Sweet Potato Biscuit

# Oysters Rockefeller

*Created at Antoine's restaurant in New Orleans in 1899, this classic dish was named after one of the wealthiest men in America at the time, John D. Rockefeller, because of its rich-tasting sauce. This streamlined version, though, is rich in taste, not calories.*

1 cup fat-free milk

1 tablespoon cornstarch

1/2 tablespoon unsalted butter

1 shallot, finely chopped

1/2 teaspoon salt

1/4 teaspoon freshly ground pepper

1 (10-ounce) box frozen chopped
    spinach, thawed and squeezed dry

1 tablespoon grated light Jarlsberg
    cheese

1 tablespoon chopped fresh tarragon

8 large oysters, scrubbed, shucked,
    and on the half shell

Lemon wedges

1. Preheat the oven to 450°F.

2. Combine the milk and the cornstarch in a bowl. Set aside. Melt the butter in a saucepan, then add the shallot. Cook, stirring, until softened, about 3 minutes. Stir in the milk mixture, salt, and pepper; bring to a boil. Remove the saucepan from the heat. Stir in the spinach, cheese, and tarragon; set aside.

3. Place the oysters in a baking pan and top each with about 2 tablespoons of the spinach mixture. Bake just until the oysters are heated through, about 10 minutes. Serve with lemon wedges.

*Per serving  (2 oysters): 99 Calories, 3 g Total Fat, 1 g Saturated Fat, 15 mg Cholesterol, 447 mg Sodium, 12 g Total Carbohydrate, 2 g Dietary Fiber, 7 g Protein, 237 mg Calcium.*

*POINTS per serving: 2.*

★ *American Way*  To shuck an oyster, hold it in a towel, large shell down, and insert an oyster knife between the shells at the hinge. Twist the knife to pry open the shell. Discard the top shell and loosen the oyster from the bottom shell with the tip of the knife, but don't remove the oyster from the shell.

# Pickled Shrimp

MAKES 8 SERVINGS

*Shrimping is a big industry in the U.S., especially the South. It's no wonder that shrimp rank as America's number-two favorite seafood (second only to canned tuna). These lemony shrimp, a favorite along the Southern coast, are great make-ahead nibbles for any gathering.*

1 pound large shrimp

1 cup white vinegar

1 cup water

2 garlic cloves, sliced

2 teaspoons coriander seeds

1 teaspoon mustard seeds

1 teaspoon black peppercorns

2 bay leaves

1/2 teaspoon crushed red pepper

1 lemon, cut in half

1/2 yellow bell pepper, seeded and thinly sliced

1 small red onion, thinly sliced

1 tablespoon olive oil

1 tablespoon chopped fresh parsley

1/4 teaspoon salt

4 leaves Boston lettuce

1. Cook the shrimp in a large pot of boiling water until cooked through, 2–3 minutes. Drain, then rinse under cold water until cool. Peel and de-vein the shrimp.

2. To make the marinade, combine the vinegar, water, garlic, coriander seeds, mustard seeds, peppercorns, bay leaves, and crushed red pepper in a saucepan. Bring the marinade to a boil. Reduce the heat and simmer 5 minutes. Set aside to cool 15 minutes.

3. Thinly slice 1 lemon half. Place the shrimp and lemon slices in a medium bowl, pour the marinade over, and allow to cool completely. Refrigerate the shrimp, in an airtight container, at least 2 hours or up to 1 day.

4. Drain the shrimp, reserving the lemon slices. Squeeze the juice from the remaining lemon half into a medium bowl. Add the lemon slices, shrimp, bell pepper, onion, olive oil, parsley, and salt. Arrange the lettuce on a large plate and spoon the shrimp mixture on top.

*Per serving   72 Calories, 3 g Total Fat, 0 g Saturated Fat, 70 mg Cholesterol, 142 mg Sodium, 3 g Total Carbohydrate, 1 g Dietary Fiber, 10 g Protein, 33 mg Calcium.*

*POINTS per serving: 1.*

★ *American Way*   Cooking shrimp in the shell increases their flavor. Prepare the shrimp a day ahead and refrigerate them in the marinade until ready to serve. Assemble the salad just before serving.

# Peanut Soup

MAKES 4 SERVINGS

*The peanut was originally cultivated in South America, then introduced to Africa by Spanish explorers, and eventually brought to North American soil by slaves. Initially, peanuts were used to fatten animals, but they became popular after George Washington Carver began his research on this nutritious legume (strictly speaking, the peanut is not a nut). Carver promoted peanut soup as one of the many ways to use the peanut, and in some places it is called Tuskegee Soup, in honor of the institution where he performed his experiments. The soup is deliciously rich, so small portions are plenty.*

½ teaspoon olive oil
1 small onion, finely chopped
2 celery stalks, finely chopped
1 garlic clove, minced
¼ cup peanut butter
2 tablespoons all-purpose flour
Pinch cayenne
2½ cups low-sodium chicken broth
½ cup fat-free milk
¼ teaspoon salt
1 tablespoon chopped peanuts

Heat the oil in a large nonstick saucepan then add the onion, celery, and garlic. Sauté until the vegetables are softened, about 10 minutes. Stir in the peanut butter, flour, and cayenne; cook 1 minute. Gradually stir in the broth and bring to a boil. Reduce the heat, cover, and simmer 15 minutes, stirring occasionally. Stir in the milk and salt and sprinkle with the peanuts.

*Per serving* 175 Calories, 11 g Total Fat, 3 g Saturated Fat, 4 mg Cholesterol, 342 mg Sodium, 12 g Total Carbohydrate, 2 g Dietary Fiber, 9 g Protein, 69 mg Calcium.

*POINTS per serving: 4.*

# The African-American Culinary Legacy

From countries, which later became known as Zanzibar, Kenya, Nigeria, Ethiopia, Ghana, and the Congo, many Africans became immigrant-slaves to America. African cooks contributed many of the products, seasonings, and cooking styles of their homelands to make Southern cooking. They added their own traditional ingredients—peanuts, sesame seeds, sweet potatoes, okra, black-eyed peas, chickpeas, rice, a variety of greens, watermelon, spicy sauces, and hot peppers—as well as ingredients borrowed from their Native American neighbors, like hominy and filé powder. The results of their ingenuity? Creamy peanut soup, Hoppin' John, gumbo, jambalaya, candied sweet potatoes, and benne (sesame) seed cookies are just a few of the dishes that define Southern cuisine.

The foods that African-American cooks created for their own families were different, though. Dishes served at home consisted primarily of ingredients rejected by their employers and foods they farmed or hunted on their own land. Chitterlings, fried chicken, fish, game, barbecued ribs, and ham hocks cooked with any available vegetable are just a few examples of the home-concocted "soul food"—and an equally delicious part of the Southern culinary tradition.

# White Bean Soup

*This simple, yet flavorful, and satisfying soup makes use of a Southern staple, beans. Leftover ham bone or smoked pork neck bones can be used instead of the ham hock for flavoring. Other dried beans, such as navy, cannellini, black-eyed peas, or pinto beans also work nicely.*

1/2 pound dried great Northern beans, picked over, rinsed, and drained

1 smoked ham hock

About 4 cups water

1/2 large onion, chopped

1/2 bay leaf

1/2 teaspoon dried salt-free herb blend

1 celery stalk, chopped

1 large carrot, peeled and chopped

1 garlic clove, crushed through a press

1/2 teaspoon salt

Freshly ground pepper, to taste

1. Combine the beans and enough cold water to cover by 3 inches in a large bowl; let stand overnight.

2. Drain the beans and place in a Dutch oven. Add the ham hock, water, onion, bay leaf, and herb blend; bring to a boil. Reduce the heat, cover, and simmer 1 hour. Add the celery, carrot, and garlic. Simmer, covered, until the beans are tender, $1^1/2$–2 hours, adding more water as needed if beans become too dry.

3. Remove the ham hock and set aside. Discard the bay leaf. Stir in the salt and pepper. Remove the meat from the ham hock and chop. Return the meat to the pot and stir to combine.

*Per serving* 275 Calories, 4 g Total Fat, 1 g Saturated Fat, 21 mg Cholesterol, 827 mg Sodium, 41 g Total Carbohydrate, 13 g Dietary Fiber, 21 g Protein, 103 mg Calcium.

*POINTS per serving: 3.*

★ *American Way* Don't worry if some of the beans fall apart; they will help thicken the soup.

# Warm Dandelion Salad

## MAKES 6 SERVINGS

*After a long winter, the tangy bite of dandelion greens is a flavorful springtime addition to any salad. Cooking dandelion and other wild greens with bacon, vinegar, onion, and a bit of sugar is a Southern tradition.*

2 (¹/2-pound) bunches dandelion greens, trimmed and cleaned
1 slice bacon, chopped
1 tablespoon olive oil
1 small red onion, thinly sliced
¹/4 cup cider vinegar
2 tablespoons honey or sugar
¹/4 teaspoon salt
Freshly ground pepper, to taste
1 hard-cooked egg, peeled and chopped

1. Tear the greens and place them in a large bowl.

2. Cook the bacon in a nonstick skillet until crisp, about 5 minutes. With a slotted spoon, transfer the bacon to a paper towel–lined plate to drain.

3. Discard the fat from the skillet. Heat the oil in the skillet, then add the onion and sauté until softened, about 4 minutes. Add the vinegar, honey, salt, and pepper and bring to a boil. Pour the hot dressing over the greens and toss. Sprinkle with the bacon and egg, toss gently, and serve.

*Per serving  100 Calories, 4 g Total Fat, 1 g Saturated Fat, 36 mg Cholesterol, 182 mg Sodium, 15 g Total Carbohydrate, 3 g Dietary Fiber, 4 g Protein, 149 mg Calcium.*

*POINTS per serving: 2.*

★ *American Way*   Small, tender dandelion greens are the most desirable, since their flavor is typically less bitter. If you can't find dandelion greens try using chicory, frisée, or mizuna.

# She-Crab Soup

*Both Charleston, South Carolina, and Savannah, Georgia, lay claim to the creation of this decadent, creamy soup. Traditionally, the roe of female crabs is what gives the soup its distinctive flavor and name. We substitute hard-cooked egg yolk for the roe here, but if you have access to live female crabs use them: Steam the crabs, then remove the meat and roe. Omit the hard-cooked egg from the recipe and stir the roe into the soup just before serving. Since the soup is so rich, serve it in small portions. It also makes an ideal first course for an elegant dinner.*

2 teaspoons olive oil

1 small onion, finely chopped

1 celery stalk, finely chopped

2 scallions, sliced

4 cups low-fat (1%) milk

3 tablespoons all-purpose flour

1/2 pound lump crabmeat, picked over

1 teaspoon grated lemon zest

3/4 teaspoon salt

Pinch cayenne

Freshly ground pepper, to taste

3 tablespoons dry sherry

1 hard-cooked egg yolk, pressed through a sieve

2 tablespoons chopped fresh parsley

1/2 teaspoon paprika

1. Heat the oil in a large saucepan, then add the onion, celery, and scallions. Sauté until the vegetables are softened, about 5 minutes. Add the milk and flour and whisk until smooth. Bring to a simmer and cook, stirring frequently, 5 minutes.

2. Stir in the crab, lemon zest, salt, cayenne, and pepper. Cook until the crab is heated through, about 3 minutes. Stir in the sherry. Ladle into 6 soup bowls and sprinkle with the egg yolk, parsley, and paprika.

*Per serving 163 Calories, 5 g Total Fat, 2 g Saturated Fat, 80 mg Cholesterol, 488 mg Sodium, 13 g Total Carbohydrate, 1 g Dietary Fiber, 14 g Protein, 256 mg Calcium.*

*POINTS per serving: 3.*

# Hoppin' John

MAKES 4 SERVINGS

*Black-eyed peas have long been associated with the mystical power to bring good luck. It's no surprise, then, that in the South New Year's Day menus feature some variation of this dish, to ensure prosperity for the coming year. On southern plantations, this combination of beans and rice was a staple of African slaves.*

1 slice bacon, chopped
1 small onion, chopped
1/2 red bell pepper, seeded and chopped
1 celery stalk, chopped
2 scallions, sliced
2 garlic cloves, crushed through a press
1/4 teaspoon dried thyme
1/8 teaspoon crushed red pepper
1/2 cup long-grain rice
1 (10-ounce) box frozen black-eyed peas (or one 10 1/2 ounce can)
1 1/4 cups low-sodium chicken broth
2 tablespoons chopped fresh parsley

1. Cook the bacon in a large skillet until crisp, about 5 minutes. With a slotted spoon, transfer the bacon to a paper towel–lined plate to drain. Discard the fat in the skillet. Combine the onion, bell pepper, celery, scallions, garlic, thyme, and crushed red pepper in the skillet; sauté over medium heat until softened, about 5 minutes.

2. Stir in the rice, peas, and broth; bring to a boil. Reduce the heat, cover, and simmer until the rice is tender and the broth has been absorbed, about 20 minutes. Remove from the heat and let stand 5 minutes. Stir in the bacon and parsley.

*Per serving   222 Calories, 3 g Total Fat, 1 g Saturated Fat, 3 mg Cholesterol, 91 mg Sodium, 42 g Total Carbohydrate, 5 g Dietary Fiber, 10 g Protein, 50 mg Calcium.*

*POINTS per serving: 4.*

★ *American Way*   For a vegetarian version, replace the bacon with 1/2 teaspoon olive oil and use vegetable broth instead of the chicken broth.

# Ozark Barbecued Beans

MAKES 6 SERVINGS

*In Arkansas' Ozarks, barbecue is usually accompanied by baked beans touched with the flavor of salty ham and sweet molasses. This slightly spicy version doesn't require hours to bake; in fact, you can have them on the dinner table in about an hour.*

½ cup chopped smoked ham

1 onion, finely chopped

1 jalapeño pepper, seeded and minced
    (wear gloves to prevent irritation)

1 garlic clove, minced

1 (8-ounce) can tomato sauce

¼ cup cider vinegar

¼ cup molasses

1 tablespoon packed brown sugar

¼ teaspoon freshly ground pepper

2 (15-ounce) cans great Northern or
    pinto beans, rinsed and drained

1. Preheat the oven to 350°F. Spray a nonstick skillet with nonstick spray and set over medium-high heat. Add the ham and onion and sauté until the onion is golden brown, about 8 minutes. Add the jalapeño and garlic and sauté 1 minute. Add the tomato sauce, vinegar, molasses, brown sugar, and pepper; bring to a boil.

2. Transfer the mixture to a deep 1½-quart casserole and add the beans; stir until blended. Bake until hot and bubbling, 60–70 minutes. Let stand 10 minutes before serving.

*Per serving   180 Calories, 1 g Total Fat, 0 g Saturated Fat, 8 mg Cholesterol, 703 mg Sodium, 33 g Total Carbohydrate, 7 g Dietary Fiber, 10 g Protein, 133 mg Calcium.*

*POINTS per serving: 2.*

# Cornmeal-Fried Catfish

MAKES 4 SERVINGS

*Catfish, now farm-raised across the South (primarily in Mississippi), has a fresh, mild flavor and a firm, low-fat flesh. Coating the fish with cornmeal and pan- or deep-frying it is the preferred method of preparation. Round out this true Southern specialty with Hush Puppies (page 171), the traditional partner.*

¹/₄ cup yellow cornmeal

2 tablespoons plain dried bread crumbs

¹/₄ teaspoon salt

¹/₄ teaspoon freshly ground pepper

¹/₈ teaspoon cayenne

1 large egg

1 tablespoon water

1 pound catfish fillets

1 tablespoon olive oil

Lemon wedges

1. Combine the cornmeal, bread crumbs, salt, pepper, and cayenne in a shallow dish or pie plate. Beat the egg and water with a fork in another shallow dish. Dip the fillets in the egg, then dredge them in the cornmeal mixture, coating both sides; shake off the excess.

2. Spray a large nonstick skillet with nonstick spray and set over medium-high heat. Add 2 teaspoons of the oil to the skillet and swirl to coat. Add the catfish and cook 3 minutes. Turn the fish and drizzle the remaining 1 teaspoon oil around the fillets. Cook until the fish is opaque in the center, 3–4 minutes more. Serve with the lemon wedges.

*Per serving  247 Calories, 14 g Total Fat, 3 g Saturated Fat, 106 mg Cholesterol, 248 mg Sodium, 9 g Total Carbohydrate, 1 g Dietary Fiber, 20 g Protein, 22 mg Calcium.*

*POINTS per serving: 6.*

*Cornmeal-Fried Catfish*

# Fish Muddle

MAKES 6 SERVINGS

*Fish Muddle, a simple fish stew from the coastal areas of North Carolina, takes advantage of whatever fish is available. It's similar to a chowder, but it uses broth instead of milk or cream.*

2 slices lean bacon, chopped

1 onion, chopped

2 celery stalks, chopped

3 scallions, sliced

2 garlic cloves, crushed through a press

3/4 teaspoon dried thyme

1/2 teaspoon salt

1/4 teaspoon crushed red pepper

1 1/2 cups low-sodium chicken broth

4 large all-purpose potatoes, peeled and cut into chunks

1 1/2 pounds firm-fleshed white fish (such as cod, haddock, striped bass, or snapper), cut into large chunks

2 tablespoons chopped fresh parsley

Lemon wedges

1. Cook the bacon in a Dutch oven until crisp, about 5 minutes. With a slotted spoon, transfer to a paper towel–lined plate to drain. Discard the fat in the Dutch oven. Combine the onion, celery, scallions, garlic, thyme, salt, and crushed red pepper in the Dutch oven; sauté until the vegetables are softened, about 5 minutes.

2. Add the broth and potatoes; bring to a boil. Reduce the heat, cover, and simmer until the potatoes are tender, about 15 minutes. Stir in the fish; bring to a boil. Reduce the heat and simmer, stirring occasionally, until the fish is cooked through, 6–8 minutes. With the back of a large spoon, mash some of the potatoes against the side of the pot to thicken the stew. Sprinkle with the bacon and parsley. Serve with the lemon wedges.

*Per serving   225 Calories, 2 g Total Fat, 1 g Saturated Fat, 53 mg Cholesterol, 355 mg Sodium, 26 g Total Carbohydrate, 3 g Dietary Fiber, 24 g Protein, 53 mg Calcium.*

*POINTS per serving: 4.*

# Kentucky Hot Brown

MAKES 4 SERVINGS

*In the late 1920s, this hot open-faced turkey sandwich was created by a chef at the famed Brown Hotel in Louisville, Kentucky. It was added to the menu as a quick and delicious way to feed hungry travelers. Add a tossed salad and you have a satisfying and easy-to-prepare dinner.*

1 cup low-fat (1%) milk

2 tablespoons all-purpose flour

1/2 cup shredded light cheddar cheese

3 tablespoons grated Parmesan cheese

1/2 teaspoon spicy brown mustard

1/4 teaspoon hot pepper sauce

4 slices whole-grain bread, toasted

2 tomatoes, sliced

1/2 pound sliced cooked turkey breast

4 slices crisp-cooked turkey bacon, cut in half

1. Combine the milk and flour in a small saucepan. Cook, stirring frequently, until the sauce thickens and comes to a boil. Reduce the heat and simmer 3 minutes. Remove from the heat and stir in the cheddar, 2 tablespoons of the Parmesan, the mustard, and pepper sauce.

2. Preheat the broiler. Place the toast into 4 individual casserole or ovenproof dishes. Arrange the tomato slices on the bread, then top with the turkey. Spoon some sauce over the top and sprinkle with the remaining Parmesan. Place the dishes on a baking sheet and broil, 5 inches from the heat, until the sandwiches are hot and the sauce begins to brown in spots. Top each sandwich with 2 pieces of the bacon.

*Per serving* 324 Calories, 11 g Total Fat, 5 g Saturated Fat, 45 mg Cholesterol, 947 mg Sodium, 33 g Total Carbohydrate, 4 g Dietary Fiber, 25 g Protein, 246 mg Calcium.

*POINTS per serving: 7.*

# Oven-Fried Chicken

MAKES 4 SERVINGS

*Fried chicken is a Southern staple. While purists wince at the thought of baking, rather than frying, this classic dish, our version uses cracker crumbs to give it a crunchy texture without the fat. You can buy cracker meal in the store, or make your own by crushing any firm low-fat crackers (like saltines) with a rolling pin.*

3/4 cup low-fat buttermilk

2 teaspoons salt

1 teaspoon freshly ground pepper

4 (1/2-pound) bone-in chicken breasts, skinned

1 cup cracker meal

2 tablespoons grated Parmesan cheese

1 tablespoon paprika

1 teaspoon dried thyme

1 teaspoon dried oregano

1. Preheat the oven to 350°F. Line a baking sheet with foil and spray with nonstick spray.

2. Combine the buttermilk, 1 teaspoon of the salt, and 1/2 teaspoon of the pepper in a zip-close plastic bag; add the chicken. Squeeze out the air and seal the bag; turn to coat the chicken. Refrigerate, turning the bag once, at least 20 minutes.

3. Combine the cracker meal, cheese, paprika, thyme, and oregano in a shallow plate or pie pan. Add the remaining 1 teaspoon salt and 1/2 teaspoon pepper. Remove the chicken from the buttermilk and dredge in the cracker meal mixture. Place the chicken on the baking sheet and bake 30 minutes. Remove the baking sheet from the oven and lightly spray the chicken with nonstick spray. Return the baking sheet to the oven and bake until the chicken is cooked through, about 15 minutes more.

*Per serving  314 Calories, 6 g Total Fat, 2 g Saturated Fat, 93 mg Cholesterol, 740 mg Sodium, 26 g Total Carbohydrate, 1 g Dietary Fiber, 38 g Protein, 102 mg Calcium.*

*POINTS per serving: 7.*

FLASHBACK >> 1955

Corbin, Kentucky restaurateur Harland Sanders takes to the highways in his car loaded with pots, pans, and "a secret blend of herbs and spices," in search of prospective franchisees for his Colonel Sander's Kentucky Fried Chicken restaurants.

# Country Ham and Red-Eye Gravy

*Ham and red-eye gravy, served with grits or biscuits, is a breakfast favorite in the South, but don't expect the traditional flour-thickened gravy here; this is a thin gravy, used sparingly. The name is derived from the appearance of a "red-eye" which forms in the middle of the gravy as it reduces.*

1/2 teaspoon vegetable oil

1 (12-ounce) slice lean hickory-smoked ham, about 3/8-inch thick

3/4 cup brewed coffee

1/4 cup water

3/4 teaspoon cornstarch

Freshly ground pepper, to taste

1. Heat a large nonstick skillet. Swirl in the oil, then add the ham and cook until browned, about 4 minutes each side. Transfer to a warm plate.

2. Combine the coffee, water, and cornstarch in a cup and stir until the cornstarch has dissolved. Pour the mixture into the skillet and bring to a boil. Cook, stirring, until slightly thickened, about 2 minutes; add the pepper. Divide the ham into 4 pieces and drizzle with the gravy.

*Per serving   141 Calories, 5 g Total Fat, 2 g Saturated Fat, 47 mg Cholesterol, 1,130 mg Sodium, 1 g Total Carbohydrate, 0 g Dietary Fiber, 21 g Protein, 7 mg Calcium.*

*POINTS per serving: 3.*

FLASHBACK>>1994

Hog farmers in the U.S. produce a record 15.7 billion pounds of pork. Pork producers expand their operations, primarily in North Carolina and Missouri.

# Pork Barbecue

*Barbecue-lovers from coast to coast debate which state lays claim to the best barbecue in the land. North Carolina chimes in with this flavorful sauce, packed with vinegar and red pepper flakes. Depending on where you live in the state, tomato may be included. But there's no variation when it comes to meat—it's always pork.*

3 tablespoons packed brown sugar

2 teaspoons paprika

3/4 teaspoon freshly ground pepper

1/2 teaspoon salt

1/4 teaspoon ground cumin

1/4 teaspoon chili powder

1 1/2 pounds pork tenderloin

1 teaspoon vegetable oil

2/3 cup cider vinegar

1/3 cup water

1/4 cup ketchup

2 tablespoons minced onion

1 garlic clove, minced

1/4 teaspoon crushed red pepper

4 hamburger rolls

1. Preheat the oven to 450°F. Combine 1 tablespoon of the brown sugar, the paprika, 1/2 teaspoon of the pepper, 1/4 teaspoon of the salt, the cumin, and chili powder in a small cup. Place the pork on a piece of wax paper. Sprinkle the spice mixture over the pork, patting the meat to help the spices adhere.

2. Heat a large nonstick skillet. Swirl in the oil, then add the pork. Cook, turning occasionally, until the pork is well browned, about 5 minutes. Transfer the pork to a shallow roasting pan. Roast until the meat reaches an internal temperature of 160°F, about 15 minutes. Let stand 10 minutes.

3. Meanwhile, combine the remaining 2 tablespoons brown sugar, 1/4 teaspoon pepper, and 1/4 teaspoon salt, the vinegar, water, ketchup, onion, garlic, and red pepper in a saucepan; bring to a boil. Reduce the heat slightly and boil until reduced to 3/4 cup, about 15 minutes.

4. Thinly slice the pork. Combine the pork and 1/4 cup of the sauce in a large bowl. Serve on the rolls with the remaining sauce on the side.

*Per serving  411 Calories, 10 g Total Fat, 3 g Saturated Fat, 101 mg Cholesterol, 808 mg Sodium, 39 g Total Carbohydrate, 2 g Dietary Fiber, 40 g Protein, 89 mg Calcium.*

*POINTS per serving: 9.*

## The Battle of the Barbecue

Barbecue was a Western Hemisphere tradition long before America even got its name. According to legend, Spanish explorers observed Native Americans cooking on a grid of green branches, called a *barbacoa*, which was placed over a pit of glowing coals.

Lured by the flavor and aroma of cooking over an open fire, modern barbecue enthusiasts from every state have devised their own rules for making *the* quintessential barbecue. It seems like there is a right way and a wrong way to "Q" from coast to coast and, in some cases, in every part of the state. While some areas concentrate on the sauce—and are apt to use it on everything from buffalo to Cornish hens—others focus on the meat, usually pork, dressing it as lightly as possible.

BBQ devotees take their task seriously. In fact, some would say that the debate over the ultimate barbecue can resemble a second civil war! And while the subject is "hot" in almost every state, the biggest battle seems to be among the barbecue masters of Texas, North Carolina, and Kansas. What comprises their individual barbecue prowess? Texans favor beef dressed with two kinds of sauce—one broth-based mop sauce used during cooking and another ketchup and vinegar based sauce to serve with it. North Carolina does barbecue two ways: Eastern North Carolinian's pick is pork, usually a whole pig lightly spiced and cooked for 16 to 18 hours over a low fire. The surface is basted very lightly with a vinegar solution during cooking and the resulting meat is pulled, never sliced. In western North Carolina, pork shoulder is preferred and doused with a serious ketchup, sugar, and vinegar sauce. As for Kansas, the secret is in the sauce. Known for its barbecue restaurants, the cooks of Kansas City credit their success to a phenomenal sauce. Whatever your personal choice for the best in barbecue, there's no contest when it comes to sampling the edibles of the contenders—it's a delicious chore.

# Frogmore Stew

MAKES 4 SERVINGS

*This seafood boil is named for a town on St. Helena Island, South Carolina. Shrimp, caught by local fishermen, and sausage mingle with spicy seasonings to produce a tasty meal.*

8 cups water

2 tablespoons crab-boil seasoning

1/4 teaspoon crushed red pepper

1 pound small red potatoes, halved

1/2 pound turkey sausage, cut into
    1-inch slices

2 celery stalks, cut into 1-inch slices

1 pound large shrimp

4 ears of corn, shucked and cut into
    3 pieces each

Lemon wedges

Cocktail sauce (optional)

1. Combine the water, crab seasoning, and red pepper in a Dutch oven; bring to a boil. Add the potatoes, sausage, and celery and return to a boil. Reduce the heat, cover, and simmer until the potatoes are tender, about 12 minutes.

2. Meanwhile, with kitchen scissors, cut through the back of each shrimp just deeply enough to expose the vein; remove the vein, leaving the shell intact.

3. Add the shrimp and corn to the Dutch oven; bring to a boil. Reduce the heat and simmer until the shrimp are just cooked through, 1–2 minutes. Using a slotted spoon, transfer the shrimp to a bowl and remove the shells. Add the peeled shrimp to the stew, serve with lemon wedges, and cocktail sauce, if using.

*Per serving  371 Calories, 9 g Total Fat, 3 g Saturated Fat, 184 mg Cholesterol, 517 mg Sodium, 42 g Total Carbohydrate, 5 g Dietary Fiber, 34 g Protein, 100 mg Calcium.*

*POINTS per serving: 7.*

★ *American Way*  Crab boil seasoning—found in the spice section of the supermarket—is a mixture of mustard seeds, peppercorns, bay leaves, allspice, cloves, ginger, and red chiles. Use it to season the water for boiling crab and other shellfish.

# Kentucky Burgoo

MAKES 14 SERVINGS

*Burgoo, a rich, thick soup brimming with a variety of vegetables and meats (including squirrel in more traditional recipes), is usually cooked in large quantities at public gatherings, like the Kentucky Derby. Theories about the origin of the name abound, but the most likely is that* burgoo *is simply a mispronunciation of* barbecue.

6 cups water

1 pound boneless beef chuck, trimmed and cut into chunks

1 (1¼-pound) lamb shank, trimmed of all visible fat

½ teaspoon dried thyme

2 bay leaves

1½ pounds bone-in chicken breasts, skinned

1 (14½-ounce) can whole tomatoes in juice

1 large onion, chopped

2 carrots, peeled and sliced

1 green bell pepper, seeded and chopped

3 large all-purpose potatoes, peeled and cut into chunks

4 garlic cloves, minced

¼ teaspoon crushed red pepper

¾ teaspoon salt

Freshly ground pepper, to taste

1 (10-ounce) box frozen succotash

1 (10-ounce) box frozen sliced okra

¼ cup chopped fresh flat-leaf parsley

1. Combine the water, beef, and lamb in a Dutch oven and bring to a boil. Reduce the heat and skim any foam. Add the thyme and bay leaves. Cover and simmer 30 minutes. Add the chicken and simmer gently, covered, until the meats are tender, about 1 hour 30 minutes. Transfer the beef, lamb, and chicken to a plate and keep warm.

2. Add the tomatoes, onion, carrots, bell pepper, potatoes, garlic, red pepper, ½ teaspoon of the salt, and the pepper to the Dutch oven; bring to a boil. Reduce the heat, cover, and simmer 30 minutes.

3. Meanwhile, remove the lamb and chicken meat from the bones and cut into chunks. Discard the bones. Add the lamb, chicken, beef, and succotash to the Dutch oven; bring to a boil. Reduce the heat and simmer 30 minutes. Add the okra and simmer until tender, about 20 minutes more. Discard the bay leaves, stir in the parsley and remaining ¼ teaspoon salt, and serve.

*Per serving* 209 Calories, 6 g Total Fat, 3 g Saturated Fat, 49 mg Cholesterol, 236 mg Sodium, 17 g Total Carbohydrate, 3 g Dietary Fiber, 21 g Protein, 51 mg Calcium.

*POINTS per serving: 4.*

★ *American Way* The flavors of the burgoo blend nicely if you allow the stew to sit for a day or two.

FLASHBACK ›› 1863

Kentucky chef Gus Jaubbert feeds the Confederate troops his meat and vegetable stew creation, burgoo.

# Brunswick Stew

MAKES 10 SERVINGS

*A few states—Virginia, North Carolina, and Georgia—claim this stew as their own. From wherever it hails, the meaty stew should contain game and fresh corn; the remaining ingredients depend on seasonal availability or personal preference.*

6 cups cold water

1 small (2-pound) rabbit, cut into pieces

2 pounds chicken parts, skinned

1 large onion, sliced

1 teaspoon dried thyme

2 bay leaves

1 (14$1/2$-ounce) can diced tomatoes

$1/2$ pound smoked ham, cut into chunks

2 large all-purpose potatoes, peeled and cut into chunks

3 carrots, peeled and sliced

2 celery stalks, chopped

$3/4$ teaspoon salt

1 (10-ounce) box frozen corn

1 (10-ounce) box frozen lima beans

$1/4$ teaspoon crushed red pepper

Freshly ground pepper, to taste

$1/4$ cup chopped fresh flat-leaf parsley

1. Combine the water, rabbit, chicken, and onion in a Dutch oven; bring to a boil. Reduce the heat and skim any foam. Add the thyme and bay leaves. Cover and simmer until the rabbit and chicken are tender, about 1 hour.

2. Transfer the rabbit and chicken to a plate and keep warm. Add the tomatoes, ham, potatoes, carrots, celery, and $1/2$ teaspoon of the salt to the Dutch oven; bring to a boil. Reduce the heat, cover, and simmer 30 minutes.

3. Remove the rabbit and chicken meat from the bones and cut into chunks. Discard the bones. Add the chicken, rabbit, corn, lima beans, red pepper, and black pepper to the Dutch oven. Simmer until the vegetables are tender, about 30 minutes. Discard the bay leaves. Stir in the parsley and remaining salt.

*Per serving (generous 1 cup): 227 Calories, 4 g Total Fat, 1 g Saturated Fat, 75 mg Cholesterol, 618 mg Sodium, 23 g Total Carbohydrate, 4 g Dietary Fiber, 25 g Protein, 48 mg Calcium.*

*POINTS per serving: 4.*

★ *American Way* If you can't find rabbit, use a total of four pounds of chicken parts.

# Ramps and Grits

MAKES 6 SERVINGS

*Ramps are wild leeks that grow in the Appalachian Mountains, from West Virginia to north Georgia. Their leaves are similar to those of a lily of the valley and the bulb resembles a scallion's. The taste is a mixture of leek, garlic, and dandelion greens. During the short ramp season (from the end of March to May), ramp cook-offs and festivals prevail throughout the region.*

1 1/2 teaspoons olive oil

2 ramps, chopped

1/4 teaspoon salt

Freshly ground pepper, to taste

3 cups water

3/4 cup quick-cooking (not instant) grits

1 extra-large egg

3 tablespoons grated Parmesan cheese

3/4 cup shredded extra-sharp cheddar cheese

1. Preheat the oven to 375°F. Spray a 1 1/2-quart deep baking dish with nonstick spray. Heat a medium nonstick skillet. Swirl in the oil, then add the ramps. Sauté until the ramps are softened, about 8 minutes. Stir in the salt and pepper.

2. Bring the water to a boil in a large saucepan. Gradually whisk in the grits. Reduce the heat, cover, and simmer, stirring occasionally, until thickened, about 8 minutes.

3. Beat the egg with a fork in bowl and slowly stir in 1/3 of the cooked grits. Gradually stir the egg mixture back into the grits in the saucepan. Stir in the ramps, Parmesan, and 1/2 cup of the cheddar.

4. Pour the grits into the baking dish and sprinkle with the remaining cheddar. Place the dish in a roasting pan and place the pan in the oven. Fill the roasting pan with enough boiling water to come halfway up the side of the dish. Bake until the grits are puffed and browned, about 1 hour.

*Per serving* 170 Calories, 8 g Total Fat, 4 g Saturated Fat, 61 mg Cholesterol, 249 mg Sodium, 18 g Total Carbohydrate, 1 g Dietary Fiber, 8 g Protein, 156 mg Calcium.

*POINTS per serving: 4.*

★ *American Way* If it's not ramp season, or your farmer's market doesn't have them, substitute one sliced leek, white and pale green part only, two sliced scallions, and two minced garlic cloves.

# Yellow Squash Casserole

MAKES 6 SERVINGS

*In the South, the yellow squash of choice is called crookneck. When buying crookneck, look for pale yellow squash with thin skin—they will be the most tender. This squash is well cooked to bring out its somewhat mild flavor, and blended with creamy cheese and crushed crackers to render a soul-warming accompaniment to any meal.*

4 large yellow squash

1 small onion, chopped

1/2 cup water

1 garlic clove, crushed through a press

1/4 cup nonfat cream cheese, at room temperature

1/2 cup shredded sharp cheddar cheese

1 large egg, lightly beaten

1/4 teaspoon salt

Freshly ground pepper, to taste

6 unsalted soda crackers

1. Preheat the oven to 350°F. Spray a 1 1/2-quart shallow baking dish with nonstick spray.

2. Combine the squash, onion, water, and garlic in a large saucepan; bring to a boil. Reduce the heat, cover, and simmer until the squash is very tender, about 12 minutes. Drain well in a colander. Return the vegetables to the saucepan and mash with a potato masher. Stir in the cream cheese, 6 tablespoons of the cheddar, the egg, salt, and pepper. Pour into the baking dish. Crush the crackers in a small bowl and add the remaining cheddar; toss to combine. Sprinkle the crumbs on top of the casserole. Bake until bubbling at the edges and browned, about 30 minutes. Allow to stand 10 minutes before serving.

*Per serving   105 Calories, 5 g Total Fat, 2 g Saturated Fat, 46 mg Cholesterol, 263 mg Sodium, 10 g Total Carbohydrate, 3 g Dietary Fiber, 7 g Protein, 116 mg Calcium.*

*POINTS per serving: 2.*

# Fresh Peach Chutney

MAKES 15 SERVINGS

*One hallmark of the South is the ingenuity of its cooks, and the chutneys and relishes that are fixtures of the Southern table are evidence of that fact. This sweet-tart chutney is especially tasty with roasted meats, such as turkey, ham, or pork.*

6 large ripe but firm peaches, peeled, cored, and sliced

2 tablespoons fresh lime juice

3/4 cup golden raisins

2/3 cup sugar

1/2 cup cider vinegar

2 tablespoons finely chopped onion

2 tablespoons finely chopped red bell pepper

2 teaspoons grated peeled fresh ginger

3 garlic cloves, minced

1/2 teaspoon salt

1/4 teaspoon crushed red pepper

Toss the peaches and lime juice together in a large bowl. Combine the raisins, sugar, vinegar, onion, bell pepper, ginger, garlic, salt, and red pepper in a large saucepan; bring to a boil. Reduce the heat and simmer 5 minutes. Stir in the peaches; bring to a boil. Reduce the heat and simmer 1 minute. Let cool. Refrigerate in an airtight container for up to 1 week.

*Per serving* (1/3 cup): 122 Calories, 0 g Total Fat, 0 g Saturated Fat, 0 mg Cholesterol, 80 mg Sodium, 31 g Total Carbohydrate, 3 g Dietary Fiber, 1 g Protein, 13 mg Calcium.

*POINTS per serving: 2.*

# Low-Country Pilau

MAKES 6 SERVINGS

*The number of names for this rice dish is perhaps a reflection of its widespread popularity: perlew, perloo, plaw, pullao, perlow, pilaf, pilaff, pelav, pilaw, and pelos. This variation is native to Charleston, South Carolina, where rice was once the primary export and the base of many great fortunes. If you add some sliced okra, it's known as Limping Susan.*

1 slice bacon, chopped

1 onion, chopped

1/2 red bell pepper, seeded and chopped

1 garlic clove, minced

1 cup long-grain rice

1 large tomato, chopped

13/4 cups low-sodium chicken broth

1/4 teaspoon salt

Pinch cayenne

Freshly ground pepper, to taste

2 tablespoons chopped fresh flat-leaf parsley

2 tablespoons chopped fresh basil

Cook the bacon in a large skillet until crisp, about 5 minutes. With a slotted spoon, transfer the bacon to a paper towel–lined plate to drain. Discard the fat in the skillet. Add the onion, bell pepper, and garlic to the skillet and sauté over medium heat until softened, about 5 minutes. Stir in the rice, tomato, broth, salt, cayenne, and pepper; bring to a boil. Reduce the heat, cover, and simmer until the liquid has been absorbed and the rice is tender, about 20 minutes. Stir in the bacon, parsley, and basil.

*Per serving  147 Calories, 1 g Total Fat, 1 g Saturated Fat, 3 mg Cholesterol, 166 mg Sodium, 29 g Total Carbohydrate, 1 g Dietary Fiber, 4 g Protein, 24 mg Calcium.*

*POINTS per serving: 3.*

★ *American Way*  Adding chicken, shrimp, or ham transforms this side dish into a satisfying main dish.

# Spoonbread Soufflé

MAKES 6 SERVINGS

*Spoonbread is commonly served instead of rice or potatoes at the Southern table. We fold beaten egg whites into a traditional spoonbread batter to make an almost-lighter-than-air soufflé. Southerners prefer stone-ground white cornmeal for its more delicate texture, but yellow cornmeal can be substituted.*

1 cup fresh or thawed frozen corn kernels

2 cups fat-free milk

1/2 cup stone-ground white cornmeal

2 tablespoons unsalted butter

1/2 teaspoon salt

Freshly ground pepper, to taste

3 large eggs, separated

1 1/2 teaspoons baking powder

1. Puree the corn and 1/4 cup of the milk in a blender or food processor. Place the remaining milk in a large saucepan and bring to a boil. Reduce the heat and gradually whisk in the cornmeal. Cook, stirring occasionally, until thick, about 5 minutes. Stir in the pureed corn, butter, 1/4 teaspoon of the salt, and the pepper. Transfer the mixture to a large bowl and set aside to cool for 10 minutes.

2. Preheat the oven to 375°F. Spray a shallow 2-quart baking dish with nonstick spray and place in the oven while preheating.

3. With an electric mixer on high speed, beat the egg whites and the remaining 1/4 teaspoon salt in a medium bowl just until stiff peaks form. Stir the yolks and baking powder into the cornmeal mixture. Fold in the whites. Remove the baking dish from the oven. Pour the mixture into the dish. Bake until the spoonbread is puffed and browned, 35–40 minutes. Serve hot.

*Per serving   169 Calories, 7 g Total Fat, 4 g Saturated Fat, 119 mg Cholesterol, 375 mg Sodium, 19 g Total Carbohydrate, 2 g Dietary Fiber, 8 g Protein, 133 mg Calcium.*

*POINTS per serving: 4.*

★ *American Way*   Two ears of corn will yield one cup of kernels.

# Hush Puppies

MAKES 6 SERVINGS

*Legend has it that hush puppies—deep-fried cornmeal fritters—got their name when cooks fried up dough scraps in the fish skillet and threw them to yapping dogs in an effort to quiet them. Outside the Carolinas, they frequently appear at barbecues—but few Carolina cooks would dream of serving them with anything but fish. These puppies are a bit nontraditional, since they're baked rather than fried.*

³/4 cup yellow cornmeal

¹/4 cup all-purpose flour

¹/2 teaspoon sugar

¹/2 teaspoon baking powder

¹/2 teaspoon salt

¹/4 teaspoon baking soda

¹/8 teaspoon freshly ground pepper

¹/8 teaspoon cayenne

³/4 cup low-fat buttermilk

1 large egg

2 scallions, finely chopped

2 tablespoons finely grated onion

1. Preheat the oven to 450°F. Place two 12-cup mini-muffin tins in the oven while preheating. Combine the cornmeal, flour, sugar, baking powder, salt, baking soda, pepper, and cayenne in a bowl. Beat the buttermilk, egg, scallions, and onion in another bowl. Add the buttermilk mixture to the cornmeal mixture and stir until just blended.

2. Remove the hot tins from the oven and spray with nonstick spray. Spoon the batter into the cups, filling each about ³/4 full. Bake until the tops spring back when gently pressed, about 10 minutes. Run a knife around the sides of the hush puppies and turn them out onto a wire rack. Serve warm.

*Per serving* (4 hush puppies): *112 Calories, 1 g Total Fat, 0 g Saturated Fat, 36 mg Cholesterol, 323 mg Sodium, 20 g Total Carbohydrate, 2 g Dietary Fiber, 4 g Protein, 52 mg Calcium.*

*POINTS per serving: 2.*

# Peppery Cornsticks

MAKES 7 SERVINGS

*These cornsticks are Southern-style cornbread: not too sweet and made with more cornmeal than flour.*

1 cup yellow cornmeal

1/2 cup all-purpose flour

2 teaspoons sugar

1/2 teaspoon baking powder

1/2 teaspoon baking soda

1/2 teaspoon salt

1/2 teaspoon freshly ground pepper

1 cup low-fat buttermilk

1 large egg

1 tablespoon vegetable oil

1. Preheat the oven to 450°F. Spray a 7-mold, cast-iron cornstick pan with nonstick spray and place in the oven while preheating.

2. Combine the cornmeal, flour, sugar, baking powder, baking soda, salt, and pepper in a bowl. Beat the buttermilk, egg, and oil in another bowl. Add the buttermilk mixture to the cornmeal mixture and stir until just moistened. The batter should have lumps.

3. Spoon half of the batter into the cornstick molds, filling each about 3/4 full. Bake until the tops spring back when gently pressed, 8–10 minutes. Run a knife around the sides of the cornsticks and turn them out onto a rack. Reheat the pan, spray with nonstick spray, and repeat with the remaining batter. Serve warm or at room temperature.

*Per serving* (2 cornsticks): 152 Calories, 3 g Total Fat, 1 g Saturated Fat, 32 mg Cholesterol, 331 mg Sodium, 25 g Total Carbohydrate, 2 g Dietary Fiber, 5 g Protein, 52 mg Calcium.

POINTS *per serving:* 3.

★ *American Way*   If you don't have a cornstick pan, spoon the batter into a muffin tin, heated the same way as the cornstick pan, to make 12 muffins.

# Moravian Spice Cookies

MAKES ABOUT 6 1/2 DOZEN COOKIES

*In 1752, a sect of Protestants came from Moravia in Eastern Europe seeking religious freedom and settled around Winston-Salem, North Carolina. Among the culinary traditions they brought with them were these molasses spice cookies. Skill and patience is required to roll the dough so thin that you can almost see through it. Stored airtight they will last up to two months.*

1 1/2 cups all-purpose flour
1 teaspoon ground ginger
3/4 teaspoon cinnamon
1/2 teaspoon baking soda
1/4 teaspoon ground cloves
1/4 cup solid vegetable shortening
1/3 cup packed brown sugar
1/2 cup unsulfured molasses

1. Combine the flour, ginger, cinnamon, baking soda, and cloves in a small bowl. With an electric mixer on low speed, beat the shortening and brown sugar in a large bowl until creamy; add the molasses and beat until well blended. Beat in half of the flour mixture, then stir in the remaining flour mixture (the dough will be stiff). Divide the dough into fourths and cover with plastic wrap. Refrigerate at least 4 hours or overnight.

2. Preheat the oven to 350°F. On a lightly floured counter, with a floured rolling pin, roll 1 piece of dough at a time to a 1/16-inch thickness. Use a 2 1/2-inch fluted round cutter to cut out cookies. With a spatula, carefully place the cookies 1/2 inch apart on an ungreased baking sheet. Bake until the cookies are set but not brown, 6–8 minutes. Allow to cool on the sheet 1 minute, then transfer to a wire rack to cool completely. Repeat with the remaining dough, gathering and rerolling scraps to make 78 cookies.

*Per serving (3 cookies): 71 Calories, 2 g Total Fat, 1 g Saturated Fat, 0 mg Cholesterol, 28 mg Sodium, 13 g Total Carbohydrate, 0 g Dietary Fiber, 1 g Protein, 17 mg Calcium.*

*POINTS per serving: 2.*

★ *American Way*   To roll the thinnest dough, use a metal spatula to periodically lift the dough and sprinkle flour on the rolling surface to prevent sticking. Unsulfured molasses has a lighter, cleaner taste than molasses that is processed using sulfur.

# Pecan Lace Cookies

### MAKES ABOUT 3¹/₂ DOZEN

*Pecans, a variety of the hickory nut, are the most cherished nut in the South. Although they're used in everything from confections, like delectably sweet pralines, to savory stuffings, pecans are perhaps best appreciated in rich Southern desserts. These thin, delicate cookies are a decidedly tempting example. Store them between layers of wax paper in an airtight container for up to one week.*

¹/₄ cup all-purpose flour
¹/₂ teaspoon baking powder
Pinch salt
2 tablespoons unsalted butter, softened
1 cup packed brown sugar
1 large egg
1 teaspoon vanilla extract
³/₄ cup pecans halves, finely chopped
¹/₄ cup quick-cooking oats

1. Combine the flour, baking powder, and salt in a bowl. With an electric mixer on low speed, beat the butter and brown sugar in another bowl until combined. Beat in the egg and vanilla until well blended. Beat in the flour mixture. Stir in the pecans and oats. Cover with plastic wrap and refrigerate 1 hour.

2. Preheat the oven to 375°F. Line 3 baking sheets with foil; spray the foil with nonstick spray. Drop the dough by rounded teaspoons 4 inches apart onto the baking sheets. Bake until browned, 6–8 minutes. Allow to cool on the sheets 2 minutes, then transfer to wire racks to cool completely. Repeat with the remaining dough to make the cookies.

*Per serving (3 cookies): 134 Calories, 6 g Total Fat, 2 g Saturated Fat, 20 mg Cholesterol, 35 mg Sodium, 19 g Total Carbohydrate, 1 g Dietary Fiber, 1 g Protein, 21 mg Calcium.*

*POINTS per serving: 3.*

# Pecan Bourbon Cake

MAKES 20 SERVINGS

*This old-fashioned Southern cake is basically a fruitcake, but it's a version anyone would be thrilled to receive as a gift. Its extraordinary flavor comes from the Kentucky whiskey of choice—bourbon. If your raisins are dry, try soaking them first in a few tablespoons of bourbon.*

2 cups pecan halves, chopped

1 cup dried Calimyrna figs, finely chopped

1 cup raisins

1¹/2 cups all-purpose flour

1 teaspoon baking powder

¹/2 teaspoon ground nutmeg

1 cup sugar

¹/2 cup unsalted butter or margarine, softened

2 teaspoons vanilla extract

3 large eggs, separated

¹/2 cup bourbon

Pinch salt

1. Preheat the oven to 325°F. Grease and flour a 10-inch tube pan. Toss the pecans, figs, raisins, and ¹/2 cup of the flour in a small bowl. Combine the remaining 1 cup flour, baking powder, and nutmeg in another bowl.

2. With an electric mixer on medium speed, beat ³/4 cup of the sugar, the butter, and vanilla in a large bowl until light and fluffy. Beat in the egg yolks, one at a time, until well blended. Beat in the flour mixture, alternating with the bourbon, until blended. Stir in the pecan mixture, including any flour left in the bowl.

3. Wash and dry the beaters. With the mixer on high, beat the egg whites and salt in a medium bowl until soft peaks form. Gradually beat in the remaining ¹/4 cup sugar. Beat just until stiff peaks form. Fold the whites into the batter. Scrape the batter into the pan.

4. Bake until a toothpick inserted in the center comes out clean, about 1 hour. Cool completely in the pan on a wire rack. Run a knife around the sides of the cake and remove it from the pan. Wrap and refrigerate overnight before serving.

*Per serving   254 Calories, 13 g Total Fat, 4 g Saturated Fat, 45 mg Cholesterol, 39 mg Sodium, 31 g Total Carbohydrate, 3 g Dietary Fiber, 3 g Protein, 32 mg Calcium.*

*POINTS per serving: 6.*

★ *American Way*   A serrated knife makes quick work of slicing the cake. The cake can be stored in the refrigerator for up to three months; simply wrap it in a bourbon-soaked cheesecloth, then in foil, and store in a tin or airtight container.

FLASHBACK >> 1790

Baptist minister Elijah Craig distills the first bourbon whiskey in what is soon established as Kentucky County. Craig's corn whiskey is so refined and smooth that it soon surpasses rum and brandy as Americans' favored liquor.

## Good Water Makes Good Whiskey

Early settlers to America arrived with the know-how for making spirits, a knowledge which would one day lead to the development of whiskies unique to the United States. Until the Revolution, homemade beer and hard cider, supplemented by some imported liquor, were the alcohols served (often in place of water) at every meal. After America gained her independence, however, locally grown grains, rye, and, later, corn, were fermented and distilled for easier and more efficient transport of the grains to market. Eventually, barrels of corn whiskey waiting to be sent down the Mississippi to New Orleans to be sold were found to have improved in flavor upon aging, so this step became part of whiskey production, adding sophistication to the process and yielding a more refined product with a more mellow flavor.

Until 1791, making whiskey had been a free and legal enterprise in America. Then, to raise revenue for the new country, Alexander Hamilton proposed taxing distillers, a decision that resulted in the Whiskey Rebellion and the migration of many whiskey makers to Kentucky, which was not yet a part of the United States. There, in Bourbon County, the pure limestone spring water that has made Kentucky Bourbon famous, was discovered. In neighboring Tennessee, an equally pure source of water in the town of Lynchburg inspired distiller Jack Daniel to produce a similar product, sold as Tennessee Whiskey, through the additional step of charcoal filtering.

# Strawberry Shortcake

## MAKES 10 SERVINGS

*Although there is some debate as to whether it's a Southern original, there's no question that Southerners make a strawberry shortcake that is first-rate. Strawberries that are in season and at the peak of ripeness are the ideal, sweet partner to the biscuit-like dough and creamy whipped topping in this rendition.*

2 cups all-purpose flour

3/4 cup granulated sugar

2 teaspoons baking powder

1/2 teaspoon baking soda

1/4 teaspoon salt

3/4 cup low-fat buttermilk

1/4 cup vegetable oil

1 large egg

6 cups strawberries

1 1/2 cups thawed frozen light nondairy whipped topping

2 teaspoons confectioners' sugar

1. Preheat the oven to 400°F. Spray a 9-inch round baking pan with nonstick spray. Combine the flour, 1/2 cup of the granulated sugar, the baking powder, baking soda, and salt in a bowl.

2. Beat the buttermilk, oil, and egg in another bowl. Add the buttermilk mixture to the flour mixture; stir with a fork until the dry ingredients are just moistened. Scrape the batter into the pan and spread evenly with a spoon. Bake until the top is browned and a toothpick inserted in the center comes out clean, 18–20 minutes. Cool in the pan on a wire rack 5 minutes. Remove from the pan and cool completely on the rack.

3. Reserve 4 small strawberries for garnish. Hull the remaining strawberries. Crush 1/2 cup of the strawberries with the remaining 1/4 cup granulated sugar in a large bowl. Slice the remaining strawberries into the bowl and toss to combine.

4. With a serrated knife, split the shortcake in half horizontally. Place the bottom layer on a serving plate and spread with the whipped topping. Spoon 2/3 of the sliced strawberries over the whipped topping and cover with the remaining shortcake layer. Dust the top with the confectioners' sugar and garnish with the whole strawberries. Serve each piece with a spoonful of the remaining sliced strawberries.

*Per serving  256 Calories, 7 g Total Fat, 1 g Saturated Fat, 22 mg Cholesterol, 233 mg Sodium, 45 g Total Carbohydrate, 3 g Dietary Fiber, 4 g Protein, 54 mg Calcium.*

*POINTS per serving: 5.*

# Lady Baltimore Cake

## MAKES 12 SERVINGS

*This delicate white cake dates back to the late 1800s. It was made famous in the 1906 romance novel by Owen Wister called* Lady Baltimore, *which was set in Charleston, South Carolina. The publication of the novel, which contained a description of the luscious cake, spurred many readers to obtain the recipe.*

### CAKE

4 egg whites, at room temperature
1³/4 cups cake flour
2 teaspoons baking powder
¹/4 teaspoon salt
6 tablespoons unsalted butter, softened
1¹/4 cups sugar
1 teaspoon vanilla extract
³/4 cup low-fat (1%) milk

### FROSTING

³/4 cup sugar
2 egg whites
¹/4 cup water
¹/2 teaspoon cream of tartar
¹/8 teaspoon salt
2 teaspoons vanilla extract
¹/2 cup raisins
6 dried figs, chopped
2 tablespoons chopped pecans

FLASHBACK >> 1863

Due to the war, production is disrupted at sugar plantations throughout the South, resulting in soaring sugar prices. To meet the country's demands for sugar, farmers in the Hawaiian Islands begin planting more and more sugar cane.

1. Preheat the oven to 350°F. Spray two 9-inch round cake pans with nonstick spray. Line the bottoms of the pans with wax paper and then spray the wax paper with nonstick spray.

2. To make the cake, with an electric mixer at high speed, beat the egg whites in a bowl until stiff peaks form. Combine the flour, baking powder, and the salt in another bowl. With the mixer on medium-high, cream the butter, sugar, and vanilla in a large mixing bowl until light and fluffy. Beat the flour mixture into the butter mixture in 3 additions, alternating with the milk. Add the egg whites, in two additions, to the batter and gently fold until no white streaks remain.

3. Pour the batter into the pans. Bake until golden and a toothpick inserted in the center comes out clean, about 20 minutes. Cool in the pans on racks 10 minutes; remove the cakes from pans, discarding the wax paper, and cool completely on the racks.

4. To make the frosting, combine the sugar, egg whites, water, cream of tartar, and salt in the top of a double boiler. With an electric mixer on high, beat until the mixture is blended, about 1 minute. Place the mixture over rapidly boiling water and beat on high until soft peaks form, about 6 minutes. Beat in the vanilla and then remove the frosting from the heat.

5. Transfer ¹/3 of the frosting to a medium bowl; stir in the raisins, figs, and pecans. Place one cake layer, bottom-side up, on a cake plate, and spread with the raisin frosting. Place the remaining cake layer, bottom-side up, on top. Frost top and sides of cake with the remaining plain frosting. Refrigerate the cake until ready to serve.

*Per serving   304 Calories, 7 g Total Fat, 4 g Saturated Fat, 17 mg Cholesterol, 177 mg Sodium, 57 g Total Carbohydrate, 2 g Dietary Fiber, 4 g Protein, 53 mg Calcium.*

*POINTS per serving: 6.*

# Lemon Chess Pie

MAKES 8 SERVINGS

*A Southern favorite, chess pie is a custard pie made with buttermilk, butter, and sugar. The name may come from the chest in which pies and sweets were once stored, or from a wife's response to her husband's query about her dessert. She answered, "It's jes' pie." Top the pie with fresh raspberries, blueberries, or blackberries for a colorful garnish.*

3/4 cup reduced-fat buttermilk baking mix

3 tablespoons cornmeal

1 tablespoon + 1 cup sugar

3 tablespoons fat-free milk

1 tablespoon olive oil

2 tablespoons all-purpose flour

3 large eggs

1¼ cups low-fat buttermilk

1 tablespoon grated lemon zest

¼ cup fresh lemon juice

1 tablespoon unsalted butter, melted

1. Preheat the oven to 350°F. Combine the baking mix, cornmeal, and 1 tablespoon sugar in a bowl. Mix the milk and oil in another bowl. Add the milk mixture to the cornmeal mixture and stir with a fork until the dough forms a ball. Knead the dough on a lightly floured counter 5 times. With a floured rolling pin, roll out to an 11-inch circle. Line a 9-inch pie pan with the dough, folding the pastry rim below the edge of the pie pan, rather than over. Cover with plastic wrap and place in the freezer for 10 minutes.

2. Line the pie crust with foil, covering the rim, and fill with dried beans, rice, or pie weights. Bake until the rim is just starting to become pale brown, about 25 minutes. Remove the foil and beans and allow the crust to cool on a rack 15 minutes.

3. Whisk the remaining 1 cup sugar and the flour in a bowl until blended. Whisk in the eggs. Add the buttermilk, lemon zest, lemon juice, and butter; stir until blended. Pour the filling into the shell. Cover the rim with foil. Bake until the filling is set at edges but still soft in the center, 28–30 minutes. Allow to cool completely on a rack.

*Per serving  233 Calories, 6 g Total Fat, 2 g Saturated Fat, 85 mg Cholesterol, 191 mg Sodium, 40 g Total Carbohydrate, 0 g Dietary Fiber, 5 g Protein, 75 mg Calcium.*

*POINTS per serving: 5.*

# Apple Stack Cake

MAKES 12 SERVINGS

*This charming cake is a Tennessee mountain favorite. According to one legend, fancy wedding cakes were beyond the resources of many pioneer families, so neighboring women brought cake layers to the bride's family. As the layers arrived, they were spread with apple filling to hold them together.*

1 (36-ounce) jar apple sauce

1 cup packed dried apple slices

2³/4 cups all-purpose flour

2 teaspoons apple pie spice

³/4 teaspoon baking soda

¹/4 teaspoon salt

¹/3 cup solid vegetable shortening

³/4 cup sugar

¹/3 cup dark molasses

2 large eggs

³/4 cup low-fat buttermilk

Confectioners' sugar

1. Combine the apple sauce and dried apples in a large saucepan; bring to a boil. Reduce the heat and simmer until the mixture has thickened and the apples are tender, 35–40 minutes. Allow mixture to cool, cover with plastic wrap, and refrigerate until cold.

2. Adjust the oven racks to divide the oven into thirds; preheat the oven to 350°F. Lightly grease three 9-inch round cake pans with nonstick spray. Line the bottoms with wax paper. Lightly spray the wax paper with nonstick spray and flour the pans, tapping out the excess.

3. Whisk the flour, pie spice, baking soda, and salt in one bowl until blended. With an electric mixer on low speed, beat the shortening and sugar in another bowl until combined. Add the molasses and beat until smooth. Beat in the eggs, one at time, until blended. Beat in the flour mixture in three additions, alternating with the buttermilk. Divide the batter among the pans and spread evenly. Bake until a toothpick inserted in a center comes out clean, 18–20 minutes. Cool in the pans on racks 15 minutes; remove the cakes from the pans and cool completely on the racks.

4. Discard the wax paper. With a serrated knife, split each layer in half horizontally. Place 1 layer on a serving plate. Spread with about ¹/2 cup of the apple filling. Repeat with the remaining cake layers and filling, ending with a cake layer. Allow the cake to stand 1 hour before serving. Dust the top with confectioners' sugar.

★ *American Way*   If you can't find apple pie spice, combine 1¹/2 teaspoons cinnamon, ¹/4 teaspoon nutmeg, and ¹/4 teaspoon allspice; this is just enough spice to flavor one Apple Stack Cake.

*Per serving*   327 Calories, 7 g Total Fat, 2 g Saturated Fat, 36 mg Cholesterol, 168 mg Sodium, 63 g Total Carbohydrate, 3 g Dietary Fiber, 5 g Protein, 110 mg Calcium.

*POINTS per serving: 7.*

*Apple Stack Cake*

# Baked Apples in Phyllo Crust

### MAKES 4 SERVINGS

*Apples are widely available in the South, particularly in West Virginia. Typically they are wrapped in pie pastry, and baked. These are wrapped in phyllo dough. Rome or Cortland apples are ideal for this recipe. For the best texture, serve the dumplings the day they are made.*

3 tablespoons sugar

1/8 teaspoon cinnamon

4 large baking apples

8 (12 × 17-inch) sheets phyllo dough, thawed according to package directions

1/2 cup diced mixed dried fruit

1/4 cup apricot preserves

1. Preheat the oven to 375°F. Spray a jelly-roll pan with nonstick spray.

2. Mix the sugar and cinnamon in a cup. Peel the apples halfway down the sides. Core each apple from the top, cutting to within 1/2 inch of the bottom.

3. Carefully remove the phyllo sheets from the package, arrange in a flat stack, and cover with plastic wrap to retain moisture. Lay 1 sheet of the phyllo on a piece of wax paper. Spray lightly with nonstick spray and sprinkle with 1/4 of the sugar mixture. Top with another sheet of phyllo. Place an apple in the center. Fill the cavity with 2 tablespoons of the dried fruit, pressing it down to fit. Spoon 1 tablespoon of the jam over the fruit. Bring 1 corner of the phyllo up and over the apple. Repeat with the remaining 3 corners, so that the apple is completely enclosed. Spray with nonstick spray and place on the pan. Repeat with the remaining apples.

4. Place the apples on the pan and bake until the phyllo is browned and the apples are tender when pierced with a paring knife, 35–40 minutes. Cool slightly in the pan on a rack. Serve warm.

*Per serving*  343 Calories, 3 g Total Fat, 1 g Saturated Fat, 0 mg Cholesterol, 193 mg Sodium, 80 g Total Carbohydrate, 6 g Dietary Fiber, 4 g Protein, 26 mg Calcium.

*POINTS per serving: 6.*

# Apple Cobbler

MAKES 8 SERVINGS

*Cobbler—an old-fashioned crowd-pleasing dessert—can be made with just about any kind of fruit. Try using Granny Smith and Golden Delicious apples or a combination of your favorite apples.*

4 baking apples, peeled, cored, and sliced

1 cup apple juice

1 (21-ounce) can apple pie filling

1/4 teaspoon cinnamon

1 cup reduced-fat buttermilk baking mix

3 tablespoons sugar

1/4 cup fat-free milk

1 large egg

1 tablespoon vegetable oil

1. Preheat the oven to 400°F. Bring the apples and juice to a boil in a large skillet. Reduce the heat and simmer until just tender, about 5 minutes. Stir in the pie filling and cinnamon. Bring the mixture to a simmer, then remove from the heat.

2. Combine the baking mix and 2 tablespoons of the sugar in one bowl. Beat the milk, egg, and oil in another bowl. Add to the baking mix and stir the batter until blended.

3. Pour the hot apple mixture into a 2-quart shallow baking dish. Drop 8 spoonfuls of the batter over the apple mixture. Sprinkle with the remaining 1 tablespoon sugar. Place the baking dish on a baking sheet to catch any overflow. Bake until the fruit is bubbling and the top is browned, about 25 minutes. Cool slightly on a rack. Serve warm.

*Per serving* 232 Calories, 4 g Total Fat, 1 g Saturated Fat, 27 mg Cholesterol, 211 mg Sodium, 50 g Total Carbohydrate, 2 g Dietary Fiber, 3 g Protein, 37 mg Calcium.

*POINTS per serving:* 5.

# Sally Lunn

MAKES 16 SERVINGS

*Though surely a Southern favorite for decades, the origin of this cake-like bread is unconfirmed. Some lore says the dish was created by Sally Lunn of Bath, England, who served the bread in her tea shop. Another explanation credits the bread's appearance; the top is as golden as the sun—soleil in French—and the bottom is as pale as the moon—lune.*

¹/4 cup warm (105–115°F) water

¹/3 cup sugar

1 (¹/4-ounce) packet active dry yeast

³/4 cup fat-free milk

¹/4 cup unsalted butter or margarine

3 large eggs

4 cups all-purpose flour

1 teaspoon salt

1. Combine the warm water and a pinch of the sugar in a bowl. Sprinkle in the yeast and let stand until foamy, about 5 minutes.

2. Combine the milk and butter in a microwavable bowl and microwave on High until warm (105–115°F), 30–60 seconds. Add the milk and butter to the yeast mixture, along with the remaining sugar, the eggs, and 3 cups of the flour. Beat vigorously with a wooden spoon until smooth. Stir in the remaining 1 cup flour, ¹/2 cup at a time, until smooth. Beat well. Cover tightly with plastic wrap and let rise in a warm spot until it almost doubles in size, about 1 hour.

3. Spray a 12-cup fluted tube pan with nonstick spray. Stir the batter and turn it into the pan. Cover tightly and let rise again until it almost doubles in size, about 45 minutes.

4. Adjust a rack to the lower third of the oven; preheat the oven to 350°F. Bake the bread 30 minutes. Cover the top loosely with foil and bake 15 minutes more. Cool in the pan on a rack 5 minutes; remove the bread from the pan and cool on the rack completely.

*Per serving  175 Calories, 4 g Total Fat, 2 g Saturated Fat, 48 mg Cholesterol, 164 mg Sodium, 29 g Total Carbohydrate, 1 g Dietary Fiber, 5 g Protein, 25 mg Calcium.*

*POINTS per serving: 4.*

★ *American Way*   This is a batter bread and too soft to be kneaded, so it needs vigorous stirring.

# Benne Seed Wafers

## MAKES 3¹/₂ DOZEN WAFERS

*Benne seeds are the African name for sesame seeds, brought to America by slaves in the 17th century and cultivated in the South Carolina low country. These make ideal cocktail crackers and can be stored in an airtight container for up to two weeks.*

¹/₄ cup + 1 tablespoon sesame seeds

1 cup all-purpose flour

¹/₄ cup whole-wheat flour

¹/₂ teaspoon baking powder

¹/₄ teaspoon salt

2 tablespoons cold unsalted butter, cut into small pieces

¹/₃ cup fat-free milk

1 tablespoon olive oil

1. Preheat the oven to 350°F. Spread ¹/₄ cup of the sesame seeds on a baking sheet. Bake until golden brown, about 10 minutes. Transfer to a small bowl and allow to cool.

2. Combine the all-purpose flour, whole-wheat flour, baking powder, and salt in a bowl. With a pastry blender or 2 knives, cut in the butter until the mixture resembles fine meal. Stir in the toasted sesame seeds.

3. Combine ¹/₄ cup of the milk and the olive oil in another small bowl. Add to the flour mixture and stir until the dough comes together. If too dry, stir in the remaining milk. Gather the dough into a ball and divide in half. Roll each piece between 2 sheets of lightly floured wax paper to an ¹/₈-inch thickness. Refrigerate 30 minutes.

4. Spray 2 baking sheets with nonstick spray. Remove the top sheets of wax paper from the dough. Sprinkle the rounds with the remaining sesame seeds and roll lightly with a rolling pin to press in the seeds. With a 2-inch round cutter, cut out the wafers. With a spatula, transfer the wafers to the baking sheets. Gather the scraps into a ball, reroll once, and cut more rounds. Bake until browned, 10–12 minutes. Cool on a wire rack.

*Per serving  (4 wafers): 107 Calories, 6 g Total Fat, 2 g Saturated Fat, 6 mg Cholesterol, 76 mg Sodium, 12 g Total Carbohydrate, 1 g Dietary Fiber, 3 g Protein, 55 mg Calcium.*

*POINTS per serving: 2.*

# Beaten Biscuits

MAKES 20 BISCUITS

*Beaten biscuits were once pounded with a hammer on a tree stump until the dough was smooth, blistered, and cracked. These days, a food processor does all the hard work. The "biscuits" are really more like soda crackers in texture and taste and are flatter than baking powder biscuits. Considered to be a true Southern delicacy, they are traditionally split and served with thin slices of country ham.*

2 cups all-purpose flour
1/4 cup solid vegetable shortening
3/4 teaspoon salt
1/2 teaspoon baking powder
About 1/2 cup cold low-fat (1%) milk

1. Combine the flour, shortening, salt, and baking powder in a food processor. Pulse until the mixture resembles fine meal. With the machine running, add 1/2 cup milk. After the dough forms a ball, if too dry, add more milk, a teaspoon at a time, and continue processing, 2 minutes.

2. Adjust the racks to divide the oven into thirds; preheat the oven to 325°F. On a lightly floured counter, with a floured rolling pin, roll out the dough to a 12-inch square. Fold the dough in half. Roll out to a 1/2-inch thickness. With a floured 2-inch round cutter, cut out the biscuits. Place 1/2 inch apart on ungreased baking sheets. Press a floured fork three times on the top of each biscuit, pressing the fork all the way to the bottom. Gather and reroll the scraps once, and cut more biscuits. Bake until the biscuits are just golden brown on top, 30–35 minutes. Cool on a wire rack. Serve at room temperature.

*Per serving  (2 biscuits): 142 Calories, 5 g Total Fat, 1 g Saturated Fat, 0 mg Cholesterol, 201 mg Sodium, 20 g Total Carbohydrate, 1 g Dietary Fiber, 3 g Protein, 22 mg Calcium.*

*POINTS per serving: 3.*

★ *American Way*   The biscuits can be stored in an airtight container for up to two weeks.

# Sweet Potato Biscuits

MAKES 16 SERVINGS

*The dark-skinned orange-fleshed potato we commonly refer to as a yam is not a true yam, but a sweet potato. Discovered in Louisiana in the early 1700s by a Dutch explorer named Antoine Simon Le Page du Pratz, the sweet potato is actually a relative of the morning glory.*

2 cups all-purpose flour
1 tablespoon packed brown sugar
2 teaspoons baking powder
3/4 teaspoon salt
1/2 teaspoon baking soda
3 tablespoons solid vegetable shortening
1 cup mashed cooked sweet potato
1/2 cup fat-free milk

1. Preheat the oven to 425°F. Mix the flour, brown sugar, baking powder, salt, and baking soda in a bowl. With a pastry blender or 2 knives, cut in the shortening until the mixture resembles fine meal.

2. Combine the sweet potato and milk in another bowl until blended. Add the sweet potato mixture to the flour mixture; stir with a fork until moistened.

3. Knead the dough on a lightly floured counter until smooth, 10–12 times. The dough will be soft and wet. With a floured rolling pin, roll out the dough to an 8-inch square, about 1/2-inch thick. With a floured knife, cut the dough crosswise into 4 pieces and lengthwise into fourths, making 16 square biscuits. Place the biscuits 1 inch apart on ungreased baking sheets. Bake until golden brown, 12–15 minutes. Serve warm.

*Per serving  106 Calories, 3 g Total Fat, 1 g Saturated Fat, 0 mg Cholesterol, 205 mg Sodium, 18 g Total Carbohydrate, 1 g Dietary Fiber, 2 g Protein, 26 mg Calcium.*

*POINTS per serving: 2.*

★ *American Way*  Flouring the knife will keep it from sticking to the dough when cutting the biscuits. These can be frozen, wrapped airtight, for up to two months. Let the biscuits thaw at room temperature, then reheat them in a 400°F oven for 5 minutes.

*chapter six*
# Gulf States

★

## APPETIZERS/SOUPS/SALADS

Shrimp with Key Lime Cocktail Sauce

Tomato Vegetable Soup

Mississippi Caviar Salad (Black-Eyed Pea Salad)

Tomato Tapenade Salad

## ENTRÉES

Baked Shrimp

Sour Orange Grouper

Catfish with Peach Salsa

Seafood Gumbo

Pecan-Crusted Fish

Jambalaya

Chicken with Rum-Mango Sauce

## SIDES

Tropical Coleslaw

Marinated Vegetables

Parmesan Vidalia Onions

Pecan Wild Rice

Okra Goulash

## DESSERTS/SNACKS/BREADS

Key Lime Sorbet

Glazed Bananas

Peach Crisp

Sweet Potato Pie

# Shrimp with Key Lime Cocktail Sauce

### MAKES 4 SERVINGS

*Along with the distinguished key lime, the Florida Keys are known for their fresh seafood. In fact, it's one of the few areas in the United States where you can still buy shrimp minutes off the boat. With the rousingly tangy cocktail sauce, these crustaceans are perfect before-dinner nibbles.*

1¼ pounds medium shrimp, peeled and deveined

½ cup ketchup

2 tablespoons key lime juice, or fresh lime juice

2 teaspoons Worcestershire sauce

½ teaspoon hot pepper sauce

1. Rinse the shrimp under cold water and place them in a saucepan with enough cold water to cover them; heat just until the water begins to simmer. Remove the saucepan from the heat and set aside 1 minute, or until the shrimp are opaque in the center. Drain the shrimp, then plunge them into a bowl of ice water. Drain and pat dry with paper towels. Arrange on a serving platter.

2. To make the cocktail sauce, combine the ketchup, key lime juice, Worcestershire sauce, and pepper sauce in a small bowl. Taste and adjust the seasoning, adding more hot pepper sauce or Worcestershire sauce as desired. Serve the shrimp with the cocktail sauce.

*Per serving  158 Calories, 2 g Total Fat, 0 g Saturated Fat, 175 mg Cholesterol, 598 mg Sodium, 9 g Total Carbohydrate, 0 g Dietary Fiber, 24 g Protein, 69 mg Calcium.*

*POINTS per serving: 3.*

★ *American Way*  Key limes are yellow and look like small lemons; they have a distinctly citrus, not sweet, taste. Regular lime juice can be substituted for the key lime juice. You can also use bottled key lime juice, available in many gourmet markets.

# Tomato Vegetable Soup

MAKES 6 SERVINGS

*The most famous hot pepper sauce, the fiery Tabasco, has only 3 innocent sounding ingredients—peppers, salt, and vinegar—but watch out for that pepper! Here, it gives a zing to this simple and quick soup that's refreshing in summer, yet filling and satisfying for a winter meal.*

2 (15-ounce) cans low-sodium chicken broth

4¹/₂ cups low-sodium canned whole tomatoes with juice

1 pound red potatoes, sliced

1 large red onion, sliced

4 celery stalks, sliced

3–4 drops hot pepper sauce

2 tablespoons balsamic vinegar

4 cups triple-washed spinach (half a 10-ounce bag), rinsed

1 cup shredded Swiss cheese

¹/₄ teaspoon salt

Freshly ground pepper, to taste

1. Combine the broth, tomatoes, and potatoes in a large pot and bring to a boil. Stir in the onion and celery. Reduce the heat, cover, and simmer 15 minutes.

2. Mix the pepper sauce and vinegar together and add to the soup. Stir in the spinach and cook 2 minutes. (The potatoes should be cooked through; if not, cook a little longer.) Stir in the cheese and season with the salt and pepper. Spoon into bowls and serve.

*Per serving* (about 1¹/₂ cups): 203 Calories, 6 g Total Fat, 4 g Saturated Fat, 19 mg Cholesterol, 404 mg Sodium, 26 g Total Carbohydrate, 6 g Dietary Fiber, 13 g Protein, 228 mg Calcium.

*POINTS per serving: 3.*

# Mississippi Caviar Salad
# (Black-Eyed Pea Salad)

MAKES 4 SERVINGS

*Black-eyed peas originated in Asia and probably came to the South via the African slave trade. They're immediately recognizable by their unique appearance: small and beige with a black circle at their inner curve. Frozen black-eyed peas work exceptionally well in this recipe: They have an excellent texture and flavor and save a ton of preparation time.*

1 (10-ounce) package frozen
    black-eyed peas

2 tablespoons red-wine vinegar

1 tablespoon Dijon mustard

2 tablespoons vegetable oil

1 red onion, diced

1/2 teaspoon salt

Freshly ground pepper, to taste

2–3 drops hot pepper sauce

1 red bell pepper, seeded and diced

Red lettuce leaves

Cook the black-eyed peas in boiling water until tender, about 15 minutes; drain. Whisk together the vinegar and mustard in a large salad bowl. Add the oil and continue to whisk until smooth. Add the onion, salt, and pepper. Add the pepper sauce and whisk thoroughly. Add the black-eyed peas and bell pepper and toss to combine. Add more pepper or pepper sauce to taste. Line a small serving platter with the lettuce leaves and top with the salad.

*Per serving   188 Calories, 8 g Total Fat, 1 g Saturated Fat, 0 mg Cholesterol, 322 mg Sodium, 24 g Total Carbohydrate, 5 g Dietary Fiber, 8 g Protein, 47 mg Calcium.*

*POINTS per serving: 3.*

*Mississippi Caviar Salad (Black-Eyed Pea Salad)*

# Tomato Tapenade Salad

MAKES 4 SERVINGS

*A dressing with the piquant flavors of a tapenade—olives, capers, and garlic—mingles with Southern favorites—tomatoes, Vidalia onions, and toasted pecans—in this updated version of tomato salad.*

8 pitted green olives

2 tablespoons capers, drained

2 garlic cloves, crushed

2 teaspoons balsamic vinegar

4 ripe tomatoes, sliced

1/2 Vidalia onion, diced

1/4 teaspoon salt

Freshly ground pepper, to taste

2 tablespoons chopped toasted pecans

To make the tapenade, combine the olives, capers, garlic, and vinegar in a food processor and puree. Combine the tomatoes and onion and place on a serving platter; sprinkle with salt and pepper. Spoon the tapenade over the tomatoes and sprinkle with the pecans. Serve at room temperature.

*Per serving* 68 Calories, 4 g Total Fat, 0 g Saturated Fat, 0 mg Cholesterol, 441 mg Sodium, 9 g Total Carbohydrate, 2 g Dietary Fiber, 2 g Protein, 20 mg Calcium.

POINTS *per serving: 1.*

# Baked Shrimp

MAKES 4 SERVINGS

*Fresh seafood from the gulf has a taste that's superior to any fish bought frozen in the market. That's why many land-locked Southerners feel it's worth the trip to the Gulf for their fresh catch. Shrimp is a runaway favorite and appears in countless Southern recipes. This is one-pot cooking at its best—just add a green salad.*

1 large onion, sliced

1 green bell pepper, seeded and sliced

1 cup long-grain white rice

2 cups low-sodium chicken broth

2–3 drops hot pepper sauce

2 tomatoes, quartered

1½ pounds medium shrimp, peeled and deveined

½ teaspoon salt

Freshly ground pepper, to taste

2 tablespoons grated Parmesan cheese

1. Preheat the oven to 350°F. Spray a nonstick flameproof casserole dish with nonstick spray and set over medium-high heat. Add the onion and bell pepper and sauté until the vegetables are translucent, about 4 minutes. Add the rice, broth, and pepper sauce and bring to a simmer. Cover, place in the oven, and bake 20 minutes.

2. Remove the casserole from the oven. Add the tomatoes, shrimp, salt, and pepper. Cover and bake until the shrimp are opaque in the center and the rice is tender, about 15 minutes. Sprinkle with the cheese. Broil, inches from the heat, until the cheese is browned, 5–10 seconds.

*Per serving   385 Calories, 5 g Total Fat, 2 g Saturated Fat, 215 mg Cholesterol, 624 mg Sodium, 48 g Total Carbohydrate, 3 g Dietary Fiber, 36 g Protein, 142 mg Calcium.*

*POINTS per serving: 8.*

★ *American Way*  When placing the casserole under the broiler, watch it carefully; the cheese will brown quickly.

FLASHBACK >> 1694

Englishman and new governor of the Carolinas, John Archdale encourages colonial farmers to plant the bag of grain he received from a ship that just arrived from Madagascar. The exotic grain, rice, will soon become an important commercial crop in North and South Carolina, as well as Georgia, Alabama, Mississippi, and Florida.

# Sour Orange Grouper

## MAKES 4 SERVINGS

*Introduced to Florida from Spain when it was brought to the U.S. by Columbus, the bitter or sour orange is a hardy orange that stands up well in cooking—better than the more common sweet navel orange.*

1½ pounds grouper fillet or any other firm white fish fillet

1 cup fresh sour orange juice

¼ cup all-purpose flour

½ teaspoon salt

Freshly ground pepper, to taste

1 tablespoon canola oil

½ cup sliced scallions

3 garlic cloves, crushed

2 teaspoons sugar or equivalent sugar substitute

¼ cup chopped fresh parsley

1. Combine the fillets and sour orange juice in zip-close plastic bag. Squeeze out the air and seal the bag; turn to coat the fish. Refrigerate, 1 hour.

2. Combine the flour, salt, and pepper in a shallow dish or pie plate. Remove the fillets from the marinade and pat dry with paper towels; reserve the marinade. Dredge the fillets in the flour until evenly coated; shake off the excess.

3. Heat the oil a large nonstick skillet, then add the scallions and garlic; sauté 2 minutes. With a slotted spoon, transfer the softened scallions and garlic to a plate and set aside. Add the fillets to the skillet in a single layer and cook until the fish is opaque in the center, about 5 minutes on each side. Transfer the fish to a plate and cover with foil to keep warm.

4. Pour the marinade into the skillet, add the sugar, scallions, and garlic and boil, stirring constantly, 3 minutes. Spoon the sauce over fillets and sprinkle with the parsley.

*Per serving*  247 Calories, 5 g Total Fat, 1 g Saturated Fat, 63 mg Cholesterol, 313 mg Sodium, 14 g Total Carbohydrate, 1 g Dietary Fiber, 34 g Protein, 71 mg Calcium.

*POINTS per serving: 5.*

★ *American Way*  If you can't find bitter oranges, use one part sweet orange juice to one part lime juice as a substitute.

# Catfish with Peach Salsa

## MAKES 4 SERVINGS

*The days Mark Twain described—young Huck Finn caught large catfish from the Mississippi River—are long gone. Until about 20 years ago, however, catfish came from rivers, lakes, and estuaries, which accounted for their slightly muddy flavor. Now, most catfish is farm-raised and sold commercially throughout the U.S. In fact, catfish farming is one of Mississippi's largest industries.*

2 tablespoons chopped fresh cilantro

3 jalapeño peppers, seeded and chopped (wear gloves to prevent irritation)

1 tablespoon fresh lime juice

2 teaspoons honey

1/4 teaspoon ground cumin

2 ripe peaches, pitted and cut into 1/4-inch pieces

1/2 teaspoon salt

1/4 teaspoon cayenne

1/4 teaspoon freshly ground pepper

4 (6-ounce) catfish fillets

1. Preheat the broiler. Line a baking sheet with foil and spray with nonstick spray.

2. To make the salsa, combine the cilantro, jalapeño, lime juice, honey, and cumin in a medium bowl. Add the peaches and toss to combine; set aside.

3. Combine the salt, cayenne, and black pepper in a cup. Sprinkle the fillets with the spice mixture until evenly coated. Arrange the fillets on the baking sheet in a single layer.

4. Broil the fish 5 inches from the heat turning the fillets once, until the fish is just opaque in the center, 3–4 minutes on each side. Transfer the fish to a serving platter and top with the salsa.

*Per serving*   233 Calories, 10 g Total fat, 2 g Saturated Fat, 82 mg Cholesterol, 395 mg Sodium, 10 g Total Carbohydrate, 1 g Dietary Fiber, 24 g Protein, 19 mg Calcium.

*POINTS per serving: 5.*

★ *American Way*  This dish is excellent grilled. To grill, preheat a gas grill 5 minutes or a charcoal grill 20 minutes. Use a grill rack with small holes, spray with nonstick spray, and place the fish on grill grates. The cooking time will be the same.

# Seafood Gumbo

MAKES 4 SERVINGS

*Gumbo, an African contribution to Louisiana cookery, is a spicy cross between a soup and a stew. There are many variations of ingredients but all gumbos begin with a dark roux—a combination of flour and fat, slowly browned. As old Creole cooks used to say, "Don't hurry the roux. You'll spoil your gumbo." Gumbo also includes either okra—which produces a thickening agent when cooked—or filé powder (ground, dried sassafras leaves).*

½ pound okra, thinly sliced

1 large onion, thinly sliced

1 green bell pepper, seeded and sliced

2 celery stalks, sliced

2 garlic cloves, crushed

2 tablespoons olive oil

2 tablespoons all-purpose flour

3 cups water

2 bay leaves

1 teaspoon dried thyme

½ teaspoon cayenne

½ cup canned diced tomatoes, drained

½ pound large shrimp, peeled and deveined

½ pound lump crab meat, picked over

¼ teaspoon salt

Freshly ground pepper, to taste

1. Spray a large nonstick skillet with nonstick spray and set over medium-high heat. Add the okra, onion, bell pepper, celery, and garlic and sauté until translucent, 5 minutes. Transfer the vegetables to a bowl and set aside.

2. To make the roux, add the oil to the skillet and then the flour; stir until well blended. Cook, stirring, until the flour is a rich brown color, but not black, about 10 minutes.

3. Add the water in a thin stream, stirring continuously to remove any lumps, and bring to a simmer. Stir in the bay leaves, thyme, and cayenne; then add the tomatoes. Return the vegetables to the pan and simmer 5 minutes. Add the shrimp and crab meat and simmer just until the shrimp are opaque in the center, 2–3 minutes. Discard the bay leaves. Season with the salt and pepper.

*Per serving*  236 Calories, 9 g Total Fat, 1 g Saturated Fat, 127 mg Cholesterol, 515 mg Sodium, 16 g Total Carbohydrate, 4 g Dietary Fiber, 24 g Protein, 159 mg Calcium.

*POINTS per serving:* 5.

★ *American Way*  Serve this like the locals do, with plenty of Worcestershire sauce and hot pepper sauce on the side.

---

FLASHBACK > > 1704

In search of husbands, 25 "Cassette" girls, so named because of the small trunks (cassettes) they have brimming with gifts from Louis XIV, land in Mobile, Alabama, from France. These unlikely pioneers will spur the beginning of Cajun cuisine, by combining French ingredients (roux) with staples from Congolese slaves (okra) and Choctaw Indians (crawfish, crabs, pepper, and sassafras leaves, or filé) to develop such current-day classics as gumbo and jambalaya.

*Seafood Gumbo*

# THE NEW ORLEANS MELTING POT

The vibrant ethnic mix of New Orleans has always stood out from the rest of the country. In addition to the French and Spanish, who alternately tried to control the unruly port, the British, Africans, East and West Indians, Native Americans, and the Chinese lent their customs and cuisine to this colorful city. New Orleans's bustling harbor has always made abundant and exotic ingredients accessible, and the French passion for good food inspired the city's cooks to make appetizing use of them.

As early as the 18th century, ship captains went out of their way to enjoy a meal in New Orleans. Today, it remains a food lover's city where the two most prominent cuisines are Cajun and Creole. The Cajuns, or Acadians, were French settlers who were driven out of Canada in the 1750s. A poor people, they settled in the bayous far from the city. There, they integrated the plentiful game and fish of the region into the French cuisine they brought with them. The Creoles are the descendants of the French and Spanish who settled within the city. Their more sophisticated cuisine is essentially a combination of French, Spanish, and African cooking. Two characteristic components of this more cosmopolitan fare are the triumvirate of celery, onion, and sweet pepper, which forms the basis of most sauces, and the roux of flour and butter that is used to thicken them.

# Pecan-Crusted Fish

MAKES 4 SERVINGS

*The pecan, America's only indigenous nut, is a popular addition to many Gulf recipes, as Pecan trees are common throughout the area, where the temperate climate keeps them thriving and awash with the sweet nuts. Not only are pecans loaded with flavor, but they're also a healthy source of protein, as well as oleic acid, and other monoun-saturated fats.*

½ cup plain dried bread crumbs

¼ cup finely chopped pecans

½ teaspoon salt

¼ teaspoon freshly ground pepper

4 (6-ounce) grouper fillets or any other firm white fish fillet

2 egg whites, lightly beaten

1 tablespoon olive oil

1. Preheat the oven to 400°F. Line a baking sheet with foil.

2. Combine the bread crumbs, pecans, salt, and pepper in a shallow dish or pie pan. Dip the fish fillets into the egg whites and then dredge each fillet in the pecan mixture, coating both sides evenly.

3. Heat the oil in a large nonstick skillet, then add the fish in a single layer and cook turning once, until browned, about 2 minutes. Transfer the fillets to the baking sheet and bake until the fish is opaque in the center, about 8 minutes.

*Per serving   289 Calories, 10 g Total Fat, 1 g Saturated Fat, 60 mg Cholesterol, 491 mg Sodium, 11 g Total Carbohydrate, 1 g Dietary Fiber, 36 g Protein, 50 mg Calcium.*

*POINTS per serving: 6.*

# Jambalaya

MAKES 4 SERVINGS

*"Jambalaya and a crawfish pie and file gumbo. . ." sang Hank Williams in the song, "Jambalaya on the Bayou," immortalizing the hearty Cajun country specialty served on the bayous and prairies throughout Louisiana. This is a frontier-style dish that uses anything that is on hand—although chicken, tomatoes, and rice are considered essential.*

2 teaspoons canola oil

1 pound skinless boneless chicken breasts, cut into pieces

1 onion, sliced

1 celery stalk, sliced

2 green bell peppers, seeded and diced

4 garlic cloves, crushed

1 cup long-grain white rice

2 teaspoons dried thyme

1/2 teaspoon cayenne

1/2 teaspoon freshly ground pepper

2 bay leaves

3 cups low-sodium chicken broth

1/2 pound medium shrimp, peeled and deveined

2 tomatoes, diced

2 tablespoons red-wine vinegar

1/2 teaspoon salt

1. Heat the oil in a nonstick skillet, then add the chicken and cook until browned on all sides, about 5 minutes. Transfer the chicken to a plate.

2. Add the onion, celery, bell pepper, and garlic to the skillet and sauté until soft, about 10 minutes. Stir in the rice, thyme, cayenne, pepper, and bay leaves. Add the broth and stir. Reduce the heat, cover, and simmer 10 minutes.

3. Return the chicken to the skillet and simmer 5 minutes. Add the shrimp and cook until the shrimp are just opaque in the center, the chicken is cooked through, and the rice is tender, about 3 minutes more. Stir in the tomatoes and vinegar and heat through. Season with salt.

*Per serving* 419 Calories, 8 g Total Fat, 2 g Saturated Fat, 118 mg Cholesterol, 532 mg Sodium, 51 g Total Carbohydrate, 4 g Dietary Fiber, 35 g Protein, 96 mg Calcium.

*POINTS per serving: 8.*

★ *American Way* For a truly authentic jambalaya, sprinkle each serving with a liberal amount of hot pepper sauce.

# Chicken with Rum-Mango Sauce

MAKES 6 SERVINGS

*Rum was brought to the Gulf states by Caribbean travelers as early as the 1600s. As this dish shows, it partners well with mangoes, which have been cultivated in South Florida since the 19th century. There are many varieties of mangoes and, from May until September, many fortunate residents of South Florida can pick the luscious fruits from their backyard trees.*

1 large ripe mango, pitted, peeled, and sliced

2 teaspoons vegetable oil

6 (1/4-pound) skinless boneless chicken breast halves

1/4 cup light rum

1 tablespoon chopped peeled fresh ginger

1 garlic clove, crushed

1/4 teaspoon salt

Freshly ground pepper, to taste

1. Puree the mango in a food processor. Heat the oil in a nonstick skillet, then add the chicken breasts. Cook until the chicken is browned, about 2 minutes on each side. Reduce the heat and cook, turning occasionally, until the chicken is cooked through, about 10 minutes. Transfer the chicken to a plate and cover to keep warm.

2. Add the rum, ginger, garlic, salt, and pepper to the skillet and cook about 30 seconds. Stir in the mango puree and cook until heated through. Spoon the sauce over the chicken and serve.

*Per serving  266 Calories, 5 g Total Fat, 1 g Saturated Fat, 99 mg Cholesterol, 258 mg Sodium, 11 g Total Carbohydrate, 1 g Dietary Fiber, 40 g Protein, 27 mg Calcium.*

*POINTS per serving: 6.*

★ *American Way*  To pit and peel a mango, halve the mango, cutting from the pointed end to the stem end, and remove the pit. Then peel off the skin from both halves.

# Tropical Coleslaw

MAKES 8 SERVINGS

*Coleslaw gets an exotic kick from Florida grapefruit and chayote (also called christophene), a tropical squash that looks like a gnarled green pear. A member of the squash and cucumber family, chayote has a crisp texture, can be eaten either raw or cooked, and need not be peeled.*

4 cups thinly sliced green cabbage

2 carrots, peeled and grated

1 red onion, thinly sliced

1 chayote, grated

1 pink grapefruit, peeled

1 cup light mayonnaise

1 cup nonfat yogurt

2 tablespoons key lime juice,
      or fresh lime juice

1 teaspoon Dijon mustard

1/2 teaspoon salt

Freshly ground pepper, to taste

1. Combine the cabbage, carrots, onion, and chayote in a large serving bowl. Working over the bowl of vegetables, cut the grapefruit into sections, allowing the juice and flesh to fall into the bowl.

2. Combine the mayonnaise, yogurt, key lime juice, mustard, salt, and pepper in a small bowl. Add the dressing to the vegetables and toss well. Cover and refrigerate at least 2 hours or overnight.

*Per serving   103 Calories, 2 g Total Fat, 0 g Saturated Fat, 1 mg Cholesterol, 465 mg Sodium, 19 g Total Carbohydrate, 2 g Dietary Fiber, 3 g Protein, 92 mg Calcium.*

*POINTS per serving: 2.*

★ *American Way*  If you can't find chayote, jicama would be a good substitute.

FLASHBACK >> 1833

On his land in South Miami, horticulturist Henry Perrine plants Mexican varieties of avocado, commonly referred to as alligator pear. However, uninterested farmers will not grow them commercially until 1901.

# Marinated Vegetables

MAKES 6 SERVINGS

*Hot sauce is an integral part of the culture and fabric of Louisiana. There are countless varieties, offering different degrees of heat and nuances of flavor, and all have their devotees. The amount of hot sauce called for in this recipe yields a tangy dressing with mild heat. If you like more kick, feel free to add more sauce.*

3 tablespoons red-wine vinegar

3 tablespoons Dijon mustard

1/4 cup water

1/4 cup diced red onion

1 tablespoon olive oil

2–3 drops hot pepper sauce

1/2 teaspoon salt

Freshly ground pepper, to taste

1 small head cauliflower, trimmed and cut into small florets

4 carrots, peeled and thinly sliced

1 zucchini, thinly sliced

2 cups thawed frozen lima beans

1. Combine the vinegar and mustard in a bowl and whisk until smooth. Whisk in the water until blended. Whisk in the onion, olive oil, pepper sauce, salt, and pepper. Add more pepper sauce, if desired.

2. Add the cauliflower, carrots, zucchini, and lima beans to a large pot of boiling water. When the water returns to a boil, immediately drain and rinse the vegetables under cold water to stop the cooking. Toss the vegetables with the dressing until well coated. Refrigerate, stirring occasionally, at least 2 hours or overnight.

*Per serving   123 Calories, 3 g Total Fat, 0 g Saturated Fat, 0 mg Cholesterol, 298 mg Sodium, 20 g Total Carbohydrate, 6 g Dietary Fiber, 6 g Protein, 51 mg Calcium.*

*POINTS per serving: 2.*

# Parmesan Vidalia Onions

## MAKES 4 SERVINGS

*Vidalia, Georgia, supplied the name for these sweet, juicy onions that are so mild, a simple drizzling with Worcestershire sauce and a few minutes in the microwave is really all they need. The area's soil and climate produce large, pale yellow onions that were one of the first sweet onions produced. Keep an eye out for them in your supermarket, or look for other sweet onions. These are delicious with roasted or grilled meat.*

4 large Vidalia onions, sliced
1 cup low-sodium chicken broth
2 teaspoons olive oil
1 tablespoon all-purpose flour
1 cup fat-free milk
1/4 teaspoon ground nutmeg
1/4 teaspoon salt
1/8 teaspoon freshly ground pepper
1 cup plain dried bread crumbs
1/4 cup grated Parmesan cheese

1. Spray a skillet with nonstick spray and set over medium-high heat. Add the onions and sauté 1 minute. Add the broth and bring the mixture to a boil. Reduce the heat, cover, and simmer gently until the liquid has evaporated and the onions have begun to color, about 10 minutes. With a slotted spoon, transfer the onions to a shallow ovenproof baking dish.

2. Preheat the broiler. Add the oil to the skillet and whisk in the flour. Add the milk in a thin stream, whisking continuously to remove lumps. When the milk begins to thicken and bubble, remove the skillet from the heat, and stir in the nutmeg, salt, and pepper.

3. Pour the sauce over the onions and stir gently. Combine the bread crumbs and cheese and sprinkle over the onions. Broil, 5 inches from the heat, until the top is golden, 2–3 minutes.

*Per serving  355 Calories, 8 g Total Fat, 2 g Saturated Fat, 6 mg Cholesterol, 775 mg Sodium, 58 g Total Carbohydrate, 4 g Dietary Fiber, 14 g Protein, 303 mg Calcium.*

*POINTS per serving: 7.*

# Pecan Wild Rice

MAKES 6 SERVINGS

*Rice is a big player in Louisiana cooking—from jambalaya to dirty rice, a Cajun specialty that consists of cooked rice mixed with ground poultry livers and gizzards. Wild rice, which is really the seed of an aquatic grass, is also widely used. In true Cajun style, this dish is finished with pecans that have been toasted with cayenne, adding a little punch to the crunchiness.*

2 tablespoons pecan pieces
1/8 teaspoon cayenne
1 1/2 cups water
1/2 cup wild rice, rinsed
1 tablespoon olive oil
1 large red onion, sliced
4 garlic cloves, crushed
1/2 cup long-grain white rice
1 1/2 cups low-sodium chicken broth
1/2 teaspoon salt
Freshly ground pepper, to taste

1. Preheat the oven to 350°F. In a shallow baking pan, toss the pecans with the cayenne and bake until the pecans begin to brown, 2–4 minutes; set aside to cool.

2. Combine the water and wild rice in a saucepan and bring to a boil. Reduce the heat, cover, and simmer until the rice is just tender and the grains are beginning to split open, 35–45 minutes.

3. Meanwhile, heat the oil in a nonstick skillet, then add the onion and garlic and sauté 3 minutes. Stir in the white rice and sauté 2 minutes. Pour in the broth and bring to a boil. Reduce the heat, cover, and simmer gently until the rice is tender and the broth is absorbed, about 15 minutes.

4. Combine the wild rice, white rice, salt, and pepper in a bowl. Sprinkle with the toasted pecans just before serving.

*Per serving*   *159 Calories, 5 g Total Fat, 1 g Saturated Fat, 1 mg Cholesterol, 231 mg Sodium, 26 g Total Carbohydrate, 2 g Dietary Fiber, 5 g Protein, 20 mg Calcium.*

*POINTS per serving: 3.*

# Okra Goulash

MAKES 4 SERVINGS

*Okra, which traveled to America with the Ethiopian slaves, is a staple in many Gulf Coast kitchens. Available in the South throughout the year, it is a mild tasting, green, ridged pod. When buying fresh okra, select smaller pods, which are usually more tender than the larger pods. Okra, when cooked, produces a thickening substance that gives the vegetable its characteristic slippery texture.*

1 large onion, chopped
$1/2$ cup water
2 tablespoons Hungarian or hot paprika
2 teaspoons all-purpose flour
1 cup low-sodium chicken broth
2 teaspoons tomato paste
3–4 sprigs fresh flat-leaf parsley
1 bay leaf
1 teaspoon dried thyme
1 pound okra, trimmed and cut into 1-inch slices
2 garlic cloves, crushed
2 large tomatoes, each cut into 8 wedges
1 red bell pepper, seeded and finely chopped
$1/4$ teaspoon salt
Freshly ground pepper, to taste
2 tablespoons light sour cream

1. Heat a nonstick skillet, then add the onion and water. Cook until the onion softens, 5 minutes. Add the paprika and cook 30 seconds. Stir in the flour and cook 30 seconds more. Add the broth, tomato paste, parsley, bay leaf, and thyme; stir until blended. Add the okra and garlic; reduce the heat, cover, and simmer 15 minutes.

2. Chop half of the tomato wedges and add to the skillet. Add half the bell pepper and cook the mixture 5 minutes. Season with the salt and pepper. Discard the parsley sprigs and bay leaf. Serve the goulash topped with the remaining tomato wedges, bell pepper, and the sour cream.

*Per serving* 117 Calories, 2 g Total Fat, 1 g Saturated Fat, 4 mg Cholesterol, 208 mg Sodium, 23 g Total Carbohydrate, 7 g Dietary Fiber, 6 g Protein, 133 mg Calcium.

*POINTS per serving: 1.*

FLASHBACK >> 1953

Bon Ton Café, showcasing Cajun cooking, opens in New Orleans. Some 35 years later, chef Paul Prudhomme's K-Paul Louisiana Kitchen opens, introducing this robust cuisine to the rest of the world.

# Key Lime Sorbet

## MAKES 4 SERVINGS

*Key limes, with their fragrant and fresh flavor, are the culinary star of the Florida Keys. Bottled key lime juice, which can be found in many gourmet markets, will make this recipe authentic, but using fresh lime juice will taste delicious too!*

3/4 cup sugar
3/4 cup water
1/2 cup key lime juice
1 egg white

1. To make the sugar syrup, combine the sugar and water in a saucepan and cook until the sugar has dissolved, about 5 minutes. Bring the syrup to a boil and immediately remove the pan from the heat. Set aside to cool.

2. Stir in the key lime juice, cover, and refrigerate until thoroughly chilled. Partially freeze the mixture in an ice cream maker according to the manufacturer's instructions. When the mixture is partly frozen, beat the egg white to stiff peaks, and fold it into the mixture. Continue to freeze until the sorbet is firm. Serve immediately or freeze in an airtight container until ready to serve.

*Per serving   152 Calories, 0 g Total Fat, 0 g Saturated Fat, 0 mg Cholesterol, 14 mg Sodium, 39 g Total Carbohydrate, 0 g Dietary Fiber, 1 g Protein, 4 mg Calcium.*

*POINTS per serving: 3.*

★ *American Way*  Homemade sorbet is best when stored in an airtight container and eaten within two days. If it becomes partially melted and then frozen again it will lose its soft texture; simply pulse the sorbet a few times in a food processor. The sugar syrup can be prepared ahead and refrigerated in an airtight container until you are ready to make the sorbet.

## Exclusive Commodities

The tropical climate of the Gulf States creates ideal conditions for some unique foods. Key limes, crawfish, and a special hot pepper—all regional ingredients—thrive in the balmy weather and have gained popularity throughout the United States for their unmatched flavors.

Key limes, a special variety of the citrus fruits that are small, yellowish (not the vibrant green of other limes) globes, refuse to grow outside their exclusive South Florida home. Despite its widespread unavailability, countless clamor for this tangy fruit for one reason and one reason alone: the Key lime pie, which gets its intense flavor from this distinguished lime. Fortunately for lovers of the tangy pie, more and more of the fruit are now grown on the Keys, and the canned or frozen juice is now shipped nationwide, so an authentic Key lime pie can be enjoyed in practically every state.

Although other parts of the world call these freshwater crustaceans crayfish or écrevisses, everyone in Louisiana knows them as crawfish, crawdads, or even mud bugs. As the primary producers and consumers of crawfish, Louisianans have discovered that they are a perfect second crop that can be reaped from fields that have been flooded for rice production. As a result, there are plenty to share with the rest of America. If you're lucky enough to find them in your local fish market, just boil them and eat them with your fingers, as they do in Louisiana.

Since the mid-19th century, the McIlhenny family of Avery Island, Louisiana, has been growing Tabasco peppers for the exclusive production of the hot sauce that bears the pepper's name. Fermented for 3 years before being processed, these peppers deliver both flavor and punch to America's most famous hot sauce.

# Glazed Bananas

MAKES 4 SERVINGS

*New Orleans is a banana-importing city, making the fruit a popular addition to many main dishes and desserts there. Bananas Foster, a famous New Orleans dessert, was named after Dick Foster, who was in charge of cleaning up crime in the famous Latin Quarter in the 1950s. This glazed banana dish is lighter, but still conveys the sweet taste of the original.*

1 tablespoon unsalted butter

¼ cup packed brown sugar

½ teaspoon cinnamon

½ cup orange juice

4 ripe bananas, peeled and cut on the diagonal into ½-inch–thick slices

Heat the butter, brown sugar, and cinnamon in a nonstick skillet until the sugar dissolves, but do not boil, about 5 minutes. Add the orange juice and mix well. Add the bananas and gently cook, turning once or twice, until the bananas are just soft, 3–5 minutes. Serve the bananas with the glaze spooned on top.

*Per serving  202 Calories, 4 g Total Fat, 2 g Saturated Fat, 8 mg Cholesterol, 7 mg Sodium, 44 g Total Carbohydrate, 3 g Dietary Fiber, 1 g Protein, 27 mg Calcium.*

*POINTS per serving: 4.*

# Peach Crisp

MAKES 6 SERVINGS

*Georgia is the Peach State, so it's no surprise that the sweet fruit infiltrates many parts of life there. The word peach is in the name of nearly every main thoroughfare and dozens of buildings in Atlanta. The peach tree originated in China in the fifth century B.C., and made its way to Japan, France, and then the U.S. Georgia's climate is ideal for growing peaches, which are best when tree-ripened, since they stop developing sweetness after they are picked.*

4 peaches, pitted and sliced

1 tablespoon fresh lemon juice

1 (.035-ounce) package sugar substitute, or 1 tablespoon sugar

³/4 teaspoon cinnamon

¹/4 cup all-purpose flour

¹/4 cup old-fashioned rolled oats

¹/4 cup packed brown sugar

2 tablespoons unsalted butter, cut into small pieces

1. Preheat the oven to 400°F. Arrange the peaches in an 10 × 7-inch oval baking dish or 8-inch pie pan. Add the lemon juice and toss until the fruit is well coated. Mix together the sugar substitute and ¹/4 teaspoon of the cinnamon in a bowl. Sprinkle over the peaches, and toss to combine.

2. Combine the flour, oatmeal, brown sugar, and the remaining ¹/2 teaspoon of cinnamon in another bowl. Add the butter and rub the mixture with your fingertips to form a crumbly mixture. Sprinkle over the peaches. Bake until browned and bubbling, about 30 minutes.

*Per serving   132 Calories, 4 g Total Fat, 3 g Saturated Fat, 11 mg Cholesterol, 5 mg Sodium, 23 g Total Carbohydrate, 2 g Dietary Fiber, 2 g Protein, 18 mg Calcium.*

*POINTS per serving: 3.*

★ *American Way*  Peaches are either freestone—the pit comes away from the flesh easily—or, clingstone—the pit sticks to the fruit. With either type of peach, select fragrant fruit that gives a little to the touch.

FLASHBACK ›› 1513

Ponce de Leon, the onetime governor of Puerto Rico, discovers Florida and finds the natives sustaining themselves on venison, wild turkeys, fish, shellfish, and corn and beans they cultivate. De Leon plants orange and lemon trees. The same year, Spanish travelers plant peaches which will eventually work their way up the Atlantic Coast and westward to the Mississippi.

*Peach Crisp*

# Sweet Potato Pie

MAKES 12 SERVINGS

*Though many Americans only enjoy sweet potatoes as part of their Thanksgiving spread, the tuber plays an important and broader role the cooking of the South, especially in traditional African-American recipes. Sweet potato pie is the epitome of classic soul food.*

1 cup all-purpose flour

1/2 teaspoon salt

4 tablespoons unsalted butter

1 tablespoon solid vegetable shortening

About 1/4 cup cold water

1 1/4 pounds sweet potatoes, peeled and chopped

1/4 cup fat-free milk

3 tablespoons packed brown sugar

1 tablespoon liquid margarine

3/4 teaspoon cinnamon

3/4 teaspoon ground nutmeg

1 egg

1. Sift the flour and salt together into a bowl. With a pastry blender or 2 knives, cut the butter and shortening into the flour until the mixture resembles coarse crumbs. Make a well in the center of the mixture and add 1 tablespoon water. Mix with a fork, adding the remaining water as needed to moisten the dough. Shape the dough into a ball, wrap in plastic, and refrigerate at least 30 minutes or overnight.

2. Meanwhile, combine the sweet potatoes with enough water to cover in a large saucepan. Bring the water to a boil. Partially cover and boil until the potatoes are soft, 20 minutes. Drain and mash the potatoes; let stand until cool.

3. On a lightly floured counter, roll the dough to a 1/4-inch thickness. Line a 9-inch pie pan with the dough and trim off the excess pastry along the edge.

4. Adjust the racks to divide the oven in half; preheat the oven to 400°F. Stir the milk, brown sugar, margarine, cinnamon, and nutmeg into the potatoes. Add the egg and mix well. Spoon the filling into the pie shell. Bake until a toothpick inserted just off center comes out clean, about 45 minutes. Allow to cool on a rack, 15–20 minutes. Serve warm.

*Per serving  153 Calories, 7 g Total Fat, 3 g Saturated Fat, 29 mg Cholesterol, 121 mg Sodium, 21 g Total Carbohydrate, 1 g Dietary Fiber, 2 g Protein, 25 mg Calcium.*

*POINTS per serving: 3.*

*chapter seven*
# Southwest

## APPETIZERS/SOUPS/SALADS

Layered Refried Bean Dip

Corn, Tomato, and Basil Soup

Watermelon Salad with Lime, Cumin, and Fresh Cilantro

Orange, Jicama, and Radish Salad

Spinach and Avocado Salad with Cumin Vinaigrette

Black Bean Salad with Chipotle Salsa

## ENTRÉES

Corn and Tomatillo Burritos

Vegetable Quesadillas for Two

Low-Fat Spicy Bowl o' Red

Black Bean Soup with Chicken, Tomatoes, and Lime

Soft Chicken Tacos

Spicy Shrimp Fajitas with Radish and Tomato Salsa

Chicken Enchiladas with Tomatillo Sauce

Grilled Tequila-Lime Chicken

Poblano Posole with Grilled Chicken

Grilled Beef Filets with Chive Butter

Grilled Beef Burritos with Warm Vegetable Salsa

## SIDES

Carrots with Cumin

Hopi-Style Spinach with Pine Nuts and Cider Vinegar

Pinto Beans with Green Chiles

Roasted Poblanos Stuffed with Coriander Rice

## DESSERTS/SNACKS/BREADS

Watermelon Granita

Strawberry Margarita Sorbet

Rice Pudding with Lemon and Coriander

Café con Leche Flan

Mexican-Style Chocolate Pudding

Corn Muffins with Chiles

# Layered Refried Bean Dip

## MAKES 8 SERVINGS

*This decidedly new American recipe is destined to become a snacking classic. The real star of the dish is canned refried beans, a terrifically versatile and tasty convenience food (a fat-free version is widely available). Depending on your family's tolerance for spicy fare, choose mild, medium, or hot salsa.*

1 cup bottled thick and chunky salsa

1 (16-ounce) can fat-free refried beans

1 cup finely chopped romaine lettuce

2 scallions, thinly sliced

3 plum tomatoes, finely chopped

1 small red onion, finely chopped

1/4 cup light sour cream

1/2 Haas avocado, peeled and finely chopped

1 tablespoon finely chopped fresh cilantro

1/4 pound baked tortilla chips (about 8 chips per serving)

1. Combine $3/4$ cup of the salsa with the beans in a small bowl. Layer the ingredients in a $1^1/2$-quart clear glass bowl in this order: the refried bean mixture, lettuce, scallions, tomatoes, red onion, and the remaining $1/4$ cup salsa.

2. Just before serving, place the sour cream in the center of the dip, top with the avocado, and sprinkle with cilantro. Serve with tortilla chips.

*Per serving  ($1/2$ cup dip with 8 chips): 150 Calories, 4 g Total Fat, 1 g Saturated Fat, 3 mg Cholesterol, 542 mg Sodium, 26 g Total Carbohydrate, 4 g Dietary Fiber, 6 g Protein, 92 mg Calcium.*

*POINTS per serving: 3.*

★ *American Way*  Assemble this recipe up to 8 hours ahead of serving, wrap in plastic, and refrigerate, but wait to top with sour cream and avocado until just before serving.

# Corn, Tomato, and Basil Soup

## MAKES 6 SERVINGS

*Corn is still the staff of life in the Southwest and this dish is a great way to showcase it. Perfect in the summertime, it highlights the best of the seasonal produce—with no need to turn on a burner or heat your oven.*

4 cups low-fat buttermilk

4 tomatoes, seeded and chopped

2 cups fresh corn kernels
   (from about 4 ears)

1 cup finely chopped seeded
   English cucumber

1/2 teaspoon salt

Freshly ground pepper, to taste

12 basil leaves

1. Combine the buttermilk, tomatoes, corn, cucumber, salt, and pepper in a large bowl. Refrigerate, covered, until chilled, at least 2 hours.

2. Just before serving, finely shred the basil leaves. Serve the soup sprinkled with the basil.

*Per serving  (1 generous cup): 145 Calories, 2 g Total Fat, 1 g Saturated Fat, 6 mg Cholesterol, 382 mg Sodium, 26 g Total Carbohydrate, 3 g Dietary Fiber, 8 g Protein, 200 mg Calcium.*

*POINTS per serving: 2.*

★ *American Way*  We prefer English cucumbers, because they have better flavor and texture. Unlike other cucumbers, their peels aren't waxed, so you can leave them on, adding a bit more fiber. In a pinch, you can use a regular cucumber, but peel it first. The soup can be made up to 6 hours ahead of serving time.

# Watermelon Salad with Lime, Cumin, and Fresh Cilantro

### MAKES 6 SERVINGS

*Nothing says summertime like a refreshing, sweet slice of watermelon. If you've never thought to try watermelon in a savory dish, give this recipe a whirl. It's fabulous as a first course or paired with a hearty entrée, like grilled steak or chops.*

¼ teaspoon ground cumin

¼ teaspoon ground coriander

¼ teaspoon chili powder

¼ teaspoon salt

Pinch cayenne

2 pounds watermelon, rind discarded, seeded if desired, and cut into chunks (about 4 cups)

¼ cup fresh cilantro leaves

3 tablespoons fresh lime juice

1. Combine the cumin, coriander, chili powder, salt, and cayenne in a small bowl.

2. Just before serving, combine the watermelon with the spice mixture, the cilantro, and lime juice; toss gently and serve.

*Per serving* 33 Calories, 0 g Total Fat, 0 g Saturated Fat, 0 mg Cholesterol, 102 mg Sodium, 8 g Total Carbohydrate, 1 g Dietary Fiber, 1 g Protein, 10 mg Calcium.

*POINTS per serving: 0.*

★ *American Way* Don't combine all the ingredients until just before serving, otherwise the salt will draw out the liquid from the melon. To save seeding time, select seedless watermelon.

# Orange, Jicama, and Radish Salad

## MAKES 4 SERVINGS

*Many Southwesterners have adopted the Mexican tradition of coupling jicama and oranges for a Christmas Eve salad called* Ensalada de Noche Buena. *It's a wonderful holiday dish, but the combination is refreshing all year round. You might prefer it served on greens—watercress, romaine, or a combination of the two. We also like the salad when the jicama is cut into julienne strips or matchsticks.*

1 tablespoon vegetable oil

1 tablespoon fresh lime juice

1/4 teaspoon salt

Freshly ground pepper, to taste

1 jicama, peeled and chopped

4 oranges, peeled and cut into segments

4 scallions, thinly sliced

2 large radishes, halved lengthwise and thinly sliced

1/3 cup fresh cilantro leaves

1. To make the dressing, combine the oil, lime juice, salt, and pepper in a bowl.

2. Combine the jicama, oranges, scallions, and radishes in another bowl. Drizzle the dressing over the salad, add the cilantro, gently toss, and serve immediately.

*Per serving   127 Calories, 4 g Total Fat, 0 g Saturated Fat, 0 mg Cholesterol, 156 mg Sodium, 24 g Total Carbohydrate, 7 g Dietary Fiber, 2 g Protein, 80 mg Calcium.*

*POINTS per serving: 1.*

★ *American Way*  Jicama, a tropical root vegetable, looks like a rough brown turnip and tastes like a cross between water chestnuts and apples. It has crisp flesh that complements spicy dishes. Choose small, relatively smooth-skinned jicama bulbs, and store in the refrigerator for up to two weeks.

# Spinach and Avocado Salad with Cumin Vinaigrette

## MAKES 6 SERVINGS

*Lime, tequila, cilantro, and avocado are classic Southwestern ingredients. They meld together wonderfully in this recipe, adding zesty flavor and color to this spinach-based salad.*

3 tablespoons fresh lime juice

2 tablespoons tequila or vegetable broth

1 tablespoon olive oil

1 tablespoon finely chopped fresh cilantro

1 teaspoon sugar

1/4 teaspoon ground cumin

1/4 teaspoon salt

Freshly ground pepper, to taste

1 Haas avocado, peeled and thinly sliced

1 small red onion, thinly sliced

1 (10-ounce) bag triple-washed spinach, rinsed and torn

Combine the lime juice, tequila, olive oil, cilantro, sugar, cumin, salt, and pepper in a serving bowl. Stir in the avocado and red onion. Add the spinach and toss to combine. Serve immediately.

*Per serving   94 Calories, 7 g Total Fat, 1 g Saturated Fat, 0 mg Cholesterol, 157 mg Sodium, 4 g Total Carbohydrate, 6 g Dietary Fiber, 2 g Protein, 44 mg Calcium.*

*POINTS per serving: 1.*

### FLASHBACK >> 1987

Santa Fe's Coyote Café opens, touting fresh, creative Southwestern fare with a sophisticated edge. The trend for Tex-Mex is off and running; thousands of miles away in Chicago, Frontera restaurant opens the same year. Both restaurants are still going strong.

# Black Bean Salad with Chipotle Salsa

MAKES 6 SERVINGS

*A chipotle chile is simply a smoked, dried jalapeño—in fact, the word* chipotle *is a combination of the Aztec words for* chile *and* smoked. *Serve this quick prep, pretty salad on a bed of greens—try shredded romaine or spinach leaves. Add rice, grilled chicken, or shrimp to make a complete meal.*

2 (19-ounce) cans black beans, rinsed and drained

1 small yellow bell pepper, seeded and finely chopped

2 small tomatoes, seeded and chopped

1 small white onion, finely chopped

1/4 cup finely chopped fresh cilantro

2 scallions, thinly sliced

2 tablespoons fresh lime juice

1 tablespoon olive oil

1–2 chipotles from canned chipotles en adobo, seeded and minced (or 1–2 chipoltes, soaked in 1 cup hot water)

1–2 teaspoons adobo sauce (or 1–2 teaspoons soaking liquid)

1–2 garlic cloves, minced

1/4 teaspoon salt

Combine the beans, bell pepper, tomatoes, onion, cilantro, scallions, lime juice, olive oil, chipotles, adobo sauce or soaking liquid (if using), garlic, and salt in a bowl. Serve at room temperature or chilled.

*Per serving*  145 Calories, 3 g Total Fat, 0 g Saturated Fat, 0 mg Cholesterol, 511 mg Sodium, 30 g Total Carbohydrate, 10 g Dietary Fiber, 8 g Protein, 71 mg Calcium.

*POINTS per serving: 1.*

★ *American Way*  Chipotles are available in many supermarkets. Smoke-dried—they look like a wrinkled dried mushroom—or canned in adobo sauce—*chipotles en adobo*—their heat level ranges from hot to fiery. The chile and the tomato-based adobo sauce add an incomparable smoky flavor to salsa, sauces, and stews.

# Corn and Tomatillo Burritos

MAKES 4 SERVINGS

*Even though they are not related to tomatoes, tomatillos are sometimes called* tomate de bolsa *(tomato in a bag) because they resemble green tomatoes with husks. Also like green tomatoes, they are tart, citric, and have a deliciously different flavor. The tomatillo sauce can be made ahead and will retain its intense green color for several days. Try this dish for a casual bunch.*

10 fresh tomatillos (about 1 pound), husked, rinsed, and quartered

1 white onion, finely chopped

1/2 cup finely chopped fresh cilantro

1 tablespoon vegetable oil

1 teaspoon sugar

1 garlic clove, minced

1/2 teaspoon salt

1 small fennel bulb, finely chopped

3 cups fresh corn kernels (from about 6 ears)

1 jalapeño pepper, seeded and minced (wear gloves to prevent irritation)

Pinch cayenne

3 tomatoes, seeded and chopped

4 (10-inch) flour tortillas

1/4 cup light sour cream

1. Combine the tomatillos, 1/2 cup of the onion, cilantro, 1 teaspoon of the oil, the sugar, garlic, and 1/4 teaspoon of the salt in a food processor. Pulse until the tomatillos are coarsely chopped.

2. Heat the remaining 2 teaspoons oil in a nonstick skillet, then add the remaining onion and the fennel and sauté until the fennel is softened, about 5 minutes. Stir in the corn, jalapeño, the remaining 1/4 teaspoon salt, and the cayenne. Sauté until the corn is softened. Stir in 1 cup of the tomatillo mixture and the tomatoes and sauté until heated through.

3. Meanwhile, warm each tortilla in a dry skillet, about 1 minute on each side. Place about 1 cup corn mixture in the center of each tortilla and fold in the sides. Top each burrito with 1 tablespoon of the sour cream and serve with the tomatillo sauce.

*Per serving  383 Calories, 8 g Total Fat, 2 g Saturated Fat, 5 mg Cholesterol, 710 mg Sodium, 74 g Total Carbohydrate, 18 g Dietary Fiber, 12 g Protein, 109 mg Calcium.*

*POINTS per serving: 5.*

# Vegetable Quesadillas for Two

## MAKES 2 SERVINGS

*A quesadilla is essentially a Mexican grilled cheese sandwich; in New Mexico, flour tortillas serve as the bread. This makes a super-satisfying, quick, and easy snack or* antojito *(light meal) at anytime of day—even breakfast. To serve more people simply double or triple the recipe.*

2 plum tomatoes, chopped

1 small zucchini, halved lengthwise and thinly sliced

1 small yellow bell pepper, seeded and finely chopped

1 scallion, thinly sliced

1 jalapeño pepper, seeded and minced (wear gloves to prevent irritation)

1 tablespoon finely chopped fresh cilantro

2 (10-inch) flour tortillas

$^1$/$_3$ cup shredded reduced-fat *queso blanco* or Monterey Jack cheese

2 tablespoons plain nonfat or low-fat yogurt

4 fresh cilantro sprigs, for garnish

1. Combine the tomatoes, zucchini, bell pepper, scallion, jalapeño, and chopped cilantro in a bowl.

2. Warm a tortilla in a dry skillet for 1 minute. Turn the tortilla over, scatter $1^1$/$_2$ cups of the tomato mixture over it, add the cheese, and top with the remaining tortilla. Cook, turning once, with a spatula, until the tomato mixture is hot and the cheese is melted, 1–2 minutes on each side.

3. Cut the quesadilla in half and top each serving with some of the remaining tomato mixture. Spoon 1 tablespoon of yogurt over each quesadilla and serve with 2 cilantro sprigs.

*Per serving  245 Calories, 5 g Total Fat, 3 g Saturated Fat, 13 mg Cholesterol, 485 mg Sodium, 39 g Total Carbohydrate, 13 g Dietary Fiber, 13 g Protein, 229 mg Calcium.*

*POINTS per serving: 3.*

★ *American Way*  These can easily be prepared in the microwave. Just cook until the cheese is melted, which should about 30 seconds.

# Low-Fat Spicy Bowl o' Red

MAKES 4 SERVINGS

*In 1977 Texas declared chili con carne its state dish, although there are those Texans who insist on calling it the national dish of Texas. Chili purists contend that the chili doesn't taste right unless it is cooked in an iron pot, which will also add iron to your diet.*

2 tablespoons chili powder

1 tablespoon ancho chile powder (optional)

2 teaspoons ground cumin

2 teaspoons ground coriander

1 teaspoon dried oregano

1 teaspoon salt

Freshly ground pepper, to taste

1 tablespoon vegetable oil

2 pounds top sirloin, round, or chuck steak, trimmed of all visible fat and cut into 1/2-inch pieces

1 large white onion, finely chopped

6 garlic cloves, minced

1 (12-ounce) can light beer

1 (141/2-ounce) can diced tomatoes

1 cup water

1 cup nonfat sour cream

Thinly sliced scallions

Fresh cilantro leaves

1. Combine the chili powder, ancho chile powder, if using, cumin, coriander, oregano, salt, and pepper in a small bowl. Set aside.

2. Heat the oil in a Dutch oven. In batches, add the beef and sauté until browned; with a slotted spoon, transfer each batch to a bowl and keep warm. Add the onion to the Dutch oven and sauté until browned, then add the garlic and sauté until fragrant.

3. Add 1/4 cup of the beer to the chili powder mixture and stir to make a paste. Add the paste to the onion mixture and sauté just until fragrant. Add the remaining beer and stir, scraping up any browned bits. Add the beef, tomatoes, and water and bring to a boil. Reduce the heat and simmer, stirring occasionally, until the meat is tender, about 1–11/2 hours.

4. Serve the chili with sour cream and sprinkle with the scallions and cilantro.

*Per serving (11/2 cups): 455 Calories, 13 g Total Fat, 3 g Saturated Fat, 104 mg Cholesterol, 1,223 mg Sodium, 26 g Total Carbohydrate, 4 g Dietary Fiber, 54 g Protein, 180 mg Calcium.*

*POINTS per serving: 9.*

★ *American Way* The ancho chile, a dried poblano, has an earthy and mild flavor; it can be used in relatively large quantities, providing the depth of chile flavor without scalding heat. If you can't find ancho chile powder, look for whole anchos (they're worth the search) and grind them in a spice grinder. Serve the chili with warmed pinto beans. Or, you can order ancho chile powder by mail from: El Paso Chile Company, 909 Texas Avenue, El Paso, Texas 79901; 800-274-7468.

FLASHBACK >> 1828

A visitor to San Antonio writes about a tasty dish that's popular in Mexico's Texas territory: chili con carne.

# Chili: A National Food Fight

Nothing arouses the passion of a chili lover as much as defending the integrity of his or her chili recipe. The simple matter of a bit of tomato in the chili's sauce can send some Texans into a frenzy, while just further west, tomato—and beans—is perfectly acceptable. In Cincinnati, it's served over spaghetti. And the affair grows more complicated all the time, with new chili recipes being invented every day.

Across the country the enthusiasm for the dish has led to a mounting interest in chili contests. Local competitions send winners to regional competitions, which then send winners on to the national competition held each year on Halloween weekend. There, grown men and women stir huge cauldrons of their own secret recipe, vying to be recognized for the ultimate chili.

One thing is certain in these chili wars: There likely will never be a national consensus on chili. However, here are some of the chilies that have captured the hearts of aficionados within their regional domains.

**New Mexico Chili**—A combination of ground meat, garlic, onions, chicken broth, crushed dried red chile peppers, and herbs.

**Texas-style Chili Con Carne**—Chunks of meat sautéed with garlic, onions, dried chile peppers, salt, and water; sometimes called "bowl of red."

**Cincinnati Chili**—Often called Five-Way and served as a stack of spaghetti, chili sauce, beans, chopped onion, and shredded cheese.

# Black Bean Soup with Chicken, Tomatoes, and Lime

## MAKES 6 SERVINGS

*Through the ages, beans have been a staple ingredient in many regions of the country, including in the Southwest. Paired with rice or tortillas, they have been enjoyed in everything from breakfast to lunch to dinner fare. This is a grand version of a black bean soup, with lots of spices and plenty of chicken.*

1 tablespoon vegetable oil

1 onion, finely chopped

1 jalapeño pepper, seeded and minced (wear gloves to prevent irritation)

2 garlic cloves, minced

1/2 teaspoon chili powder

1/2 teaspoon ground cumin

1/2 teaspoon ground coriander

1/4 teaspoon salt

3 cups low-sodium chicken broth

2 (19-ounce) cans black beans, rinsed and drained

1 pound cooked skinless boneless chicken breasts, shredded

2 cups cherry tomatoes, quartered

1/4 cup finely chopped fresh cilantro

2 scallions, thinly sliced

1/4 teaspoon finely grated lime zest

1 tablespoon fresh lime juice

6 tablespoons light sour cream or plain low-fat yogurt

6 (8-inch) flour tortillas, warmed

Lime wedges

1. Heat the oil in a Dutch oven, then add the onion. Sauté until the onion is translucent. Stir in the jalapeño, garlic, chili powder, cumin, coriander, and salt; sauté until fragrant. Stir in the broth and beans. Transfer 1 cup of the mixture to a blender or food processor and puree; return the puree to the Dutch oven. Stir in the chicken and cook, stirring occasionally, until heated through, about 5 minutes.

2. Meanwhile, combine the cherry tomatoes, 1 tablespoon of the cilantro, 1 tablespoon of the scallions, the lime zest, and lime juice in a bowl.

3. Stir the remaining cilantro and scallions into the soup. Serve the soup hot, topped with the tomatoes and sour cream, and the tortillas and lime wedges on the side.

*Per serving (generous 1 cup plus 1 tortilla): 441 Calories, 11 g Total Fat, 3 g Saturated Fat, 72 mg Cholesterol, 921 mg Sodium, 53 g Total Carbohydrate, 11 g Dietary Fiber, 38 g Protein, 184 mg Calcium.*

*POINTS per serving: 8.*

★ *American Way* Feel free to poach, grill, or broil the chicken. We call for ground spices, which are readily available in supermarkets, but for the best flavor, buy whole cumin and coriander seeds and grind them yourself. The difference in flavor is comparable to pre-ground pepper and freshly ground peppercorns. Grind the spices with a mortar and pestle, or use a clean coffee grinder.

# Soft Chicken Tacos

### MAKES 4 SERVINGS

*If flour tortillas are the heart of Southwestern cooking, corn tortillas are the soul. They were the original tortilla, created by Native Americans long before the Spanish arrived. The conquerors called them tortillas because of their shape, similar to the omelets that went by the same name in Spain. Soft corn tortillas are found in restaurants and markets throughout the Southwest and have the smoky flavor of maize.*

1 1/2 pounds skinless boneless chicken breasts

1 small white onion, finely chopped

1/2 cup fresh cilantro leaves

1/2 teaspoon chili powder

Pinch anise seeds, lightly crushed (optional)

1/2 teaspoon salt

Hot pepper sauce

12 (6-inch) corn tortillas

4 tomatoes, cut into chunks

2 scallions, thinly sliced

1 tablespoon fresh lime juice

1 Haas avocado, peeled and finely chopped

2 cups finely shredded romaine lettuce

4 radishes, halved lengthwise and thinly sliced

Lime wedges

1. Bring the chicken and enough cold water to cover to a boil in a large pot. Reduce the heat and simmer for 15 minutes. Remove the pot from the heat and let the chicken cool in the cooking liquid 20 minutes. Transfer the chicken to a cutting board. When cool enough to handle, finely shred the chicken with your fingers. Combine the chicken, onion, cilantro, chili powder, anise seeds, if using, 1/4 teaspoon of the salt, and a dash of the hot pepper sauce in a bowl. Keep warm.

2. Preheat the oven to 400°F. Wrap the tortillas in foil and warm them in the oven, about 10 minutes.

3. Meanwhile, combine the tomatoes, scallions, and 1/2 tablespoon of the lime juice in a bowl; season with a pinch of salt and a dash of hot pepper sauce. Combine the avocado and the remaining 1/2 tablespoon lime juice in another bowl; season with a pinch of salt and another dash of hot pepper sauce.

4. To serve the tacos, arrange the lettuce, tomatoes, avocado, radishes, and lime wedges on a platter. Transfer the chicken mixture to a serving bowl. Stack the warm tortillas and cover with a towel to keep them warm and moist. Have diners assemble their own tacos.

*Per serving   458 Calories, 13 g Total Fat, 2 g Saturated Fat, 84 mg Cholesterol, 443 mg Sodium, 49 g Total Carbohydrate, 9 g Dietary Fiber, 39 g Protein, 190 mg Calcium.*

*POINTS per serving: 8.*

★ *American Way*  For an almost-instant dinner, bring home some cooked chicken—you'll need about 4 cups shredded—and the tacos will be ready in the time it takes to assemble them.

# Spicy Shrimp Fajitas with Radish and Tomato Salsa

## MAKES 4 SERVINGS

*Fajitas began appearing on Texas menus in the 1970s. Fajita translates from Spanish as little strip, a reference to the slices of marinated skirt steak that are stuffed into flour tortillas. Today, the word refers to the dish itself, not skirt steak, and fajitas are made with just about any marinated meat (including chicken), fish, or, as here, shrimp.*

2 scallions, thinly sliced

3 tablespoons fresh lime juice

1 teaspoon vegetable oil

1 garlic clove, minced

1/2 teaspoon ground cumin

1/2 teaspoon ground coriander

1/2 teaspoon chili powder

1/4 teaspoon cayenne

1/2 teaspoon salt

1 pound medium shrimp, peeled and deveined

3 tomatoes, seeded and chopped

2 large radishes, quartered lengthwise and thinly sliced

1 small white onion, finely chopped

1 jalapeño pepper, seeded and minced (wear gloves to prevent irritation)

1 tablespoon finely chopped fresh cilantro

Pinch cayenne

8 (8-inch) flour tortillas

1 small Haas avocado, peeled and chopped

1/4 cup light sour cream

1. To marinate the shrimp, combine the scallions, lime juice, oil, garlic, cumin, coriander, chili powder, cayenne, and 1/4 teaspoon of the salt in a zip-close plastic bag; add the shrimp. Squeeze out the air and seal the bag; turn to coat the shrimp. Refrigerate, turning the bag occasionally, 20 minutes.

2. To make the salsa, combine the tomatoes, radishes, onion, jalapeño, cilantro, the remaining 1/4 teaspoon salt, and the cayenne in a bowl. Set aside.

3. Preheat the oven to 400°F. Wrap the tortillas in foil and place in the center of the oven to warm for 10 minutes.

4. Meanwhile, heat a nonstick skillet, then add the shrimp and the marinade and sauté until the shrimp are just opaque in the center, about 4 minutes.

5. To serve the fajitas, place the salsa, shrimp, avocado, and sour cream in separate bowls. Stack the warm tortillas and cover with a towel to keep them warm and moist. Have diners assemble their own fajitas by placing the shrimp in the middle of a warm tortilla, then topping with salsa, avocado, and sour cream and rolling up the tortilla.

*Per serving* (2 fajitas): 484 Calories, 17 g Total Fat, 4 g Saturated Fat, 145 mg Cholesterol, 1,077 mg Sodium, 55 g Total Carbohydrate, 5 g Dietary Fiber, 28 g Protein, 226 mg Calcium.

*POINTS per serving: 10.*

★ *American Way* To save time, substitute store-bought salsa for the Radish and Tomato Salsa—you'll need a little over 2 cups. Haas avocados, the ones with the black, pebbly skin, are common in the Southwest and Mexico. Westerners prefer their firmer, denser texture over the smooth-skinned, bright green Florida, or Fuerte, avocado, typically found on the East Coast.

*Spicy Shrimp Fajitas with Radish and Tomato Salsa*

# Chicken Enchiladas with Tomatillo Sauce

## MAKES 6 SERVINGS.

*Although tomatillos look like green cherry tomatoes with papery brown husks, they are actually more closely related to kiwifruit than to tomatoes. They are native to Mexico, but widely available in North American supermarkets.*

1 1/2 pounds skinless boneless chicken breasts

25 fresh tomatillos (about 2 1/2 pounds), husked, rinsed, and quartered

1 jalapeño pepper, seeded and halved (wear gloves to prevent irritation)

2 teaspoons sugar

1/2 teaspoon salt

Freshly ground pepper, to taste

1 tablespoon vegetable oil

1 small white onion, finely chopped

2 garlic cloves, minced

12 (6-inch) corn tortillas

1 cup shredded reduced-fat *queso blanco* or Monterey Jack cheese

3/4 cup light sour cream

1/3 cup minced fresh cilantro

1. Bring the chicken and enough cold water to cover to a boil in a large pot. Reduce the heat and simmer 15 minutes. Remove the pot from the heat and let the chicken cool in the cooking liquid for 20 minutes. Transfer the chicken to a cutting board. When cool enough to handle, finely shred the chicken with your fingers.

2. Preheat the oven to 350°F. Spray a 9 × 13-inch glass baking dish with nonstick spray.

3. Combine the tomatillos, jalapeño, sugar, salt, and pepper in a food processor and pulse until the tomatillos are coarsely chopped. Heat the oil in a large nonstick skillet. Add the onion and garlic and sauté until translucent. Remove the skillet from the heat and stir in the tomatillo mixture.

4. Soak 1 tortilla in the warm tomatillo sauce for 1 minute, then fill it with about 1/3 cup shredded chicken, 2 teaspoons cheese, and 1 teaspoon sour cream; roll up the tortilla. Set the enchilada, seam-side down, in the baking dish. Repeat with the remaining tortillas to make 12 enchiladas. Combine the remaining sour cream with the remaining tomatillo mixture and spoon over the top of the enchiladas. Sprinkle with the remaining cheese and the cilantro. Cover with foil and bake 20 minutes. Uncover and bake until the edges just begin to brown and the cheese melts, about 10 minutes more. Let stand 5 minutes before serving.

*Per serving* (2 enchiladas): *404 Calories, 14 g Total Fat, 5 g Saturated Fat, 78 mg Cholesterol, 454 mg Sodium, 38 g Total Carbohydrate, 6 g Dietary Fiber, 33 g Protein, 312 mg Calcium.*

*POINTS per serving: 8.*

★ *American Way* Choose very firm tomatillos that are pale green, not yellow; they are best if the husks are just beginning to split but remain firmly attached. Tomatillos will last up to 10 days in the refrigerator.

# Grilled Tequila-Lime Chicken

## MAKES 4 SERVINGS

*Tequila—made from the agave plant—imparts an authentic Southwestern flavor when used in cooking. Southwestern cooks love the flavor so much that they use tequila in everything, from ice cream to fish to chicken. Our version of tequila-and-lime spiked chicken is a refreshing and simple entrée that's ideal on a hot summer day.*

¼ cup fresh lime juice

¼ cup tequila

1 fresh jalapeño pepper, seeded and minced (wear gloves to prevent irritation)

2 tablespoons triple sec or orange juice

1 tablespoon vegetable oil

1 teaspoon ground coriander

4 sprigs fresh cilantro

1 garlic clove, halved

¼ teaspoon salt

¾ pound skinless boneless chicken breasts

2 teaspoons minced fresh cilantro

1. Combine the lime juice, tequila, jalapeño, triple sec or orange juice, oil, coriander, cilantro sprigs, garlic, and salt in a zip-close plastic bag; add the chicken. Squeeze out the air and seal the bag; turn to coat the chicken. Refrigerate, turning the bag occasionally, 20 minutes.

2. Spray a nonstick ridged grill-pan with nonstick spray and heat over medium heat. Grill the chicken, turning once, until cooked through, 5–6 minutes on each side. Serve, sprinkled with the minced cilantro.

*Per serving   131 Calories, 3 g Total Fat, 1 g Saturated Fat, 54 mg Cholesterol, 120 mg Sodium, 1 g Total Carbohydrate, 0 g Dietary Fiber, 20 g Protein, 11 mg Calcium.*

*POINTS per serving: 3.*

★ *American Way*  We suggest pairing this chicken with warm tortillas and a crunchy slaw of green cabbage, jicama, and red pepper slivers.

# Poblano Posole with Grilled Chicken

## MAKES 8 SERVINGS

*Posole, a thick, hominy soup, is the original New Mexican comfort food and holds a revered position similar to the admiration that chili holds in Texas. It is a feast day dish for Mexicans, so you'll find it on many Southwestern tables at Christmas time and New Year's day.*

3/4 pound skinless boneless chicken breasts

1 tablespoon vegetable oil

1 large white onion, finely chopped

3 garlic cloves, minced

2 teaspoons cumin seed, coarsely ground, or ground cumin

1 teaspoon dried oregano

6 cups low-sodium chicken broth

1 (19-ounce) can posole or hominy

6 poblano chiles, roasted, peeled, seeded, and chopped

1/2 teaspoon salt

Freshly ground pepper, to taste

1 tablespoon fresh lime juice

8 thin lime slices

Thinly sliced scallions

Thinly sliced radishes

Fresh cilantro leaves

1. Spray a nonstick ridged grill pan with nonstick spray and heat over medium heat. Grill the chicken, turning once, until cooked through, 5–6 minutes on each side. Transfer to a cutting board and let cool. When cool enough to handle, finely shred the chicken with your fingers.

2. Heat the oil in a Dutch oven, then add the onion. Sauté until the onion is translucent. Stir in the garlic, cumin, and oregano and sauté until fragrant. Stir in the broth, posole, poblanos, salt, and pepper. Simmer, stirring occasionally, until reduced slightly, about 30 minutes.

3. Add the chicken and lime juice to the posole and heat through, about 3 minutes. Serve the soup topped with the lime slices, scallions, radishes, and cilantro.

*Per serving  (1 cup): 180 Calories, 5 g Total Fat, 1 g Saturated Fat, 31 mg Cholesterol, 421 mg Sodium, 19 g Total Carbohydrate, 3 g Dietary Fiber, 15 g Protein, 47 mg Calcium.*

*POINTS per serving: 3.*

★ *American Way*  Posole is also the name for the kind of hominy that is the base of this soup. Canned *posole* is available in the Latin foods sections of large supermarkets. Canned hominy can be substituted, if you like. Other options for garnishing *posole* are red or green salsa, finely shredded cabbage, avocado, and grated cheese.

*Poblano Posole with Grilled Chicken*

# Grilled Beef Filets with Chive Butter

## MAKES 2 SERVINGS

*This dish is "all beef and no bull," as they'd say in Texas, where they love their beef and never mince their words.*

2 teaspoons unsalted butter, softened

1 teaspoon finely minced scallion

2 teaspoons snipped fresh chives

1/2 teaspoon salt

Freshly ground pepper, to taste

2 (3-ounce) filets mignons (1/2-inch thick), trimmed of all visible fat

1. Combine the butter, scallion, chives, and a pinch each of salt and pepper in a small bowl.

2. Spray the broiler rack with nonstick spray; preheat the broiler. Season the filets with the remaining salt and pepper. Broil the steak, inches from the heat, until done to taste, 3–4 minutes on each side for medium-rare. Top each filet with the chive butter and serve immediately.

*Per serving   171 Calories, 10 g Total Fat, 5 g Saturated Fat, 65 mg Cholesterol, 622 mg Sodium, 0 g Total Carbohydrate, 0 g Dietary Fiber, 18 g Protein, 7 mg Calcium.*

*POINTS per serving: 4.*

★ *American Way*  When you're using top-quality beef like filet mignon, keep the rest of the meal simple—a salad of Bibb lettuce tossed with an oil and vinegar dressing and plain baked potatoes—will allow the beef's flavor to shine. Make the chive butter ahead, wrap in plastic, and freeze until ready to use.

> FLASHBACK ›› 1863
>
> Cattle theft (or rustling) sweeps the Texas plains due to an unusually harsh winter.

*Grilled Beef Filets with Chive Butter*

# Grilled Beef Burritos with Warm Vegetable Salsa

MAKES 4 SERVINGS

*Served with an icy limeade or Mexican beer, the burrito is a classic. The word is Spanish for "little donkey."*

4 (10-inch) flour tortillas

1 pound boneless top sirloin steak, trimmed of all visible fat

3/4 teaspoon salt

Freshly ground pepper, to taste

1 teaspoon vegetable oil

1 onion, thinly sliced

1 small zucchini, halved lengthwise and thinly sliced

1 small yellow squash, halved lengthwise and thinly sliced

8 mushroom caps, thinly sliced

1 red or orange bell pepper, seeded and cut into thin strips

1 jalapeño pepper, seeded and minced (wear gloves to prevent irritation)

1 garlic clove, minced

2 tomatoes, seeded and chopped

2 scallions, thinly sliced

2 tablespoons finely chopped fresh cilantro

1/4 cup light sour cream

1. Preheat the oven to 400°F. Wrap the tortillas in foil and place in the oven to warm for 10 minutes.

2. Spray a nonstick ridged grill pan with nonstick spray and set over medium heat. Season the beef with 1/4 teaspoon of the salt and the pepper. Grill the steak, turning once, until done to taste, about 5 minutes on each side for medium-rare. Transfer to a cutting board and let stand 5 minutes.

3. Heat the oil in a nonstick skillet, then add the onion. Sauté until translucent, about 5 minutes. Stir in the zucchini, yellow squash, mushrooms, bell pepper, jalapeño, garlic, and the remaining 1/2 teaspoon salt. Cover and cook, stirring occasionally, until the vegetables are softened, 5–7 minutes. Stir in the tomatoes, scallions, and cilantro; remove the pan from the heat and let stand, covered, until ready to use.

4. Cut the steak into 1/4-inch–thick slices and divide evenly among the warm tortillas. Fill each burrito with 3/4 cup salsa, and fold the sides over to enclose the filling. Serve each burrito topped with salsa and 1 tablespoon of the sour cream.

*Per serving   376 Calories, 10 g Total Fat, 4 g Saturated Fat, 81 mg Cholesterol, 866 mg Sodium, 39 g Total Carbohydrate, 14 g Dietary Fiber, 34 g Protein, 107 mg Calcium.*

*POINTS per serving: 6.*

# Carrots with Cumin

MAKES 4 SERVINGS

*This dish is one of the simplest ways to get Southwestern flavors onto your table—it literally takes minutes. Experiment by adding cilantro, lime, and ground coriander to the carrots. Cumin, a predominant spice in Southwestern and in Mexican cuisine, adds a nutty, earthy flavor.*

1 pound peeled baby carrots
1/4 cup low-sodium vegetable broth
1 teaspoon packed brown sugar
1/4 teaspoon cumin seeds
Pinch salt
Freshly ground pepper, to taste

1. Cook the carrots in large pot of boiling salted water until tender when pierced with a fork, about 5 minutes. Drain.

2. Combine the carrots, broth, brown sugar, cumin, salt, and pepper in a nonstick skillet and cook, stirring, until the carrots are heated through and the broth is evaporated, 5–10 minutes.

*Per serving   50 Calories, 1 g Total Fat, 0 g Saturated Fat, 0 mg Cholesterol, 122 mg Sodium, 11 g Total Carbohydrate, 2 g Dietary Fiber, 1 g Protein, 29 mg Calcium.*

*POINTS per serving: 1.*

★ *American Way*   You can blanch the carrots up to a day ahead of time and store them in an airtight container in the refrigerator. Simply sauté them just before serving.

# Hopi-Style Spinach with Pine Nuts and Cider Vinegar

MAKES 4 SERVINGS

*The piñon is the state tree of New Mexico. This tree—which grows in the desert throughout much of the Southwest—bears the precious pine nut, small jewels of flavor that ripen in the crevices of the piñon's pine cones. The nuts must be harvested by hand, which explains their high price tag.*

1 tablespoon vegetable oil

2 (10-ounce) bags triple-washed spinach, rinsed and torn

1 tablespoon cider vinegar

1/4 teaspoon salt

Pinch cayenne

2 tablespoons toasted pine nuts

Heat the oil in large deep skillet over medium-high heat. Add the spinach, in batches if necessary, and cook, turning constantly with tongs, just until wilted. Stir in the vinegar, salt, and cayenne. With a slotted spoon, transfer the spinach to a bowl and sprinkle with the pine nuts.

*Per serving  57 Calories, 4 g Total Fat, 0 g Saturated Fat, 0 mg Cholesterol, 172 mg Sodium, 4 g Total Carbohydrate, 3 g Dietary Fiber, 3 g Protein, 94 mg Calcium.*

*POINTS per serving: 1.*

★ *American Way*  Pine nuts are best toasted: Simply place in a dry skillet set over medium-high heat and toast, tossing occasionally, until the nuts are lightly browned, about 5 minutes. Because of the very high fat content of pine nuts, they go rancid quickly, so store them in the freezer.

# Pinto Beans with Green Chiles

## MAKES 4 SERVINGS

*Pinto beans are the leading legume in New Mexico and the bean of choice in Santa Fe. The nutrient-rich pinto (which means* painted *in Spanish) gets its name from its mottled reddish-brown color and the cream colored spots of the raw bean—although when cooked, the color of the beans changes to a uniform pinkish tan. A relative of the kidney bean, it makes a great side dish or pot of chili beans.*

2 teaspoons vegetable oil

1 small red onion, finely chopped

¼ teaspoon chili powder

1 (19-ounce) can pinto beans, rinsed
   and drained

1 (4½-ounce) can chopped green
   chiles, drained

Pinch salt

Pinch cayenne

Heat the oil in a nonstick skillet, then add the onion. Sauté until the onion is translucent, about 5 minutes. Add the chili powder and sauté until fragrant, 1 minute more. Stir in the beans, chiles, salt, and cayenne; sauté until heated through. Serve warm, at room temperature, or chilled.

*Per serving   145 Calories, 3 g Total Fat, 0 g Saturated Fat, 0 mg Cholesterol, 353 mg Sodium, 23 g Total Carbohydrate, 7 g Dietary Fiber, 7 g Protein, 90 mg Calcium.*

*POINTS per serving: 2.*

★ *American Way*  Canned roasted green chiles are very mild. Using them is the next best thing to being in New Mexico during early autumn, the immensely fragrant outdoor-chile-roasting season. Consider serving the beans with rice or cornbread as a main course.

FLASHBACK ﹥﹥ 1835

Mexico's Texas Territory English settlers mix a variety of ground peppers to create chili powder.

## NATIVE AMERICAN FOODS

When Columbus landed in the Caribbean in 1492, he didn't find gold or a spice route to India, as promised. He did, however, unwittingly add a wealth of new foods to the European diet. Avocados, beans, chiles, chocolate, corn, papayas, peanuts, peppers, pineapple, potatoes, pumpkins, squash, tapioca, tomatoes, and wild rice are just some of the foods that were being cultivated, harvested, or foraged in countless Native American communities.

Supplemented with game and fish whenever possible, these plant foods were the staples of the Native American diet. However, great regional variation existed, depending upon the foods that could be grown well, their proximity to water, and the hunting traditions of the group. In the Northeast, women raised corn, squash, beans, and other vegetables on cleared land while the men hunted small game and birds. Meat was roasted on a spit over an open flame, making these Native Americans the first to barbecue. In the South, the men tended vegetables raised in uncleared fields while the women cared for the children and cooked. In the Southwest, pine nuts, berries, cactus fruit, and yucca were collected to add to corn and beans, the staple foods. Pacific Northwest tribes enjoyed a wide variety of fish, which they attached to a board and roasted at the side of a fire. Today, elements of these New World traditions continue to enrich our menus.

# Roasted Poblanos Stuffed with Coriander Rice

MAKES 4 SERVINGS

*The poblano chile, grown throughout the Southwest, has a shiny dark green skin and is wide at the stem end and tapered like a valentine heart. They are just the right size for stuffing and serving as a side dish.*

⅓ cup long-grain white rice

4 fresh poblano peppers, roasted and peeled

1 tablespoon toasted pumpkin seeds, chopped

1 tablespoon finely chopped fresh cilantro

2 teaspoons vegetable oil

¼ teaspoon ground coriander

¼ teaspoon ground cumin

¼ teaspoon salt

⅛ teaspoon chili powder

1 cup prepared salsa

1. Prepare rice according to package directions. Drain in a sieve and spread the rice on a plate lined with paper towels to cool.

2. Meanwhile, make a 2-inch long lengthwise slit in each poblano, leaving the stems intact. Carefully remove and discard the seeds. Pat the peppers dry.

3. Combine the rice, pumpkin seeds, cilantro, oil, coriander, cumin, salt, and chili powder in a bowl. Gently stuff each poblano with about ⅓ cup of the mixture. Serve the poblanos, slit-side down, at room temperature with the salsa.

*Per serving* 128 Calories, 4 g Total Fat, 1 g Saturated Fat, 0 mg Cholesterol, 381 mg Sodium, 20 g Total Carbohydrate, 3 g Dietary Fiber, 3 g Protein, 14 mg Calcium.

*POINTS per serving: 2.*

★ *American Way* Poblanos take on a terrific smoky quality when roasted. We like to char chiles over a gas flame—or better yet, a charcoal fire—turning as needed. Even placing the chiles on a rack directly over an electric burner works fine. All are preferable to a broiler, where the peppers can easily get overcooked.

# Watermelon Granita

*A granita is a coarse-textured, (typically fruit-flavored) frozen ice native to Africa. Granitas were eaten in Egypt well before 2000 BC. Unlike ice cream and sorbet, granitas are never churned. They capture the very essence of ripe fruit and are refreshing—especially as dessert after an outdoor barbecue. The strawberries aren't absolutely necessary, but they do enhance the flavor of the watermelon. Serve the granita in a pretty, long-stemmed goblet or tall glass.*

1 cup water

4 strawberries, hulled and sliced (optional)

1/3 cup sugar

Pinch salt

2 1/2 pounds watermelon, rind discarded and flesh chopped

1 tablespoon fresh lime juice

1. To make the syrup, combine the water, strawberries, if using, sugar, and salt in a saucepan. Bring the mixture to a boil, then reduce the heat to low, and simmer 10 minutes. Transfer the syrup to a bowl.

2. Puree the watermelon in a food processor, working in batches if necessary. Puree the syrup and combine with the watermelon puree. Strain the puree through a fine sieve set over a bowl. Stir in the lime juice. Cover and refrigerate until chilled. Transfer the mixture to an 8-inch square metal pan.

3. Freeze the mixture, stirring and crushing the lumps with a fork every 30 minutes or so, until the granita is firm but not frozen solid, about 2 hours.

★ *American Way*  Ideally, the granita should be prepared just two hours before serving. However, if you'd like to freeze it longer, simply pulse the frozen granita in a food processor a few times to soften just before serving. There's no need to seed the watermelon, since the sieve will strain them out. When you're picking out watermelon, look for one that's heavy and shiny. Check the underside where it has rested on the ground—it should have a yellowish cast; an unripe watermelon will have a white cast. Tap the watermelon gently with your knuckles; a ripe melon sounds hollow.

4. Just before serving, scrape the granita with a fork to lighten the texture. Serve at once.

*Per serving  (3/4 cup): 79 Calories, 0 g Total Fat, 0 g Saturated Fat, 0 mg Cholesterol, 26 mg Sodium, 20 g Total Carbohydrate, 1 g Dietary Fiber, 1 g Protein, 8 mg Calcium.*

*POINTS per serving: 1.*

FLASHBACK >> 1929

A mutated, red-fleshed grapefruit, later called a ruby, is discovered on a farm in McAllen, Texas.

*Watermelon Granita*

# Strawberry Margarita Sorbet

## MAKES 6 SERVINGS

*This potent dessert—spiked with tequila—is for adults only. Tequila is a strong, colorless spirit distilled from the agave plant. Originally, the Aztec concocted the drink, but the Spanish later refined the process of making tequila in a town of the same name, near Guadalajara. If you're serving children, simply omit the tequila and use the orange juice instead of the triple sec.*

4 cups fresh strawberries, hulled
    and halved

1/4 cup sugar

Pinch salt

1 cup water

3 tablespoons fresh lime juice

2 tablespoons triple sec or orange juice

2 tablespoons tequila

1. Puree the strawberries in a food processor. Add the sugar and salt and process for 10 seconds. Transfer the mixture to a bowl and whisk in the water, lime juice, triple sec, and tequila.

2. Freeze the mixture in an ice cream maker according to manufacturer's instructions. Serve immediately or freeze in an airtight container for up to 7 weeks.

*Per serving* (3/4 cup): 86 Calories, 0 g Total Fat, 0 g Saturated Fat, 0 mg Cholesterol, 24 mg Sodium, 17 g Total Carbohydrate, 2 g Dietary Fiber, 1 g Protein, 14 mg Calcium.

*POINTS per serving:* 1.

★ *American Way* If the sorbet is frozen solid, it can be thawed slightly in the refrigerator before serving. If it is very hard, pulse a few times in a food processor.

# Rice Pudding with Lemon and Coriander

MAKES 6 SERVINGS

*Desserts of the Southwesterners are sweet and solidly comforting, so this Spanish-influenced rice pudding, also called* arroz con leche, *fits right in. The coriander enhances the subtle, citrusy lemon flavor.*

½ cup + 2 tablespoons long-grain white rice

2 cups fat-free milk

2 large eggs, lightly beaten

⅓ cup sugar

1 teaspoon vanilla extract

1 teaspoon finely grated lemon zest

1 teaspoon ground coriander

Pinch salt

½ cup golden raisins

1. Cook the rice in a saucepan of boiling salted water until very tender, about 17 minutes. Drain in a sieve and transfer to a bowl.

2. Combine the milk, eggs, sugar, vanilla, lemon zest, coriander, and salt in a heavy saucepan. Cook, whisking constantly, until the mixture is thick enough to coat the back of a spoon, about 12 minutes. Do not allow the mixture to come to a boil; the eggs will curdle.

3. Add the rice and raisins to the milk mixture and cook, stirring constantly with a wooden spoon, until the mixture resembles cooked oatmeal; do not allow the mixture to come to a boil. Transfer immediately to a bowl. Serve hot, warm, or chilled. Refrigerate, in an airtight container, for up to 2 days.

*Per serving  (¾ cup): 211 Calories, 2 g Total Fat, 1 g Saturated Fat, 72 mg Cholesterol, 91 mg Sodium, 41 g Total Carbohydrate, 1 g Dietary Fiber, 7 g Protein, 124 mg Calcium.*

*POINTS per serving: 4.*

# Café con Leche Flan

MAKES 12 SERVINGS

*This elegant, silky-smooth custard dons a caramel coating that glistens across the top, runs down the side, and pools around the flan when it is unmolded. It is a luscious finale to any meal.*

3/4 cup sugar

5 tablespoons water

2 (12-ounce) cans fat-free evaporated milk

1 (14-ounce) can fat-free sweetened condensed milk

2 large eggs

3 egg whites

1 1/2 tablespoons instant espresso powder

1 teaspoon vanilla extract

1/4 teaspoon salt

1. Adjust the racks to divide the oven in half. Preheat the oven to 325°F.

2. To make the caramel, combine the sugar and water in a saucepan and bring to a boil. Cook, stirring and washing down any sugar crystals clinging to the side of the pan with a brush dipped in cold water, until all of the sugar is dissolved. Cook the syrup, without stirring, until it becomes a deep caramel color. Pour the caramel into a 9-inch round cake pan, tilting the pan, to coat it evenly.

3. To make the custard, combine the evaporated milk, condensed milk, eggs, egg whites, espresso powder, vanilla, and salt in a medium bowl. Stir until all of the coffee is dissolved and the mixture is smooth. Strain the mixture into a large glass measure. Set the cake pan inside a roasting pan and then place the roasting pan on the center oven rack. Pour the custard into the cake pan, then pour hot water into the roasting pan until it comes halfway up the side of the cake pan. Bake the flan until a toothpick inserted in the center of the custard comes out clean, 1–1 1/2 hours.

4. Carefully remove the cake pan from the hot water and transfer to a rack. Let the flan cool to room temperature, then cover it with plastic wrap, and refrigerate at least 6 hours before serving.

5. To serve, run a thin knife around the edge of the flan and invert it onto a large platter deep enough to hold the caramel.

*Per serving  203 Calories, 1 g Total Fat, 0 g Saturated Fat, 40 mg Cholesterol, 172 mg Sodium, 39 g Total Carbohydrate, 0 g Dietary Fiber, 9 g Protein, 255 mg Calcium.*

*POINTS per serving: 4.*

★ *American Way*  Flan is always baked in a water bath, but it is tricky getting the pans in the oven. We recommend placing the cake pan inside the roasting pan, then placing the roasting pan in the oven. Only then should you pour the custard into the cake pan and the hot water into the roasting pan.

# Mexican-Style Chocolate Pudding

MAKES 6 SERVINGS

*Mexican chocolate (most often the Ibarra brand from Oaxaca) is flavored with cinnamon and is grainy from ground almonds; it makes a truly spectacular hot chocolate. Since it's loaded with sugar, we created this simulation using almond and cinnamon flavors, less sugar, and a rich, deep chocolate flavor.*

½ cup packed brown sugar

⅓ cup unsweetened cocoa powder

2 (1-ounce) squares semi-sweet
    chocolate, chopped

3 tablespoons cornstarch

⅛ teaspoon cinnamon

Pinch salt

2½ cups fat-free chocolate milk

1 teaspoon vanilla extract

¼ teaspoon almond extract

1 tablespoon toasted sliced almonds
    (optional)

1. Combine the brown sugar, cocoa, chocolate, cornstarch, cinnamon, and salt in a saucepan. Whisk in 1 cup of the chocolate milk and cook the mixture, whisking until the chocolate melts and the mixture is smooth. Gradually stir in the remaining chocolate milk and cook, stirring constantly, until large bubbles pop on the surface and the pudding is thick and smooth, about 8 minutes. Remove the pan from the heat and stir in the vanilla and almond extracts.

2. Serve the pudding hot, at room temperature, or chilled with the almonds, if using. Refrigerate, in an airtight container, with a piece of plastic wrap touching the surface of the pudding, for up to 2 days.

*Per serving (½ cup without almonds): 216 Calories, 4 g Total Fat, 3 g Saturated Fat, 3 mg Cholesterol, 96 mg Sodium, 40 g Total Carbohydrate, 3 g Dietary Fiber, 5 g Protein, 142 mg Calcium.*

*POINTS per serving: 4.*

★ *American Way*  Be sure to use semi-sweet, not unsweetened, chocolate.

# Corn Muffins with Chiles

## MAKES 12 SERVINGS

*Throughout New Mexico families roast green chiles by the bushel in early autumn. Fresh picked chiles fill large wire cages that rotate on a spit over an open fire—they exude a heady, spicy aroma that fills the air. These are not the sweet, dessert-like breakfast muffins you're probably familiar with. They make great accompaniments to supper and pair well with grilled, broiled, or roasted meats and poultry—the roasted chiles and the corn lend a fabulous, but savory, flavor.*

1 cup all-purpose flour

1 cup stone-ground yellow cornmeal

1 tablespoon baking powder

1/2 teaspoon salt

1 cup low-fat buttermilk

1 (7-ounce) can reduced-sodium corn, drained

1 (41/2-ounce) can chopped green chiles, drained

2 large eggs

2 tablespoons vegetable oil

1. Preheat the oven to 425°F. Spray a 12-cup muffin tin with non-stick spray.

2. Combine the flour, cornmeal, baking powder, and salt in a bowl. Combine the buttermilk, corn, chiles, eggs, and oil in another bowl. Add the buttermilk mixture to the flour mixture; stir just until blended.

3. Spoon the batter into the cups, filling each about 2/3 full. Bake until a toothpick inserted in a muffin comes out clean, 18–20 minutes. Cool in the pan on a rack 5 minutes, then remove from the pan and cool completely on the rack. Store in an airtight container for up to 1 week.

*Per serving   131 Calories, 4 g Total Fat, 1 g Saturated Fat, 36 mg Cholesterol, 282 mg Sodium, 20 g Total Carbohydrate, 1 g Dietary Fiber, 4 g Protein, 57 mg Calcium.*

*POINTS per serving: 3.*

★ *American Way*  You can find stone-ground cornmeal in large supermarkets or health-food stores.

★

## APPETIZERS/SOUPS/SALADS

Scallops with Warm Cherry Tomatoes and Toasted Couscous

Spicy Asian Broth

Yellow Pepper Soup with Cilantro Puree

Cream of Zucchini Soup

Potato and Cheese Soup

Chorizo Sausage and Kale Soup

Fennel and Orange Salad

Celeriac Remoulad Salad

## ENTRÉES

Capellini with Asparagus and Shaved Parmesan

Artichoke, Shrimp, and Potato Salad

Mountain Trout in Tomato, Carrot, and Onion Sauce

Grilled Mountain Trout with Herbs and Garlic

Mango, Kiwi, and Chicken Salad

Sage Chicken with Peppers and Chickpeas

Basque Chicken with Rice

Chicken Swiss Steak–Style

Grilled Spiced Pork with Orange-Lime Glaze and Sugar-Snap Peas

Pheasant Stir-Fry with Ginger and Orange

Beer-Braised Country Style Beef Short Ribs

Elk Tenderloins with Green Peppercorn Sauce

Peppered Bison Tenderloin Steaks with Merlot and Cherry Sauce

Bison Burgers with Shiitake Mushrooms

## SIDES

Caramelized Bell Pepper Sauté

Butternut Squash and Swiss Chard Risotto

Minted Lemon-Glazed Carrots

Roasted Winter Vegetables

Savoy Cabbage with Torpedo Onions

Lentils with Leeks and Carrots

Tabbouleh with Black Quinoa

Warm Basil Potato Salad

Twice-Baked Potatoes with Goat Cheese and Parsnips

Scalloped Potatoes with Jarlsberg and Smoked Gouda

## DESSERTS/BREADS

Gingered Idared Apple Crisp

Huckleberry Pie

Raspberry Cobbler

Frozen Raspberry-Peach Torte

Basque Sheepherder's Bread

# Scallops with Warm Cherry Tomatoes and Toasted Couscous

MAKES 4 SERVINGS

*Sea scallops live in deep water and have a sweet, moist meat that is best appreciated with only minimal cooking. These large scallops are an ideal appetite-whetting first course. Remember to pull off the small, tough muscle on the side of each. Fresh tarragon lends a French elan to this dish.*

1 scant cup toasted couscous or
    acini di pepe pasta
2 tablespoons minced red onion
2 tablespoons olive oil
1 tablespoon white-wine vinegar
3/4 teaspoon salt
Freshly ground pepper, to taste
1 garlic clove, minced
2 cups red cherry or grape tomatoes
2 cups yellow cherry or grape tomatoes
 tablespoon finely chopped fresh tarragon
3/4 pound sea scallops

1. Cook the couscous according to package directions. Combine with the onion, 1/2 tablespoon of the oil, 1/2 tablespoon of the vinegar, 1/4 teaspoon of the salt, and a pinch pepper in a bowl. Set aside.

2. Heat 1 tablespoon oil in a nonstick skillet, then add the garlic. Sauté until the garlic is fragrant. Add the tomatoes and sauté just until they start to split, 1–2 minutes. Stir in the tarragon, the remaining 1/2 tablespoon vinegar, 1/4 teaspoon of the remaining salt, and pinch of pepper. Transfer the tomatoes to a bowl. Wipe out the skillet.

3. Sprinkle the scallops with the remaining 1/4 teaspoon salt and pepper to taste. Heat the remaining 1/2 tablespoon oil in the same skillet, then add the scallops. Sear until the scallops are just opaque in the center, about 2 minutes on each side.

4. Serve the scallops over the couscous topped with the tomatoes.

*Per serving  347 Calories, 8 g Total Fat, 1 g Saturated Fat, 28 mg Cholesterol, 593 mg Sodium, 46 g Total Carbohydrate, 4 g Dietary Fiber, 22 g Protein, 43 mg Calcium.*

*POINTS per serving: 7.*

★ *American Way*  Toasted couscous is a kind of Israeli couscous, which is characterized by larger grains than regular couscous. It is available in many supermarkets; however, if you cannot find it, any Israeli couscous or acini di pepe—tiny peppercorn shaped pasta—will work well.

*Scallops with Warm Cherry Tomatoes and Toasted Couscous*

# Spicy Asian Broth

MAKES 4 SERVINGS.

*Chinese and Japanese workers arrived in California in the mid-19th century to help construct the railroads. When their descendents opened Chinese restaurants in the early part of the twentieth century, they offered a westernized version of Chinese food. This Spicy Asian Broth, with a touch of Thai flavors like ginger and chile pepper, is one example of a refreshing first course for an Asian-inspired meal.*

4 cups low-sodium chicken broth

Juice of 1 lime

2 plum tomatoes, cut into thin wedges

2 tablespoons shredded carrot

1 tablespoon reduced-sodium soy sauce

1 tablespoon chopped fresh cilantro

1 teaspoon grated peeled fresh ginger

1 small garlic clove, minced

1 small Thai chile, seeded and minced (wear gloves to prevent irritation)

1 small bunch watercress, leaves only, rinsed

Combine the broth, lime juice, tomatoes, carrot, soy sauce, cilantro, ginger, garlic, and chile in a saucepan. Cook, stirring occasionally, until heated through. Add the watercress and serve at once.

*Per serving  62 Calories, 2 g Total Fat, 1 g Saturated Fat, 5 mg Cholesterol, 287 mg Sodium, 7 g Total Carbohydrate, 1 g Dietary Fiber, 5 g Protein, 35 mg Calcium.*

*POINTS per serving: 1.*

★ *American Way*  This recipe uses a small Thai chile. Thai chiles are fiery—they range from green to red in color. Look for them in Asian markets.

# Yellow Pepper Soup with Cilantro Puree

## MAKES 4 SERVINGS

*The visionary cooking ideas of chef Alice Waters, most notably using fresh, locally produced ingredients, now defines California cuisine. In the last few decades, West Coast chefs have followed her lead in ways like using vegetable and fruit purees as a low-fat alternative to butter and cream in soups and sauces. This chilled soup gets its fresh taste from sweet yellow bell peppers. The cilantro puree provides an attractive flair and a refreshing flavor.*

2½ teaspoons olive oil

1 large shallot, finely chopped

1 teaspoon curry powder

3¾ cups low-sodium chicken broth

4 yellow bell peppers, seeded and coarsely chopped

2 medium Yukon gold potatoes, peeled and coarsely chopped

½ teaspoon salt

1 cup rinsed fresh cilantro leaves (do not dry)

¼ teaspoon chopped garlic

1. Heat 1 teaspoon of the oil in a saucepan and add the shallot. Cover and cook until translucent, 3–5 minutes. Add the curry powder and sauté until the shallot is coated. Add the broth, bell peppers, potatoes, and salt; bring to a boil. Reduce the heat and simmer until the vegetables are tender 12–15 minutes. Cool slightly. Puree the soup, in batches, in a blender. Cover and refrigerate until chilled.

2. To make the cilantro puree, combine 1 tablespoon of the soup in a mini food processor with the cilantro, the remaining 1½ teaspoons oil, the garlic, and a pinch of salt; puree until smooth.

3. Ladle the soup into bowls. Top each serving with 1 teaspoon of the cilantro puree, then draw a knife through the puree to swirl.

*Per serving   157 Calories, 3 g Total Fat, 0 g Saturated Fat, 0 mg Cholesterol, 366 mg Sodium, 28 g Total Carbohydrate, 4 g Dietary Fiber, 6 g Protein, 55 mg Calcium.*

*POINTS per serving: 3.*

★ *American Way*  To give the soup a silkier texture, puree the cooked peppers and potatoes in a small amount of broth at first until very smooth, then add the remaining broth.

## The New Chefs and Their Farmers

Since the construction of the railroads, California has been the source of much of America's fresh produce. So it is no surprise that the bounty from the state's farmlands and orchards has inspired a cuisine so fresh, colorful, and creative that, under the umbrella "California cuisine," it has spread to restaurants across the country.

The real impetus for looking at food in the context of its regional and seasonal parameters came in 1971, when Alice Waters could not find a restaurant that served food as fresh and flavorful as the cuisine she had enjoyed in France. So, she decided she would cook it herself. At Chez Panisse in Berkeley, Waters created menus around the fresh regional products that were available at the moment and established relationships with local organic farmers, foragers, and cheese, poultry, and meat producers to supply her with the quality raw materials that she needed. Chefs trained in her restaurant began to bring her ideas to other areas of the country, and today, quality restaurants in every state boast cuisines based on fresh, local, seasonal products. Among the positive effects of this partnership between chefs and local suppliers are a palate of new and unusual ingredients for chefs to draw from, exciting and innovative dining experiences for restaurant customers, and the survival of small family farms.

# Cream of Zucchini Soup

## MAKES 4 SERVINGS

*Hardworking Mormon pioneers relied on nourishing fare to fuel their bodies and consumed soups as a large part of their diet. This hearty soup is a modern rendition of an old favorite that uses evaporated fat-free milk to give the soup a silky texture without adding fat. Yellow squash can be used in place of the zucchini—or try a combination of the two.*

1 tablespoon unsalted butter

1 onion, chopped

2 tablespoons all-purpose flour

3 cups low-sodium chicken broth, heated

3 medium zucchini (about 3/4 pound), sliced

3/4 teaspoon salt

1/4 teaspoon freshly ground pepper

1/2 cup evaporated fat-free milk

Freshly grated nutmeg

1. Melt the butter in a saucepan, then add the onion. Sauté until the onion is almost tender, about 8 minutes. Stir in the flour and cook, stirring, 2 minutes.

2. Remove the pan from heat and stir in the broth; return to heat and bring to a boil. Stir in the zucchini, salt, and pepper. Reduce the heat, cover, and simmer until the zucchini is completely tender, about 15 minutes.

3. Transfer the soup to a blender and puree. Return the soup to the saucepan and add the evaporated milk. Cook until heated through; do not let the soup boil. Divide the soup evenly among 4 bowls and grate a dash of nutmeg over each serving. Serve immediately.

*Per serving (1 1/3 cups): 97 Calories, 3 g Total Fat, 2 g Saturated Fat, 9 mg Cholesterol, 522 mg Sodium, 12 g Total Carbohydrate, 2 g Dietary Fiber, 6 g Protein, 120 mg Calcium.*

*POINTS per serving: 2.*

# Potato and Cheese Soup

## MAKES 6 SERVINGS

*We found a version of this rich-tasting, slightly sweet soup in an old Mormon cookbook and lightened it up. The carrot lends a golden color, and the potatoes provide the illusion of cream. For the best flavor, use a very sharp cheddar cheese.*

1 tablespoon unsalted butter

1 large onion, chopped

3 garlic cloves, sliced

2 tablespoons all-purpose flour

2 cups low-sodium chicken broth, heated

1 carrot, peeled and thinly sliced

1 large Idaho potato, peeled, halved, and cut into 1/4-inch–thick slices

1/2 teaspoon salt

1/4 teaspoon freshly ground pepper

1 cup low-fat (2%) milk

1/2 cup shredded extra-sharp cheddar cheese

1 tablespoon snipped fresh chives or minced fresh parsley

1. Melt the butter in a saucepan, then add the onion and garlic. Sauté until the onion is almost tender, about 8 minutes. Stir in the flour and cook, stirring, about 2 minutes.

2. Remove the pan from heat and stir in the broth. Return to heat, bring to a boil, and stir in carrot, potato, salt, and pepper. Reduce the heat, cover, and simmer until the vegetables are completely tender, about 20 minutes.

3. Transfer the soup to a blender and puree. Return the soup to the saucepan and add the milk. Cook until heated through; do not allow the soup to boil. Add the cheese and stir just until melted. Divide the soup among 4 bowls and sprinkle with the chives.

*Per serving (1 cup): 138 Calories, 6 g Total Fat, 4 g Saturated Fat, 18 mg Cholesterol, 300 mg Sodium, 15 g Total Carbohydrate, 2 g Dietary Fiber, 6 g Protein, 136 mg Calcium.*

*POINTS per serving: 3.*

# Chorizo Sausage and Kale Soup

## MAKES 6 SERVINGS

*Today there is a very large Basque population in the Mountain states of Wyoming, Nevada, and Idaho, a result of sheepherders who emigrated from the area straddling the border of France and Spain. Chorizo sausage, flavored with garlic and paprika, is a staple in Spanish cooking. The pioneering Basques combined the zesty sausage with kale to create this classic, hearty soup. Serve it with Basque Sheepherder's Bread (page 294).*

6 cups water

1 1/2 pounds Yukon Gold potatoes, peeled and sliced

1 teaspoon salt

1 bunch kale, stems removed, cleaned, and finely shredded (about 6 cups)

1/4 pound chorizo sausage

1 tablespoon extra-virgin olive oil

1/2 teaspoon freshly ground pepper

1. Combine the water, potatoes, and salt in a large saucepan and bring to a boil. Reduce the heat and simmer until the potatoes are tender, 20–25 minutes. Do not drain.

2. Meanwhile, bring a large pot of water to a boil and add the kale. Reduce the heat, cover, and simmer until tender, about 6 minutes. Drain well.

3. Remove the skin from the chorizo and slice the sausage into 1/4-inch–thick pieces. Heat a nonstick skillet, then add the chorizo. Sauté until the sausage is browned, about 10 minutes. Drain well on paper towels, then dice.

4. When the potatoes are tender, remove the pan from heat and mash the potatoes with a potato masher, leaving some pieces a bit larger for texture. Add the kale, chorizo, olive oil, and pepper and heat through. Serve immediately.

*Per serving   195 Calories, 7 g Total Fat, 2 g Saturated Fat, 10 mg Cholesterol, 567 mg Sodium, 27 g Total Carbohydrate, 3 g Dietary Fiber, 7 g Protein, 101 mg Calcium.*

*POINTS per serving: 4.*

★ *American Way*  Do not squeeze the kale before adding it to the soup. The excess moisture will add more distinctive kale flavor.

# Fennel and Orange Salad

## MAKES 4 SERVINGS

*The orange industry has been booming in California since the 1870s and has helped make the state practically synonymous with sunshine and good health. The San Joaquin Valley is the home of many orange groves, as well as other citrus fruits. To make this a light vegetarian lunch, add a nutty-flavored cheese, such as an aged Gouda.*

4 large oranges, peeled and pith cut away

1 tablespoon olive oil

1 tablespoon white-wine vinegar

$1/4$ teaspoon salt

$1/8$ teaspoon freshly ground pepper

1 (1-pound) fennel bulb, trimmed, cored, and very thinly sliced

1 Belgian endive, thinly sliced

1 small red onion, thinly sliced

1 tablespoon chopped fresh mint

Holding an orange over a large bowl, cut between the membranes to free the segments. Repeat with the remaining oranges. Stir in the oil, vinegar, salt, and pepper. Add the fennel, endive, onion, and mint; gently toss to combine the salad, and serve.

*Per serving*  138 Calories, 4 g Total Fat, 0 g Saturated Fat, 0 mg Cholesterol, 179 mg Sodium, 27 g Total Carbohydrate, 7 g Dietary Fiber, 3 g Protein, 107 mg Calcium.

*POINTS per serving: 2.*

★ *American Way*  To segment an orange, use a small, sharp knife to cut between the membranes of the orange and carefully remove each section. Slice the fennel as thin as possible to keep the salad delicate and lend just the right amount of crunch.

# Celeriac Rémoulade Salad

MAKES 6 SERVINGS

*Celeriac, or celery root, grows well in the Mountain West. It is a knobby subterranean vegetable that many say resembles something from outer space. Underneath its peculiar-looking exterior, however, lies a crunchy, cream-colored flesh that tastes mildly of celery. This recipe's tangy, creamy rémoulade sauce is a wonderful partner with celeriac's crunch. Be sure to let the salad marinate for a few hours for the best flavor and texture.*

¾ cup light sour cream

½ cup low-fat mayonnaise dressing

1 tablespoon Dijon mustard

1 teaspoon prepared horseradish
(preserved in vinegar)

½ teaspoon salt

⅛ teaspoon freshly ground pepper

4 cups water

Juice of 1 lemon

2 pounds whole celeriac
(1–1¼ pounds peeled)

1 tablespoon minced fresh tarragon

1. Whisk the sour cream, mayonnaise dressing, mustard, horseradish, salt, and pepper in a bowl.

2. Combine the water and lemon juice in another bowl. Peel and cut the celeriac, dipping cut surfaces into the lemon-water. Cut the celeriac into matchstick-sized pieces and drop them into the lemon-water once again. Drain well and combine the matchsticks with the rémoulade dressing, add the tarragon, and fold together. Cover and refrigerate at least 2 hours before serving.

*Per serving 115 Calories, 5 g Total Fat, 2 g Saturated Fat, 12 mg Cholesterol, 501 mg Sodium, 16 g Total Carbohydrate, 1 g Dietary Fiber, 3 g Protein, 78 mg Calcium.*

*POINTS per serving: 3.*

★ *American Way* Celeriac darkens almost as soon as it is cut, so it's important to have a bowl of acidulated water, or lemon-water, nearby to retard discoloring. There's a lot of waste when you peel the celeriac, so buy twice what you think you'll need. The easiest way to cut it is with a food processor fitted with the 3mm julienne disc. Otherwise, cut the celeriac into thin slices with a sharp, heavy knife. We prefer low-fat mayonnaise dressing to low-fat mayonnaise in this salad because it contains even less fat, with little difference in taste.

# Capellini with Asparagus and Shaved Parmesan

MAKES 4 SERVINGS

*California produces 70 percent of the nation's asparagus, the tender green spears being one of the state's main crops. The lush color and unique taste make them the ideal vegetable for fresh-tasting and imaginative dishes.*

4 garlic cloves, unpeeled

3/4 pound capellini

2 tablespoons olive oil

3 tablespoons fresh lemon juice

2 1/2 cups low-sodium chicken broth

2 bunches asparagus, trimmed and cut into 2-inch pieces

10 large basil leaves, thinly sliced

2 ounces Parmigiano-Reggiano, shaved

1. Heat a large nonstick skillet, then add the garlic and toast, turning the cloves as the peels char, until the garlic feels soft when pressed, about 20 minutes. Remove from the pan and let cool.

2. Cook the capellini according to package directions. Drain and transfer the pasta to a warm serving bowl.

3. Slit the garlic peels and squeeze the garlic pulp into the same skillet. Add the oil and mash the garlic to blend. Add the lemon juice and bring to a boil; boil for 30 seconds. Add the broth and asparagus, bring to a boil, and cook until the asparagus is just tender, 4–5 minutes.

4. Stir the basil into the asparagus mixture and then pour over the capellini. Toss to combine the pasta and asparagus. Serve with the Parmesan shavings.

*Per serving  512 Calories, 13 g Total Fat, 4 g Saturated Fat, 14 mg Cholesterol, 338 mg Sodium, 74 g Total Carbohydrate, 6 g Dietary Fiber, 23 g Protein, 265 mg Calcium.*

*POINTS per serving: 10.*

★ *American Way*  Cook the asparagus until just tender; if cooked too long, they will lose their bright green color and become mushy. Toasting the garlic in a dry skillet produces results similar to roasting, but the flavor will be slightly milder and less caramelized. Use a vegetable peeler to shave the Parmesan.

*Capellini with Asparagus and Shaved Parmesan*

# Artichoke, Shrimp, and Potato Salad

MAKES 4 SERVINGS

*Nearly all of the commercially grown artichokes in the U.S. come from California, where the climate is never too hot or too cold. Most of the artichoke fields are located around Castroville, just north of Monterey, where farms border the ocean's edge. When cooked, fresh artichokes should be just tender, with a bit of resistance to the bite. Although preparing fresh artichokes just for the hearts is a labor-intensive undertaking, their fresh flavor and unique texture are worth the effort.*

1 pound new white potatoes, scrubbed

1 pound medium shrimp, peeled and deveined

2 lemons

4 medium artichokes

1 tablespoon olive oil

1 tablespoon chopped fresh oregano

2 garlic cloves, chopped

½ teaspoon salt

Freshly ground pepper, to taste

6 ounces mesclun salad greens

1 small red onion, thinly sliced

10 kalamata olives, pitted

1. Bring the potatoes and enough water to cover to a boil in a large saucepan; reduce the heat and simmer until almost fork-tender, 18–20 minutes. Add the shrimp and simmer until the shrimp are opaque in the center, 2–3 minutes more. Transfer to a colander, rinse briefly with cool water, then let drain 5 minutes. Slice the potatoes.

2. Cut 1 lemon in half and squeeze the juice into a saucepan half-filled with water; drop in the lemon halves. With a sharp knife, cut off the artichokes' sharp tips at the tops; trim the stem. Remove and discard all the leaves from artichokes. With the knife, peel the outer dark-green layer from the base and stem, leaving just the artichoke heart. As you finish trimming each, drop the artichoke hearts into the saucepan. Bring to a boil, then reduce the heat and simmer until hearts are just fork-tender, 5–6 minutes. Drain and cut each heart in half.

3. Juice the remaining lemon into a small bowl; whisk in the oil, oregano, garlic, salt, and pepper. Combine the shrimp, potatoes, and artichoke hearts in a medium bowl; add 1 tablespoon of the dressing and toss gently. Combine the mesclun, onion, and olives with the remaining dressing and gently toss. Serve the shrimp, potatoes and artichoke hearts over the greens.

*Per serving* 276 Calories, 6 g Total Fat, 1 g Saturated Fat, 140 mg Cholesterol, 580 mg Sodium, 33 g Total Carbohydrate, 6 g Dietary Fiber, 23 g Protein, 102 mg Calcium.

*POINTS per serving:* 5.

★ *American Way* If you're in a hurry, substitute a 16-ounce can of artichoke hearts.

# Mountain Trout in Tomato, Carrot, and Onion Sauce

MAKES 6 SERVINGS

*Idaho isn't just potato country; it is also known for its trout. With the state becoming home to a new wave of Russian immigrants, this recipe gets its inspiration from sturgeon in tomato sauce, a Russian specialty. Crusty bread is an essential extra for soaking up the thick sauce.*

1 pound skinless boneless trout fillets, cut into 2–inch pieces

$1/2$ teaspoon salt

$1/4$ teaspoon freshly ground pepper

$1^1/2$ tablespoons olive oil

2 carrots, peeled and shredded

1 large onion, finely chopped

1 (16-ounce) can tomato puree

$1/2$ cup dry white wine

1 tablespoon fresh lemon juice

$1/2$ teaspoon sugar

$1/4$ cup minced fresh parsley

1. Sprinkle the trout with $1/4$ teaspoon of the salt and $1/8$ teaspoon of the pepper. Heat $1/2$ tablespoon of the oil in a nonstick skillet, then add half the trout. Sauté until the fish pieces are golden brown, about 1 minute on each side. Transfer the fish to a plate. Add another $1/2$ tablespoon of the oil to the skillet and repeat with the remaining fish.

2. Remove the skillet from the heat and cool slightly, then wipe with paper towels. Add the remaining $1/2$ tablespoon oil to the skillet and heat over medium-high heat. Add the carrots and onion and sauté until softened, about 5 minutes. Add the tomato puree, wine, lemon juice, sugar, parsley, the remaining $1/4$ teaspoon salt, and the remaining $1/8$ teaspoon pepper. Bring the mixture to a boil, reduce the heat, cover, and simmer until the carrots are crisp-tender, about 10 minutes. Add the trout, stirring it very gently into the sauce. Cover and cook just until heated through.

*Per serving  191 Calories, 8 g Total Fat, 2 g Saturated Fat, 45 mg Cholesterol, 257 mg Sodium, 13 g Total Carbohydrate, 3 g Dietary Fiber, 18 g Protein, 79 mg Calcium.*

*POINTS per serving: 4.*

# Grilled Mountain Trout with Herbs and Garlic

MAKES 4 SERVINGS

*The state of Wyoming is justifiably proud of its blue-ribbon trout streams, which are jumping with rainbow, cutthroat, and brown trout—all of which make for wonderful eating. If you don't fish for your own trout, you'll likely be buying a farm-raised variety, like rainbow trout. Although not as richly flavored as its wild cousins, fresh herbs, lemon, and garlic will enhance its taste in this dish. The trout can be prepped to the point of grilling earlier in the day and refrigerated until the grill is hot.*

Finely grated zest of 1 lemon

1 tablespoon fresh lemon juice

2 garlic cloves, minced

2 tablespoons chopped fresh flat-leaf parsley

1 tablespoon chopped fresh oregano

1 tablespoon chopped fresh thyme

2 teaspoons olive oil

1/2 teaspoon salt

1/4 teaspoon freshly ground pepper

4 (3/4–1 pound each) whole trout, cleaned, rinsed, and patted dry

1. Combine the lemon zest and juice, the garlic, parsley, oregano, thyme, olive oil, salt, and pepper in a bowl. Spread the mixture in the trout cavities. Wrap the trout in plastic wrap and refrigerate at least 2 hours.

2. Spray a grill rack with nonstick spray; prepare the grill. Grill the trout, 5 inches from the heat and covered, 8–10 minutes. Using a metal spatula, carefully turn each fish. Cover and grill until the fish is just opaque at the thickest part, 8–10 minutes longer. Using the spatula, loosen the fish from the grill rack and transfer to plates.

*Per serving  293 Calories, 14 g Total Fat, 4 g Saturated Fat, 108 mg Cholesterol, 359 mg Sodium, 1 g Total Carbohydrate, 0 g Dietary Fiber, 39 g Protein, 148 mg Calcium.*

*POINTS per serving:* 7.

★ *American Way*  For the best way to grill trout, pat the fish dry before putting them on the grill rack. Be sure the rack is very clean and set the rack a few inches above the coals to heat it thoroughly before setting the fish on it. These steps greatly reduce the chance of the fish skin sticking to the rack.

# Mango, Kiwi, and Chicken Salad

## MAKES 4 SERVINGS

*Vanilla bean and salad? Yes indeed, in this colorful salad with Californian flair. The mango does double duty in this recipe, providing sweet, fruity flavor and the low-fat base of the dressing. Peppery watercress adds a crisp contrast to the fruit's sweetness. Serve the salad as a lunch, light dinner, or in smaller portions as an elegant first course.*

1 pound skinless boneless chicken breasts

1/2 teaspoon salt

Freshly ground pepper, to taste

1/4 cup water

2 tablespoons sugar

1/2 vanilla bean (about 4 inches long), split

2 mangoes, pitted, peeled, and thinly sliced

2 tablespoons rice vinegar

1 tablespoon safflower oil

1/2 teaspoon minced shallot

1 large (6-ounce) bunch watercress, trimmed and rinsed

4 kiwi fruits, peeled and sliced

1. Spray a nonstick ridged grill pan with nonstick spray and set over medium-high heat. Season the chicken with the salt and pepper. Grill the chicken until it is cooked through, about 6 minutes on each side. Wrap the chicken in foil and let stand 5 minutes, then slice.

2. To make the dressing, bring the water, sugar, and vanilla bean to a boil in a small saucepan; boil until the liquid reduces to 3 tablespoons, about 3 minutes. Cool. Scrape the seeds from the vanilla bean and return the seeds to the syrup (discard the pod or save for another use). Combine the vanilla syrup with about 1/4 of the mango, the vinegar, oil, shallot, and a pinch of the salt in a food processor; puree.

3. Arrange the watercress on a large platter. Fan the remaining mango slices on the watercress at opposite ends of the platter. Place the chicken in the center, surrounded with the kiwi. Drizzle the salad with the dressing and serve.

*Per serving   315 Calories, 7 g Total Fat, 1 g Saturated Fat, 72 mg Cholesterol, 374 mg Sodium, 36 g Total Carbohydrate, 5 g Dietary Fiber, 28 g Protein, 86 mg Calcium.*

*POINTS per serving: 6.*

★ *American Way*   If you want to add a robust, smoky flavor, you can grill the chicken on an outdoor grill.

## Immigrant Influences

California's first immigrants were Spanish-speaking Franciscan Friars who built missions from San Diego to Sonoma in an effort to convert the Native Americans to Christianity. They were avid horticulturists and the first to plant many products, such as wine grapes and citrus groves, for which California is now noted.

Spain was the primary foreign influence in the area until the early 19th century, and, in 1812, Russia developed a colony north of San Francisco. However, by 1825, the entire area had become a territory of Mexico. The discovery of gold at Sutter's Mill in 1848 brought thousands of prospectors of all nationalities west in search of their fortunes. The completion of the transcontinental railroad in 1869 continued the rush of gold-seeking settlers.

During this period, some of California's biggest fortunes weren't found in the gold mines, but rather by those who sold food and supplies to those who arrived. Chinese laborers were brought in to care for the vineyards and citrus groves in the 1880s, and by the 1890s, Italian workers arrived to do the same jobs. As each group was replaced by another wave of immigrants, the previous laborers created their own businesses in the area. Many Chinese immigrants started small vegetable farms and, in their turn, Italians began food-related operations, like groceries, import/export businesses, and restaurants. California has always been a strong provider of America's fresh food, and each of the immigrant groups who came to the state has contributed a bit of its culture to the California cuisine.

# Sage Chicken with Peppers and Chickpeas

*Nestled in the San Joaquin Valley is the town of Gilroy, the garlic capital of the U.S., where the smell of garlic permeates the air. Choose garlic bulbs that are firm and plump; use the largest clove or two small cloves in this recipe for more of its assertive flavor. To produce a crispy crust on the chicken, be sure the skillet gets hot.*

8 long Italian frying peppers

3/4 teaspoon salt

4 (5-ounce) skinless boneless chicken thighs

Freshly ground pepper, to taste

1 large garlic clove, minced

1/2 cup low-sodium chicken broth

1 plum tomato, diced

1 (19-ounce) can chickpeas, rinsed and drained

1 tablespoon chopped fresh sage

1. Adjust the oven racks within the bottom and center of the oven. Preheat the oven to 400°F. Line a baking sheet with foil and spray with nonstick spray. Put the peppers on the baking sheet, spray the tops lightly with nonstick spray, and sprinkle with 1/4 teaspoon salt. Set on the bottom oven rack and roast, turning once halfway through, until the peppers are browned, 20–25 minutes.

2. Meanwhile, season the chicken with the remaining 1/2 teaspoon salt and a pinch of pepper. Heat a nonstick skillet, then add the chicken. Sauté until the chicken is browned, about 2 minutes on each side. Add the garlic and cook until fragrant. Add the broth and top the chicken with the tomato. Transfer the skillet to the middle oven rack and roast for 15 minutes.

3. Remove the pan from the oven, add the chickpeas, and sprinkle with the sage. Return to the oven and roast until the chicken is cooked through, 5–7 minutes more.

4. Transfer the chicken to a platter and surround with the peppers. Spoon the pan juices, tomatoes, and chickpeas over the chicken and serve.

*Per serving  301 Calories, 8 g Total Fat, 2 g Saturated Fat, 118 mg Cholesterol, 897 mg Sodium, 22 g Total Carbohydrate, 8 g Dietary Fiber, 35 g Protein, 71 mg Calcium.*

*POINTS per serving: 5.*

# Basque Chicken with Rice

MAKES 6 SERVINGS

*The Basque sheepherders who settled in the Mountain West region found the land in Wyoming, Nevada, and Idaho similar to their homeland. The dry climate, cool mountain air, rivers, and acres of forage were ideal for raising their herd. Basque dishes typically make generous use of tomatoes, peppers, and onions, and they're all here, along with rice, which makes this a satisfying, one-dish meal.*

$\frac{1}{2}$ teaspoon saffron threads, crumbled

1 tablespoon hot water

2 tablespoons olive oil

6 ($\frac{1}{4}$-pound) skinless boneless chicken breast halves

1 large onion, chopped

1 large red bell pepper, seeded and chopped

1 large green bell pepper, seeded and chopped

3 garlic cloves, finely chopped

1 cup long-grain rice

6 tomatoes, peeled, seeded, and chopped

2 cups low-sodium chicken broth

$\frac{3}{4}$ teaspoon salt

$\frac{1}{4}$ teaspoon cayenne

2 tablespoons minced fresh parsley

1. Stir the saffron and hot water together in a cup and set aside. Preheat the oven to 350°F.

2. Heat the oil in a Dutch oven, then add the chicken and cook until slightly brown, about 1 minute on each side. Transfer the chicken to a plate.

3. Add the onion, bell peppers, and garlic to the skillet. Reduce the heat, cover, and cook, stirring occasionally, until the vegetables are tender but not browned, about 8 minutes. Add the rice and cook, stirring, 2 minutes.

4. Stir in the saffron, tomatoes, broth, salt, and cayenne. Add the chicken and bring the mixture to a simmer, then cover the pan, and transfer to the oven. Bake until the chicken is cooked through and the rice is tender, 35–40 minutes. Sprinkle with the parsley.

*Per serving   332 Calories, 7 g Total Fat, 1 g Saturated Fat, 66 mg Cholesterol, 400 mg Sodium, 37 g Total Carbohydrate, 2 g Dietary Fiber, 31 g Protein, 45 mg Calcium.*

*POINTS per serving: 7.*

### FLASHBACK >> 1850

Gold prospectors in California sustain themselves with sourdough bread and biscuits. The Bread is made using starter dough from the previous day's bread as a leaven to make a fresh batch daily. San Francisco soon becomes a sourdough mecca; it is believed the city's starter dough came from Basques from southern Europe or Mexican gold miners.

# Chicken Swiss Steak–Style

MAKES 6 SERVINGS

*Though it is usually made with beef, Swiss steak can be just as delicious made with chicken. Although the traditional vegetables—onions, bell pepper, celery, and tomatoes—remain, this version is easier and lighter since there is no need to pound and flour the meat and it's cooked with minimal fat. We like chicken thighs because they tend to be moister than breasts and they cook much faster than beef. Serve with rice or noodles.*

2 tablespoons all-purpose flour

1/2 teaspoon salt

1/4 teaspoon freshly ground pepper

6 (1/4-pound) skinless boneless chicken thighs

2 tablespoons vegetable oil

1 large onion, chopped

1 green bell pepper, seeded and chopped

2 celery stalks, sliced

3 garlic cloves, finely chopped

1 tablespoon tomato paste

1 teaspoon dried oregano, crumbled

1/2 teaspoon fennel seeds, crushed

3 bay leaves

2 tomatoes, chopped

1 cup low-sodium chicken broth

2 tablespoons minced fresh parsley

1. Combine the flour, salt, and pepper in a large shallow dish or pie pan. Dredge the chicken in the flour, coating completely; shake off the excess. Heat 1 tablespoon of the oil in a nonstick skillet, then add the chicken and cook until browned, about 1 minute on each side. Transfer the chicken to a plate and set aside.

2. Heat the remaining 1 tablespoon oil in the skillet. Add the onion, bell pepper, celery, and garlic and sauté until softened, about 5 minutes. Stir in the tomato paste, oregano, fennel seeds, and bay leaves. Add the tomatoes and broth and bring to a boil.

3. Add the chicken to the pan and spoon the vegetable mixture over the pieces. Reduce the heat, cover, and simmer until the chicken is cooked through and tender, about 25 minutes. Discard the bay leaves. Sprinkle with the parsley.

*Per serving   362 Calories, 10 g Total Fat, 2 g Saturated Fat, 94 mg Cholesterol, 322 mg Sodium, 39 g Total Carbohydrate, 3 g Dietary Fiber, 28 g Protein, 46 mg Calcium.*

*POINTS per serving: 7.*

# Grilled Spiced Pork with Orange-Lime Glaze and Sugar-Snap Peas

MAKES 4 SERVINGS

*California is a true melting pot for ethnic foods. It is, in fact, the birthplace of fusion cuisine. This recipe melds Chinese and Mexican ingredients, creating a rather natural partnership, since the two cuisines often overlap in the use of certain herbs and spices. In this recipe, the spicy rub gives the pork great depth of flavor, while the simple glaze, which uses orange marmalade as a short cut, adds a welcome sweetness. Serve jasmine rice as a perfectly flavored accompaniment.*

1/2 cup orange marmalade

2 tablespoons fresh lime juice

1/4 teaspoon finely chopped shallot

1 1/2 teaspoons chili powder

1 teaspoon sugar

3/4 teaspoon salt

1/4 teaspoon five-spice powder

1 (3/4-pound) pork tenderloin, trimmed of all visible fat

3/4 pound sugar-snap peas, trimmed

1 1/2 teaspoons safflower oil

1 1/2 teaspoons rice vinegar

1/4 teaspoon grated peeled fresh ginger

Freshly ground pepper, to taste

1. Spray the grill rack with nonstick spray; prepare the grill.

2. Bring the marmalade, lime juice, and shallot to a boil in a small saucepan; boil 2 minutes. Allow to cool, then transfer half of the glaze to a small bowl.

3. Blend the chili powder, sugar, 1/2 teaspoon salt, and the five-spice powder in a small bowl. Rub the spices all over the pork. Grill the pork 5 inches from the heat, turning and brushing with half of the glaze, until an instant-read thermometer inserted in the center of the pork reaches 160°F, 20–25 minutes.

4. Meanwhile, cook the sugar-snaps in a saucepan of boiling water until crisp-tender, 2–3 minutes. Rinse under cold water and drain. Toss the sugar-snap peas with the oil, vinegar, ginger, the remaining 1/4 teaspoon salt, and the pepper.

5. Gently warm the remaining glaze over low heat. Slice the tenderloin, drizzle with the glaze, and serve with the sugar-snap peas.

*Per serving  327 Calories, 7 g Total Fat, 2 g Saturated Fat, 84 mg Cholesterol, 538 mg Sodium, 35 g Total Carbohydrate, 4 g Dietary Fiber, 32 g Protein, 82 mg Calcium.*

*POINTS per serving: 6.*

★ *American Way*  Be sure to add the vinegar to the sugar-snaps just before serving; adding it too early will dull their color.

*Grilled Spiced Pork with Orange-Lime Glaze and Sugar-Snap Peas*

# Pheasant Stir-Fry with Ginger and Orange

## MAKES 4 SERVINGS

*Pheasant is especially abundant in Wyoming and other mountain states, where wild game is still popular dinner fare. Assertive, but not gamy, pheasant has a taste that can stand up to strong flavors—like the ginger—in this Asian-inspired dish. The addition of shiitake mushrooms and snow peas make this a complete meal.*

2 skinless boneless pheasant breasts (about 1 pound total), cut into 1/2-inch cubes

3 tablespoons dry sherry

3 tablespoons fresh orange juice

1/2 cup low-sodium chicken broth

2 tablespoons hoisin sauce

1 tablespoon reduced-sodium soy sauce

1 teaspoon cornstarch

1/4 teaspoon salt

4 teaspoons vegetable oil

1 (1-inch) piece fresh ginger, peeled and grated

1/2 pound fresh snow peas, trimmed

1/4 pound fresh shiitake mushrooms, stems removed and caps thinly sliced

3 scallions, sliced

3 cups cooked rice, hot

1. Combine the pheasant with 1 tablespoon of the sherry and 1 tablespoon of the orange juice in a bowl. Set aside. Combine the remaining 2 tablespoons sherry and the remaining 2 tablespoons orange juice, with 1/4 cup of the broth, the hoisin sauce, soy sauce, cornstarch, and salt in a small bowl. Stir the mixture until the cornstarch dissolves.

2. Heat 2 teaspoons of the oil in a nonstick skillet, then add the ginger, snow peas, mushrooms, and scallions. Sauté the vegetables 1 minute. Add 2 tablespoons of the remaining broth and sauté until the broth evaporates. Add the remaining 2 tablespoons broth, continue sautéing until the broth evaporates, and the snow peas are crisp-tender. Transfer the vegetables to a plate and set aside.

3. Heat the remaining 2 teaspoons oil in the skillet, then add the pheasant. Sauté until the pheasant is almost cooked through, 2–3 minutes. Stir the hoisin mixture thoroughly, then add it to the skillet; cook, stirring, until the sauce bubbles and thickens. Return the vegetables to the skillet, then stir to coat with the sauce and to heat through. Serve immediately with cooked rice.

*Per serving   386 Calories, 9 g Total Fat, 2 g Saturated Fat, 66 mg Cholesterol, 464 mg Sodium, 41 g Total Carbohydrate, 3 g Dietary Fiber, 33 g Protein, 52 mg Calcium.*

*POINTS per serving: 8.*

★ *American Way*  If pheasant isn't readily available in your area, call D'Artagnan (800-DAR-TAGN) to order. If you just can't wait to make this dish, chicken is a good substitute.

# Beer-Braised Country Style Beef Short Ribs

## MAKES 6 SERVINGS

*Short ribs—the meaty tail end of the chuck—along with ribs and beef brisket, are some of the most flavorful cuts of meat. Boneless ribs, sold in markets as country style, contain far less fat than their bone-in cousins and are used in this recipe. Since the meat can be tough, it requires plenty of cooking time. An overnight marinade in apple juice flavors the meat, and two to three hours in the oven make the ribs meltingly tender—and well worth the time and effort! Serve the ribs with boiled new potatoes.*

3¹/₂ cups apple juice

3 bay leaves

3 garlic cloves, crushed but unpeeled

6 fresh parsley sprigs

2¹/₂ pounds boneless beef short ribs (country style), trimmed of all visible fat

2 tablespoons vegetable oil

1 (14¹/₂-ounce) can low-sodium chicken broth

1 (12-ounce) bottle beer

1 (14¹/₂-ounce) can diced tomatoes

1 cup unsweetened applesauce

2 tablespoons Worcestershire sauce

1 tablespoon Dijon mustard

³/₄ teaspoon salt

1. Combine the apple juice, bay leaves, garlic, and fresh parsley in a zip-close plastic bag; add the ribs. Squeeze out the air and seal the bag; turn to coat the ribs. Refrigerate, turning the bag occasionally, at least 8 hours or overnight.

2. Adjust the racks to the divide the oven in half. Preheat the oven to 350°F. Remove the beef from the marinade and pat dry with paper towels. Discard the marinade. Heat the oil in a Dutch oven. In batches, add the meat and sauté until browned on all sides. Transfer the meat to a plate and set aside. Discard the fat from the Dutch oven, then add the broth and beer. Bring the liquid to a boil, scraping any browned bits from the pan. Return the meat to the Dutch oven, being careful not to overlap any pieces. Cover the pan and transfer it to the oven. Bake until the meat is completely tender, about 2 hours. Remove the Dutch oven from the oven and reduce the oven temperature to 300°F.

3. Transfer the meat to a plate and set aside. Pour the liquid into a heatproof measuring cup or fat separator and let stand a few minutes to allow the fat to rise. Skim off the fat and discard. Return the liquid to the Dutch oven; there should be about 3 cups.

4. Puree the tomatoes with their juice in a blender. Add the tomatoes, applesauce, Worcestershire, mustard, and salt to the Dutch oven, and bring to a boil. Cook, stirring occasionally, until the mixture thickens slightly, about 5 minutes. Add the meat, cover, return to he oven, and bake until the flavors are blended, about 1 hour more.

*Per serving* *401 Calories, 23 g Total Fat, 9 g Saturated Fat, 106 mg Cholesterol, 717 mg Sodium, 10 g Total Carbohydrate, 1 g Dietary Fiber, 36 g Protein, 31 mg Calcium.*

*POINTS per serving: 10.*

★ *American Way* Since short ribs require so much time to prepare, you'll probably want to eat this dish right away. But it also is an ideal make-ahead since the flavor improves with time. It can be made up to a day or two ahead of time: Cool to room temperature, then cover and refrigerate. When you're ready to serve, reheat slowly until the sauce and meat are piping hot.

## Cowboy Cuisine

During the days of cowboys, cattle drives, and chuck wagons, the reputations of trail cooks were nothing short of legendary. Portrayed in movies as cantankerous but good-hearted, these traveling cooks were always ready with a robust meal, despite their lack of time, ingredients, and cooking equipment.

In truth, the period in American history on which such movie legend is based was quite short. Though lasting only from the end of the Civil War until the mid 1880s, when the railroad took over the job of driving cattle to Chicago, the era of the chuck wagon cook produced recipes and cooking techniques that translate well to campfire cooking in any setting. With a larder of potatoes, beans, flour, cornmeal, coffee, dried apples, bacon, and a variety of seasonings, complemented by fresh meat along the way, these inventive chefs were able to devise a surprisingly varied menu of stews, bean dishes, barbecued or fried meats, corn bread, biscuits, and coffee.

Many chuck wagon cooks were renowned even for their baked products. Beans, biscuits, and pies were often baked over coals or hot stones in a hole in the ground. When the hole was covered, it held in the heat and served as a makeshift oven. Metal storage cans, called billycans, sometimes served as baking containers for biscuits or breads, producing cylindrical loaves, which could then be cut crosswise into slices.

# Elk Tenderloins with Green Peppercorn Sauce

## MAKES 4 SERVINGS

*Hunters from around the world flock to the Rocky Mountains for its abundant wild game, including Rocky Mountain elk and white-tailed deer. Elk has a wonderful meaty taste without being heavy and also lacks any off-putting gamy flavor. Spicy green peppercorns provide a tasty counterpoint to the elk's sweetness in this recipe. Serve the steaks with fresh peas or steamed green beans.*

4 (¼-pound) elk tenderloin steaks, 1 inch thick, trimmed of all visible fat

2 tablespoons green peppercorns in water, rinsed and drained

1 teaspoon mustard powder

1 teaspoon + 1 tablespoon olive oil

1 shallot, finely chopped

½ cup low-sodium chicken broth

1 cup Merlot

2 tablespoons minced fresh tarragon

1 teaspoon Dijon mustard

Pinch salt

1. Pat the steaks dry with paper towels. Mash the peppercorns, mustard powder, and 1 teaspoon of the oil together in a small bowl with a fork. Spread the mixture on both sides of the steaks.

2. Heat the remaining 1 tablespoon oil in a nonstick skillet, then add the steaks. Sear until the meat is nicely browned, but still rare, about 3 minutes on each side; cover the pan during the last 2 minutes of cooking. Transfer the steaks to a plate; cover and keep warm.

3. Add the shallot to the skillet, return the pan to the heat, and sauté briefly. Add the broth and cook, scraping the browned bits from the pan, until the broth is almost completely evaporated.

4. Add the Merlot, tarragon, mustard, and salt. Cook, stirring constantly, until the sauce is thickened slightly. Return the steaks with any juices to the pan and spoon the sauce over them. Heat just briefly and serve.

*Per serving   204 Calories, 6 g Total Fat, 1 g Saturated Fat, 62 mg Cholesterol, 120 mg Sodium, 5 g Total Carbohydrate, 1 g Dietary Fiber, 28 g Protein, 24 mg Calcium.*

*POINTS per serving: 4.*

★ *American Way*  Elk, available in 2-pound tenderloins, can be cut into steaks. They may be ordered from D'Artagnan (800-DAR-TAGN) or Durham Meat Company (800-233-8742). Beef fillets make a fine substitute. The steaks can be prepped up to 6 hours ahead. Cover them with the seasoning, wrap in plastic wrap, and refrigerate until cooking time.

# Peppered Bison Tenderloin Steaks with Merlot and Cherry Sauce

MAKES 4 SERVINGS

*In the 19th century, it is estimated that more than 40 million bison roamed the frontiers of America and Canada. By the turn of the century, however, only thousands were left. Thanks to Native Americans, conservation groups, and ranchers, bison are once again flourishing. In this recipe, bison's mild, sweet taste is accentuated by a sauce of sour cherries and Merlot—a mellow red wine. Take care not to overcook the bison's lean meat or the steaks will toughen. Serve with green beans and new potatoes sprinkled with parsley.*

1/4 cup dried sour cherries

1 cup hot water

2 tablespoons whole black peppercorns

4 (1/4-pound) bison tenderloin steaks, about 1 inch thick, trimmed of all visible fat

1 tablespoon vegetable oil

1 large shallot, minced

3/4 cup Merlot

3/4 cup low-sodium beef broth

2 teaspoons minced fresh thyme

1/2 teaspoon salt

1. Soak the cherries in the hot water until plumped. Drain and set aside. Place the peppercorns in one layer in a cake pan and coarsely crush with a meat mallet or the bottom of a skillet. Pat the steaks dry with paper towels, then dredge in the peppercorns, coating each side well. Press the pepper down on the steaks, then set aside.

2. Heat 1/2 tablespoon oil in a nonstick skillet, then add the steaks. Sear the steaks 2 1/2 minutes, then turn them over and add the remaining 1/2 tablespoon oil to the pan. Swirl the pan to distribute the oil evenly. Cover the pan and cook the steaks until rare to medium-rare, 2–3 minutes more. Transfer the meat to a plate; cover and keep warm.

3. Add the shallot to the skillet and cook, scraping up any browned bits from the bottom of the pan. Add the cherries, Merlot, broth, and thyme. Bring the mixture to a boil and cook until the liquid is reduced by half and slightly thickened, 2–3 minutes. Add the salt, then reduce the heat, and return the steaks to the pan. Cook, continuously spooning the juices and cherries over the steaks, until heated through, about 1 minute. Serve immediately.

*Per serving   211 Calories, 6 g Total Fat, 1 g Saturated Fat, 70 mg Cholesterol, 386 mg Sodium, 10 g Total Carbohydrate, 1 g Dietary Fiber, 27 g Protein, 38 mg Calcium.*

*POINTS per serving: 5.*

★ *American Way*  To order bison, call D'Artagnan (800-DAR-TAGN). If you like, you can substitute beef tenderloins for the bison. The steaks can be prepped up to 6 hours ahead. Cover them with the pepper, wrap in plastic, and refrigerate until cooking time.

# Bison Burgers with Shiitake Mushrooms

## MAKES 4 SERVINGS

*Many ranchers in Colorado and other Rocky Mountain states raise bison specifically for its meat, which is lean, tender, and not as gamy-tasting as some other exotic meats. Since it is very lean, it must be gently cooked to retain the meat's moisture.*

1 (¹/2-ounce) package dried shiitake
  mushrooms

1 cup hot water

1 pound ground bison

2 tablespoons Asian oyster sauce

¹/2 cup low-fat mayonnaise dressing

2 tablespoons finely chopped fresh
  cilantro

4 Kaiser rolls or hamburger buns,
  split and toasted

4 slices red onion

4 slices English cucumber

4 slices tomato

1. Soak the mushrooms in the hot water until softened, about 30 minutes. Remove the mushrooms from the water and squeeze out the excess moisture. Reserve ¹/4 cup of the soaking liquid. Trim off the tough stems and discard. Finely chop the mushrooms and combine them with the ¹/4 cup soaking liquid in a bowl. Add the ground bison and oyster sauce. Shape the meat into 4 patties about 4 inches in diameter.

2. Combine the mayonnaise dressing and cilantro and set aside. Spray a large nonstick skillet with nonstick spray and heat over medium-high heat. Add the burgers and cook until done to taste, about 3 minutes on each side for medium-rare.

3. Spread about 1 tablespoon of the mayonnaise-cilantro mixture on each roll half. Assemble the burgers with the onion, cucumber, and tomato. Serve immediately.

*Per serving   362 Calories, 7 g Total Fat, 1 g Saturated Fat, 70 mg Cholesterol, 861 mg Sodium, 43 g Total Carbohydrate, 2 g Dietary Fiber, 31 g Protein, 70 mg Calcium.*

*POINTS per serving: 7.*

★ *American Way*  This exotic burger can also be made with lean ground beef.

# Caramelized Bell Pepper Sauté

MAKES 4 SERVINGS

*Bell peppers are ubiquitous in California, partly because they flourish in the climate, but also because of the state's rich history of ethnic cuisines that used the pepper extensively. This practically effortless preparation is a melange of brilliantly colored bell peppers, chopped fresh herbs, and pungent garlic.*

2 teaspoons olive oil

5 bell peppers in assorted colors, seeded and cut into thin strips

2 large garlic cloves, minced

2 teaspoons chopped fresh thyme

1 teaspoon chopped fresh rosemary

3/4 teaspoon salt

Freshly ground pepper, to taste

2 teaspoons balsamic vinegar

1. Heat the oil in a large nonstick skillet, then add the bell peppers. Cover and cook, stirring occasionally, until just tender, about 15 minutes.

2. Stir in the garlic, thyme, rosemary, salt, and pepper. Cook, uncovered, until the peppers are caramelized, 10–12 minutes more. Stir in the vinegar and serve.

*Per serving   80 Calories, 3 g Total Fat, 0 g Saturated Fat, 0 mg Cholesterol, 440 mg Sodium, 14 g Total Carbohydrate, 3 g Dietary Fiber, 2 g Protein, 25 mg Calcium.*

*POINTS per serving: 1.*

★ *American Way*  For the most spectacular presentation, use as many different colored bell peppers as possible. The secret to this side dish is patience, since peppers take time to caramelize.

# Butternut Squash and Swiss Chard Risotto

## MAKES 6 SERVINGS

*Italians have certainly made their mark on the food of California, particularly in the North Beach neighborhood in San Francisco. This lovely risotto uses roasted squash—roasting intensifies the flavor without adding calories. The squash also imparts a golden color as bright as the warm California sun.*

1 medium (1 1/2-pound) butternut squash, peeled, seeded, and cut into 1/2-inch dice

4 cups low-sodium chicken broth

1 cup water

1 tablespoon olive oil

1 onion, finely chopped

1 1/2 cups Arborio rice

4–6 garlic cloves, finely chopped

1/2 cup dry white wine

1 medium bunch Swiss chard, stems trimmed, cleaned, and leaves coarsely chopped (about 5 cups)

3 tablespoons grated Parmesan cheese

1. Preheat the oven to 450°F. Spray a large jelly-roll pan with non-stick spray. Arrange the squash in the pan, lightly spray with nonstick spray, and roast until tender, 20–25 minutes.

2. Meanwhile, bring the broth and water to a boil. Reduce the heat and keep the liquid at a simmer. Heat the oil in a heavy saucepan, then add the onion. Sauté until the onion is lightly browned. Add the rice and garlic and cook, stirring, 2–3 minutes.

3. Add the wine and stir the rice until the wine is almost absorbed. Add 1/2 cup of the hot broth and stir the rice until the broth is absorbed. Continue adding the broth—1/2 cup at a time—and stirring until it is completely absorbed before adding more, about 15 minutes. Stir in the squash, Swiss chard, and any remaining broth. Cook until the risotto is creamy and the chard is tender, 5–6 minutes longer. Stir in the cheese and serve immediately.

*Per serving  301 Calories, 3 g Total Fat, 1 g Saturated Fat, 2 mg Cholesterol, 156 mg Sodium, 57 g Total Carbohydrate, 4 g Dietary Fiber, 8 g Protein, 114 mg Calcium.*

*POINTS per serving: 5.*

★ *American Way*  To keep the fat down, we use light cheese in this soup. If you prefer to use Vermont cheddar, select an extra-sharp variety and use only 1/4 pound. For effortless cheese shredding, cut the cheddar into chunks and use the cheese-shredding blade in your food processor.

## WINE COUNTRY

While Thomas Jefferson and others on the East Coast spent a good deal of time and money importing grape cuttings from Europe and tried making wine from local grapes grown throughout the colonies, the Spanish Friars on the West Coast found instant success.

The first grape vines planted in California were brought to present-day San Diego by Franciscan Father, Junipero Serra. Before long, wine was being produced in 19 of the 21 missions along the coast. Not every region of California provided the ideal climate for the European *Vitis vinifera* grapes, however. After experimenting with matching grape variety to climate, Sonoma became the first successful wine growing area—just in time to toast the discovery of gold in California.

It was more than a decade before the Napa Valley caught up to Sonoma, but by 1868, there were more than 25 vineyards there. Most of Napa's wine makers who settled in the area were Europeans, many of them Germans, with a prior knowledge of winemaking. Unfortunately, two monumental problems soon affected the developing industry. The 1880s brought phylloxera (a vine-killing root louse). In time, phylloxera was successfully foiled by grafting vinifera cuttings to resistant root stock. In 1920, Prohibition was enacted, curtailing the wine industry until its repeal in 1933.

# Minted Lemon-Glazed Carrots

MAKES 4 SERVINGS

*The Mormon settlers who first arrived in Utah had the daunting task of transforming an arid desert into productive farmland. Carrots were among the first of their crops that could be stored for long periods. Needless to say, they devised many uses for this Vitamin A-packed vegetable. In this recipe, carrots are boiled, then coated with a sweet-sour lemon glaze and tossed with mint and parsley. Serve with any roasted or grilled meat.*

1 (1-pound) package peeled baby carrots

Finely grated zest of 1 lemon

4 cups water

1 teaspoon salt

1 tablespoon unsalted butter

1 tablespoons sugar

2 tablespoons fresh lemon juice

1 tablespoons finely chopped fresh parsley

1 tablespoon finely chopped fresh mint

Freshly ground pepper, to taste

1. Combine the carrots, lemon zest, water, and salt in a saucepan. Cover and bring the water to a boil. Remove the cover, reduce the heat, and simmer until the carrots are almost tender, 8–10 minutes. Drain well.

2. Melt the butter in a skillet, then add the sugar, lemon juice, and carrots. Cook, stirring constantly, until the liquid is absorbed and the carrots start to sizzle, 3–5 minutes. Remove the pan from the heat and stir in the parsley, mint, and pepper.

*Per serving* 96 Calories, 4 g Total Fat, 2 g Saturated Fat, 8 mg Cholesterol, 186 mg Sodium, 16 g Total Carbohydrate, 2 g Dietary Fiber, 1 g Protein, 31 mg Calcium.

*POINTS per serving: 2.*

# Roasted Winter Vegetables

MAKES 6 SERVINGS

*Hearty root vegetables undoubtedly helped to nourish and sustain the early settlers through the long, cold winters of the mountain states. This side dish, a medley of tastes and textures, is easy to prepare and satisfying in any weather. Substitute turnips or fennel bulbs for any of the vegetables in this dish.*

2 cups diced, peeled rutabaga
   (2–3 medium)
2 cups diced, peeled parsnips (about 3)
2 cups diced, peeled butternut squash
2 onions, diced
1 tablespoon olive oil
1/2 teaspoon salt
1/4 teaspoon freshly ground pepper
1 tablespoon chopped fresh sage
1 tablespoon chopped fresh thyme

Adjust the racks to divide the oven in half. Preheat the oven to 400°F. Combine the rutabaga, parsnips, squash, and onions in a bowl. Add the oil, salt, and pepper; toss to coat. Transfer the vegetables to a large nonstick jelly-roll pan and spread them out evenly. Bake, stirring every 15 minutes, until the vegetables are tender and just beginning to take on color, about 45 minutes. Sprinkle with the herbs and serve hot or warm.

*Per serving   112 Calories, 3 g Total Fat, 0 g Saturated Fat, 0 mg Cholesterol, 211 mg Sodium, 22 g Total Carbohydrate, 5 g Dietary Fiber, 2 g Protein, 76 mg Calcium.*

*POINTS per serving: 1.*

★ *American Way*  Cut the vegetables into 1/2- to 3/4-inch dice for even cooking. Be sure to roast them only until they begin to take on color, since overbrowning will leave them with a bitter taste.

# Savoy Cabbage with Torpedo Onions

MAKES 6 SERVINGS

*This is an excellent side dish for roasted game birds, Cornish hens, or chicken. Torpedo onions are a spindle-shaped variety of onion with an especially rich flavor; look for them in specialty produce markets. If you can't find them, red onions are a suitable stand in. Be sure to use savoy cabbage, however, as it has no substitute.*

1 tablespoon olive oil

4 torpedo onions or 2 large red onions, sliced

2 tablespoons red-wine vinegar

1 tablespoon sugar

1 (1-pound) savoy cabbage, quartered, cored, and sliced

1 large tart apple, cored and thinly sliced

1/2 teaspoon salt

1/4 teaspoon freshly ground pepper

1 cup low-sodium chicken broth

Preheat the oven to 350°F. Heat the oil in a large nonstick skillet with an ovenproof handle, then add the onions, vinegar, and sugar. Sauté the vegetables 2–3 minutes. Add the cabbage, apple, salt, and pepper; sauté 2–3 minutes more. Add the broth and bring to a boil. Cover the pan and transfer to the oven. Bake until the vegetables are tender and the liquid is absorbed, about 30 minutes.

*Per serving   88 Calories, 3 g Total Fat, 0 g Saturated Fat, 0 mg Cholesterol, 223 mg Sodium, 16 g Total Carbohydrate, 4 g Dietary Fiber, 2 g Protein, 39 mg Calcium.*

*POINTS per serving: 1.*

FLASHBACK >> 1971

Chez Panisse opens in Berkeley, California. Chef Alice Waters' restaurant adheres to her philosophy of using only the freshest, finest ingredients with minimal preparation. Chez Panisse's menu changes daily to accomplish the goal of serving fresh, seasonal food to its patrons.

# Lentils with Leeks and Carrots

## MAKES 6 SERVINGS

*The fertile, rolling hills of Idaho's Palouse country (named after the appaloosa horse, which once roamed freely in those parts) produce nearly all of America's lentils. This recipe can be made ahead and calls for green lentils (also called French lentils), which don't fall apart when cooked. Lentils are terrific with cooked green vegetables or as an accompaniment to roast chicken or broiled fish.*

3 cups water

1 cup French green lentils, picked over, rinsed, and drained

2 bay leaves

3/4 teaspoon salt

2 teaspoons olive oil

1 carrot, peeled, halved lengthwise, and thinly sliced

2 leeks, white part only, cleaned and thinly sliced

1 1/2 tablespoons red-wine vinegar

Freshly ground pepper, to taste

1. Combine the water, lentils, bay leaves, and salt in a saucepan. Bring the water to a boil, then reduce the heat and cook at a brisk simmer until the lentils are tender, about 25 minutes. Set aside, but do not drain. Preheat the oven to 350°F.

2. Heat the oil in a nonstick skillet, then add the carrot and leeks and stir well. Reduce the heat, cover, and cook until the vegetables are crisp-tender and slightly browned, about 5 minutes. Add the vinegar and stir until absorbed. Remove the pan from the heat.

3. Discard the bay leaves and add the vegetables and pepper to the lentils. Transfer the mixture to a shallow 1-quart baking dish. Bake, uncovered, until most of the liquid is absorbed, about 30 minutes. Serve hot or warm.

*Per serving   144 Calories, 2 g Total Fat, 0 g Saturated Fat, 0 mg Cholesterol, 303 mg Sodium, 23 g Total Carbohydrate, 11 g Dietary Fiber, 10 g Protein, 34 mg Calcium.*

*POINTS per serving: 1.*

# Tabbouleh with Black Quinoa

## MAKES 8 SERVINGS

*Tabbouleh is a traditional Middle Eastern dish made with bulgur, tomatoes, onions, and parsley. We've added black quinoa, which grows in the San Juan Mountains of Colorado, a relatively new variety of this highly nutritious, protein-rich grain originally from South America's Andes mountains.*

1/2 cup black quinoa

1 cup water

1/2 cup bulgur wheat

1 bunch scallions, thinly sliced

2 cups chopped fresh flat-leaf parsley

3/4 cup chopped fresh mint

1 English cucumber, peeled and diced

4 plum tomatoes, diced

1/4 cup fresh lemon juice

1/4 cup extra-virgin olive oil

1 teaspoon salt

1/2 teaspoon freshly ground pepper

8 Romaine lettuce leaves, washed and dried

1. Rinse the quinoa in a fine-mesh strainer under cold running water for 1 minute. Shake the strainer to remove excess water. Bring the water to a boil in a small saucepan and stir in the quinoa. Cover, reduce the heat to the lowest setting, and cook until the water is absorbed and the quinoa tender, about 20 minutes. Set aside, uncovered, to cool to room temperature.

2. Meanwhile, soak the bulgur wheat in hot water and cover until it is tender but still firm, about 30 minutes. Drain well in a fine mesh strainer, shaking off the excess water. Combine the quinoa, bulgur, scallions, parsley, mint, cucumber, tomatoes, lemon juice, oil, salt, and pepper in a large bowl. Cover the tabbouleh and chill 1–2 hours before serving.

3. Serve the tabbouleh over the lettuce leaves.

*Per serving  159 Calories, 8 g Total Fat, 1 g Saturated Fat, 0 mg Cholesterol, 311 mg Sodium, 20 g Total Carbohydrate, 4 g Dietary Fiber, 4 g Protein, 57 mg Calcium.*

*POINTS per serving: 3.*

★ *American Way*  Many health food stores carry black quinoa, but you can also order it from White Mountain Farms in Mosca, Colorado (call 719-378-2436 to order). Regular quinoa may be substituted. Be sure to rinse quinoa *thoroughly* before cooking to remove the bitter residue that coats the grains.

# Warm Basil Potato Salad

MAKES 4 SERVINGS

*North Beach, the Italian neighborhood in San Francisco, became a mecca for Italian fisherman who settled in California during the Gold Rush, and today offers an endless array of Italian specialties. Extra-virgin olive oil has the rich fruitiness required to lend a great depth of flavor, so it's worth its higher price tag. Add it with fresh sliced basil leaves to warm potatoes and they become a special side dish.*

1½ pounds new red potatoes, halved

1 tablespoon extra-virgin olive oil

1 large garlic clove, minced

Pinch crushed red pepper

2 tablespoons white-wine vinegar

½ teaspoon salt

1 tablespoon thinly sliced basil leaves

1. Bring the potatoes and enough water to cover to a boil in a large saucepan; reduce the heat and cook until fork-tender, 20–25 minutes. Drain in a colander 5 minutes. Wipe out the saucepan.

2. Heat the oil in the saucepan, then add the garlic and crushed red pepper and sauté just until fragrant. Stir in the vinegar and salt. Transfer the potatoes to a serving bowl. Drizzle the potatoes with the vinaigrette, add the basil, and toss gently to combine.

*Per serving   179 Calories, 4 g Total Fat, 1 g Saturated Fat, 0 mg Cholesterol, 300 mg Sodium, 34 g Total Carbohydrate, 3 g Dietary Fiber, 3 g Protein, 18 mg Calcium.*

*POINTS per serving: 3.*

★ *American Way*  If you can't find new potatoes, use full-size potatoes and cut them into 3/4-inch dice.

# Twice-Baked Potatoes with Goat Cheese and Parsnips

## MAKES 6 SERVINGS

*Vegetables that grow underground fare well in the Mountain West. Parsnips make a delicious, sweet-tasting purée. Try combining them with carrots, turnips, or mix them with potatoes and add goat cheese as we have here.*

3 large (10-ounce) Idaho potatoes

1 large (8-ounce) parsnip, peeled and cut into 1/2-inch cubes

3 large garlic cloves, thinly sliced

2 ounces goat cheese

1/4 teaspoon hot pepper sauce

1/2 cup low-fat buttermilk

1 large egg white

3/4 teaspoon salt

1/4 teaspoon freshly ground pepper

Pinch freshly grated nutmeg

2 scallions, thinly sliced

2 tablespoons grated Parmesan cheese

1/4 teaspoon paprika

1. Adjust the racks to divide the oven in half. Preheat the oven to 450°F. Bake the potatoes directly on the oven rack until they are tender when squeezed, 50–60 minutes. Set the potatoes aside to cool slightly. Reduce the oven temperature to 400°F.

2. Meanwhile, cook the parsnip and garlic in a large pot of boiling water until tender, about 20 minutes. Drain well. Combine the parsnip, garlic, goat cheese, and pepper sauce in a food processor and puree.

3. Cut the warm potatoes in half lengthwise and scoop out the pulp, leaving only a thin layer of potato in the shells. Mash the potato pulp in a medium bowl and add the buttermilk. With an electric mixer on high speed, beat the potato until very smooth. Add the parsnip mixture, egg white, salt, pepper, and nutmeg. Beat until very smooth, then stir in the scallions. Pile the mixture into the potato shells, mounding in the centers, or pipe through a pastry bag fitted with a large star tip. Combine the Parmesan with the paprika and sprinkle over the potatoes. Set the potatoes on a baking sheet.

4. Bake the potatoes until the tops are lightly browned and they are heated through, about 20 minutes.

*Per serving  208 Calories, 4 g Total Fat, 2 g Saturated Fat, 10 mg Cholesterol, 416 mg Sodium, 37 g Total Carbohydrate, 4 g Dietary Fiber, 7 g Protein, 105 mg Calcium.*

*POINTS per serving: 4.*

★ *American Way* Prep the potatoes to the point of baking them twice, up to 1 day ahead of serving them; cover with plastic wrap and refrigerate until cooking time.

# Scalloped Potatoes with Jarlsberg
# and Smoked Gouda

MAKES 8 SERVINGS

*The strong flavor of smoked Gouda makes it seem as though these creamy potatoes, a splendid make-ahead dish, were baked on a smoky grill. Cooking the milk-based sauce with a little flour beforehand prevents curdling during baking. Serve these scene-stealing potatoes with any basic grilled or roasted meat.*

1 tablespoon all-purpose flour

1/2 cup low-sodium chicken broth

2 cups low-fat (1%) milk

1/2 teaspoon salt

1/4 teaspoon freshly ground pepper

Pinch freshly grated nutmeg

1/2 cup shredded smoked Gouda cheese

1/2 cup shredded Jarlsberg cheese

2 pounds Yukon Gold or Yellow Finn
   potatoes, thinly sliced

1. Adjust the racks to divide the oven in half. Preheat the oven to 425°F. Whisk the flour and broth until smooth in a medium saucepan. Add the milk, salt, pepper, and nutmeg, whisking until smooth. Bring the mixture to a boil, whisking constantly, until slightly thickened, then remove from the heat.

2. Spray a 2-quart baking dish with nonstick spray. Combine the cheeses in a bowl and set aside. Arrange half of the potatoes, overlapping slightly, on the bottom of the dish. Sprinkle with half of the cheese mixture and arrange the remaining potatoes on top. Pour the hot milk mixture over the potatoes. Bake 25 minutes. Press down on the potatoes with a metal spatula, submerging them completely in the milk mixture, then sprinkle with the remaining cheese. Bake until the potatoes are tender and the top is browned, about 20 minutes more. Allow to stand 20 minutes before serving.

*Per serving   164 Calories, 4 g Total Fat, 3 g Saturated Fat, 14 mg Cholesterol, 290 mg Sodium, 24 g Total Carbohydrate, 1 g Dietary Fiber, 8 g Protein, 190 mg Calcium.*

*POINTS per serving: 3.*

# Gingered Idared Apple Crisp

## MAKES 8 SERVINGS

*Like neighboring Washington, Idaho is apple country. Its climate—hot days and cool evenings—are ideal for raising America's favorite fruit. Idared, cross developed in Idaho from two old-time New York apples—Jonathan and Wagener—is sweetly tart, juicy, and firm-textured. It is an excellent baking apple that's especially suitable for crisps and pies. Serve this classic crisp with vanilla frozen yogurt.*

3/4 cup all-purpose flour

1/2 cup packed brown sugar

1/4 cup unsalted butter, melted

1 teaspoon cinnamon

1/2 cup quick-cooking rolled oats

5 large Idared apples, peeled, cored, and thinly sliced

1/3 cup granulated sugar

1/4 cup finely chopped crystallized ginger

Finely grated zest of 1 lemon

1 tablespoon fresh lemon juice

Pinch salt

1. Adjust the racks to divide the oven in half. Preheat the oven to 350°F.

2. Combine the flour, brown sugar, butter, cinnamon, and oats in a medium bowl.

3. Combine the apples, granulated sugar, ginger, lemon zest, lemon juice, and salt in another bowl. Transfer to a 9-inch square baking pan. Sprinkle the oatmeal mixture evenly on top, covering the apples completely, and pat it gently in place. Bake until the top of the crisp is golden brown and the apples are tender, about 1 hour. Cool on a rack. Serve warm or at room temperature.

*Per serving   282 Calories, 7 g Total Fat, 4 g Saturated Fat, 16 mg Cholesterol, 25 mg Sodium, 55 g Total Carbohydrate, 3 g Dietary Fiber, 2 g Protein, 27 mg Calcium.*

*POINTS per serving: 6.*

★ *American Way* If you can't find Idared, use Jonagold, Braeburn, or Granny Smith apples.

# Huckleberry Pie

MAKES 10 SERVINGS

*Huckleberries grow wild in the mountains of Montana, where locals spend July and August in search of the coveted fruit. The beloved berry boasts a rich, tangy taste that is unequaled in the berry world.*

2 cups all-purpose flour

1/3 cup ice water

1/2 teaspoon salt

1/4 cup chilled unsalted butter, cut into tablespoon-size pieces

1/4 cup solid vegetable shortening

1 cup + 1 tablespoon sugar

5 tablespoons quick-cooking tapioca

1 teaspoon pumpkin pie spice

Pinch salt

6 cups huckleberries or blueberries

2 tablespoons fresh lime juice

1. To make the crust, combine 1/3 cup flour with the ice water, stirring with a fork until well blended. Combine the remaining flour and the salt in a bowl; cut in the butter and shortening with a pastry blender until the mixture resembles coarse meal. Add the flour-water mixture and toss with a fork until moist. Divide the dough into two pieces, one slightly larger than the other, and place on plastic wrap. Gently press each piece of dough into a 4-inch disk; cover with the plastic wrap and refrigerate at least 1 hour or up to 24 hours.

2. Adjust the racks to the center and bottom of the oven. Set a heavy baking sheet on the lower rack and preheat the oven to 450°F. On a lightly floured counter, roll out the larger piece of dough to a 12-inch round and fit into a 9-inch pie plate. Roll the second piece of dough into an 11-inch round.

3. For the filling, combine 1 cup sugar, the tapioca, pumpkin pie spice, and salt in a large bowl. Add the huckleberries and lime juice, gently toss to combine, and let stand 15 minutes.

4. Pour the filling into the dough lined pie plate, mounding the filling slightly in the center. Brush the edge of the pastry lightly with water and place the top crust over the berries. Press the edges together, trim excess pastry, fold the edges under, and flute. Make a few slits in the top crust with a sharp knife. Brush the crust with water and sprinkle with the remaining tablespoon of sugar.

★ *American Way* If you prefer your pie filling slightly loose, use only 4 tablespoons of tapioca. The full 5 tablespoons will produce a filling that is richer and less juicy. No matter which amount you use, be sure to let the filling stand 15 minutes before transferring it into the crust so that the tapioca can absorb some of the moisture from the fruit and thicken the filling properly.

5. Set the pie on the baking sheet and bake 20 minutes at 450°F. Transfer the pie on its baking sheet to the center rack. Reduce the temperature to 350°F. Bake until the crust is golden brown and the filling bubbles up through the slits, 45–60 minutes more. Cool on a rack for at least 6 hours. Refrigerate for 2 or more hours, if you wish, and serve the pie slightly chilled.

*Per serving   313 Calories, 10 g Total Fat, 4 g Saturated Fat, 13 mg Cholesterol, 141 mg Sodium, 53 g Total Carbohydrate, 1 g Dietary Fiber, 3 g Protein, 20 mg Calcium.*

*POINTS per serving: 7.*

# Raspberry Cobbler

MAKES 8 SERVINGS

*Every August, Garden City, Utah, hosts the Bear Lake Raspberry Days, celebrating the fruit's harvest with crafts, a rodeo, chuckwagon breakfasts, and countless raspberry-laden treats. For best results, use perfectly ripe local raspberries in this easy cobbler. Top the cobbler with frozen vanilla yogurt or enjoy it all by itself.*

½ cup water

½ cup packed brown sugar

1 tablespoon cornstarch

1 teaspoon vanilla extract

½ teaspoon cinnamon

¼ teaspoon freshly grated nutmeg

6 cups raspberries

1 cup all-purpose flour

¼ cup granulated sugar

1 teaspoon baking powder

¼ teaspoon baking soda

¼ teaspoon salt

¼ cup chilled unsalted butter, cut into pieces

½ cup low-fat (1%) milk

1. Adjust the racks to divide the oven in half. Preheat the oven to 400°F.

2. Combine together the water, brown sugar, cornstarch, vanilla, cinnamon, and nutmeg in a bowl. Whisk until the mixture is smooth and the sugar dissolves. Gently fold in the raspberries. Pour the mixture into a shallow 2-quart baking dish.

3. Sift together the flour, granulated sugar, baking powder, baking soda, and salt into a bowl. Cut in the butter with a pastry blender until the mixture resembles coarse meal. Add the milk and stir together just until the mixture gathers into a very thick batter.

4. Drop spoonfuls of the batter over the raspberries in 8 mounds, with 7 around the perimeter and 1 in the center, leaving some space between the mounds. Bake until the cobbler is well browned and the raspberry juices are thick and bubbling, about 35 minutes. Cool on a rack and serve warm or at room temperature.

*Per serving   244 Calories, 7 g Total Fat, 4 g Saturated Fat, 17 mg Cholesterol, 176 mg Sodium, 44 g Total Carbohydrate, 7 g Dietary Fiber, 3 g Protein, 66 mg Calcium.*

*POINTS per serving: 4.*

# Frozen Raspberry-Peach Torte

## MAKES 8 SERVINGS

*This fat-free torte is so simple to prepare, but it has the appearance of a restaurant-style dessert. Use a sharp knife to cut the torte into wedges.*

1 pint raspberry sorbet
1 (7-ounce) package amaretti cookies
1 pint peach sorbet
1 pint raspberries
1/3 cup water
1/4 cup sugar

1. Soften the raspberry sorbet in the refrigerator for 15 minutes. Line an 8-inch cake pan with plastic wrap. Coarsely crush the cookies and set aside.

2. Spread the softened sorbet evenly in the pan, and sprinkle with half the crushed cookies, lightly pressing them into the sorbet. Cover loosely with plastic wrap and freeze until firm, about 30 minutes.

3. Soften the peach sorbet in the refrigerator 15 minutes. Spread the sorbet evenly over the cookies. Sprinkle the remaining crushed cookies over the peach sorbet, lightly pressing them into the sorbet. Cover again and freeze until very firm, about 1 hour.

4. Combine the raspberries—reserving 16 berries—the water, and sugar in a saucepan. Bring the mixture to a boil and cook 3 minutes. Puree the mixture in a blender, and then strain through a sieve.

★ *American Way* Keep the cookie crumbs fairly large and be sure to press them into the sorbet. This way, they won't pull up when you top with the second layer. The torte and sauce can be made up to three days ahead. Store the sauce in an airtight container and cover the surface of the torte with plastic wrap.

5. Remove the torte from the freezer. Place a cake plate over the cake pan; invert. Pull the edge of the plastic wrap to remove the torte from the pan, then remove the plastic. Smooth the top of the torte with the side of a knife. Cut into 8 wedges and top each wedge with 2 raspberries. Serve with the raspberry sauce on the side.

*Per serving* 267 Calories, 2 g Total Fat, 0 g Saturated Fat, 0 mg Cholesterol, 18 mg Sodium, 60 g Total Carbohydrate, 4 g Dietary Fiber, 2 g Protein, 8 mg Calcium.

*POINTS per serving: 5.*

FLASHBACK >> 1933

Grower Walter Knott rediscovers the boysenberry in Anaheim, California. The berry becomes the hallmark of his Knott's Berry Farms. Soon, he harvests five tons of the berries per acre.

*Frozen Raspberry-Peach Torte*

# Basque Sheepherder's Bread

## MAKES 12 SERVINGS

*A true pioneer recipe, this mildly sweet bread is difficult to find anywhere in the U.S. Originally, it was baked in large cast iron pots that were nestled in a pile of hot coals while Basque sheepherders tended to their flocks. Twenty-first century cooks can use a 9-inch springform pan and achieve the same scrumptious results. The texture of this bread is ideal for dunking into soups—it's perfect with Chorizo Sausage and Kale Soup (page 257)— or for sopping up your favorite sauce.*

2 cups warm (105–115°F) water

1/3 cup sugar

1 (1/4-ounce) packet active dry yeast

1/4 cup unsalted butter or margarine, melted and cooled to room temperature

1 1/2 teaspoons salt

5 cups all-purpose flour

1. Combine 1/2 cup of the water and 1 teaspoon of the sugar in a large bowl. Sprinkle in the yeast and let stand until foamy, 5 minutes. Stir in the remaining water and sugar, the butter, salt, and 3 1/2 cups of the flour. Beat with a wooden spoon to make a smooth, thick batter. Gradually stir in the remaining 1 1/2 cups of flour. Turn out the dough on a floured counter; knead until firm and elastic.

2. Spray a large bowl with nonstick spray; put the dough in the bowl and spray with nonstick spray. Cover tightly with plastic wrap and let rise in a warm spot until the dough doubles in size, about 1 1/2 hours. Knead the dough briefly in the bowl and shape it into a ball.

3. Spray a 9-inch springform pan with nonstick spray. Place the dough in the pan, spray with nonstick spray, and cover the pan loosely with plastic wrap. Let rise at room temperature until the dough domes up 1–1 1/2 inches above the center of the pan, about 1 hour.

4. Adjust the racks to divide the oven into thirds. Preheat the oven to 375°F. Bake the bread until it is golden brown and sounds hollow when tapped, about 45 minutes. Remove the loaf from the pan and cool completely on a rack.

*Per serving   281 Calories, 5 g Total Fat, 3 g Saturated Fat, 11 mg Cholesterol, 332 mg Sodium, 51 g Total Carbohydrate, 0 g Dietary Fiber, 7 g Protein, 2 mg Calcium.*

*POINTS per serving: 6.*

★ *American Way*   When working with the dough, don't worry if it's slightly sticky after kneading; the key is that it is smooth and supple.

★

*chapter nine*
# The Pacific and Northwest

## APPETIZERS/SOUPS/SALADS

Penn Cove Mussels in Herbed Tomato Broth

Dungeness Crab Cakes with Pear Chutney

Saimen Noodle Soup

Alaskan Halibut Chowder

Mixed Greens with Toasted Hazelnuts, Blue Cheese, and Currants

## ENTRÉES

Linguine with Cougar Gold Cheese and Grilled Walla Walla Onions

Macaroni with Cougar Gold Cheese and Shiitake Mushrooms

Scallop, Maui Onion, and Papaya Kebabs

Alaskan Spot Prawns with Spaghettini

Seared Ahi Tuna with Mango Salsa

Chinook Salmon with Spring Vegetables in Foil

Stuffed Whole Red Snapper with Cilantro Pesto

Pan-Roasted Copper River Salmon with Herbed Mayonnaise

Beer-Braised Chicken Thighs with Morels

Grilled Ellensburg Leg of Lamb with Apricot-Mint Compote

## SIDES

Asparagus with Goat Cheese and Lemon Vinaigrette

## DESSERTS

Golden Delicious Phyllo Apple Tart

All-American Cherry Pie

Coconut Bread Pudding with Chocolate Sauce

Huckleberry and Cranberry Pie

# Penn Cove Mussels in Herbed Tomato Broth

MAKES 6 SERVINGS

*Coupeville, Washington, a quaint town on Whidbey Island in northern Puget Sound, is the home of the Penn Cove Mussel Farm. This delicious mussel, originally brought to Washington from the Baltic Sea on the hulls of sailing ships, is farmed in the calm bays around the cove. These cultivated mussels are fatter and sweeter than the wild varieties and have a less spiny beard. If you're not in the Northwest, Eastern Blue mussels or the green-tipped New Zealand mussels are fine substitutes.*

2 fresh thyme sprigs

12 fresh parsley stems

6 large garlic cloves, peeled

1/4 teaspoon crushed red pepper

1 (28-ounce) can diced tomatoes in juice

1/2 teaspoon salt

2 teaspoons olive oil

1 small onion, finely chopped

1 cup dry white wine

3 1/2 pounds mussels, scrubbed and debearded

4 thick slices country bread, toasted

1/2 cup minced fresh parsley

1. Tie the thyme sprigs and parsley stems together with white cotton twine. Spray a saucepan with nonstick spray and set over medium heat. Add the garlic and sauté until lightly browned, about 2 minutes. Add the red pepper and sauté just until fragrant, about 1 minute. Add the tomatoes with their juice and the salt. Bring the mixture to a simmer and cook, stirring occasionally, 12 minutes. Keep warm.

2. Heat the oil in a heavy 6-quart saucepan or Dutch oven, then add the onion. Sauté until the onion is softened, about 3 minutes. Add the wine and the herb bundle and bring to a boil. Add the mussels, cover, and steam until the mussels have opened, about 5 minutes. Discard any mussels that do not open.

3. Place a slice of toasted bread in the bottom of 4 warm shallow soup bowls. Using a slotted spoon, evenly divide the mussels among the bowls. Add the cooking liquid to the tomato sauce and bring to a simmer. Discard the herb bundle and garlic cloves. Stir the parsley into the tomato broth and then ladle the broth over the mussels; serve immediately.

*Per serving  237 Calories, 5 g Total Fat, 1 g Saturated Fat, 24 mg Cholesterol, 1,214 mg Sodium, 31 g Total Carbohydrate, 2 g Dietary Fiber, 15 g Protein, 65 mg Calcium.*

*POINTS per serving: 5.*

★ *American Way*  To clean mussels, place them in a colander and rinse under cold running water. Scrub them with a stiff brush and then pull off the beards—the thick whiskers from between their shells. Discard any mussel that does not close after being rinsed or that feels heavy, which indicates it is filled with sand.

# Dungeness Crab Cakes with Pear Chutney

MAKES 6 SERVINGS

*Dungeness crab—sweet, moist, and wonderfully flavored—is a favorite among crab connoisseurs. One small seafood restaurant along the Oregon coast claims their Dungeness crabs to be so fresh, "they come crawlin' in the back door to the kitchen." During the winter, the crabs are harvested from the waters of northern California; in spring and summer they come from the Aleutian Islands. The crabs weigh up to three pounds and are eight to ten inches long.*

## PEAR CHUTNEY

2 teaspoons olive oil

1/2 teaspoon ground cumin

3 large underripe Anjou or Bosc pears, peeled, cored, and chopped

2 tablespoons fresh lemon juice

1 teaspoon salt

1/2 small white onion, finely chopped

1/2 small red bell pepper, seeded and finely chopped

Pinch crushed red pepper

2 tablespoons minced fresh cilantro

1/4 teaspoon sugar

## DUNGENESS CRAB CAKES

1/2 pound Dungeness crab meat, picked over and flaked

1/2 small red bell pepper, seeded and finely chopped

1/2 small white onion, finely chopped

2 tablespoons minced fresh flat-leaf parsley

1 tablespoon minced fresh thyme, or 1 teaspoon dried

1/4 cup light mayonnaise

3/4 cup plain dried bread crumbs

1 tablespoon olive oil

1. To make the chutney, heat the oil in a skillet, then add the cumin. Sauté just until the cumin is fragrant, about 1 minute. Add the pears, lemon juice, and salt; sauté until the pears just begin to soften, about 3 minutes. Add the onion, bell pepper, and crushed red pepper; sauté until the onions and bell pepper soften, about 3 minutes more. Remove from the heat and gently stir in the cilantro and sugar. Transfer to a bowl and allow to cool to room temperature.

2. To make the crab cakes, combine the crab meat, bell pepper, onion, parsley, and thyme in a bowl. Add the mayonnaise and stir to combine. Form the mixture into twelve 3/4-inch–thick patties. Place the bread crumbs on a shallow plate. Carefully dredge the patties in the bread crumbs, coating them evenly.

3. Heat a large nonstick skillet. Swirl in 1/2 tablespoon of the oil. Add 6 crab cakes and cook until nicely browned, 2–3 minutes on each side; Repeat with the remaining oil and crab cakes. Serve the crab cakes with the chutney.

*Per serving (2 crab cakes and 1/3 cup chutney): 226 Calories, 9 g Total Fat, 1 g Saturated Fat, 32 mg Cholesterol, 727 mg Sodium, 27 g Total Carbohydrate, 3 g Dietary Fiber, 11 g Protein, 73 mg Calcium.*

*POINTS per serving: 5.*

★ *American Way* Pear chutney is the perfect complement to the crab cakes. Try it with pork chops, too. The chutney can be prepared ahead of time and refrigerated, in an airtight container, for up to 2 days.

FLASHBACK >> 1993

Pear growers in the US have a record year: 949,000 tons (more than half are Bartletts) are harvested in northern Washington, Oregon, and northern California.

# Saimen Noodle Soup

## MAKES 6 SERVINGS

*True Hawaiian cuisine is a mixture of culinary styles that evolved from the cooking techniques and exotic flavors favored by laborers from China, Japan, Korea, and the Philippines, who worked on the sugarcane and pineapple plantations. This delicious soup melds Japanese and Chinese ingredients that can be found in most well-stocked Asian markets: Dashi—the Japanese all-purpose soup stock—is sold in instant granulated form; saimen (or somen) noodles are delicate spaghetti-like noodles made from wheat flour; and char sui—Chinese roasted pork—is available at Asian meat counters (usually hanging near the Peking duck), or vacuum-sealed in a refrigerator case.*

1 (12-ounce) package dried saimen noodles

2 teaspoons Asian sesame oil

8 cups dashi (Japanese soup stock)

6 large shiitake mushrooms, sliced

3 (quarter-size) slices peeled fresh ginger, cut into slivers

1/2 pound large shrimp, peeled and deveined

1/4 pound char sui (Chinese roasted pork), thinly sliced

1 1/2 cups packed watercress, rinsed

2 scallions, thinly sliced

1. Cook the noodles according to package directions. Drain and place in a large bowl. Drizzle with the sesame oil and toss to combine. Set aside.

2. While the noodles are cooking, bring the dashi to a boil in a saucepan. Reduce the heat, add the mushrooms and ginger, and simmer until the mushrooms are tender, about 5 minutes. Add the shrimp, char sui, watercress, and scallions. Simmer just until the shrimp turn pink and are opaque in the center, about 3 minutes. Ladle the soup into warm bowls and serve immediately.

*Per serving  349 Calories, 5 g Total Fat, 1 g Saturated Fat, 84 mg Cholesterol, 1,481 mg Sodium, 51 g Total Carbohydrate, 5 g Dietary Fiber, 23 g Protein, 203 mg Calcium.*

*POINTS per serving: 6.*

*Saimen Noodle Soup*

# Alaskan Halibut Chowder

## MAKES 6 SERVINGS

*Fish chowders are a popular and warming choice during the many months of cold weather in America's last frontier. From Seward to Sitka, the mighty Alaskan halibut is a favorite of seafood-loving Alaskans. The snow-white flesh is fine-grained and firm, and the flavor is mild yet slightly sweet. It is best grilled, sautéed, baked, or, in this case, cubed and added to a chowder.*

1 cup fresh corn kernels
(from about 2 ears)

1/4 teaspoon salt

1 strip bacon, finely chopped

1 onion, chopped

2 medium russet potatoes, peeled
and cut into 1/2-inch cubes

2 cups bottled clam juice

2 cups fat-free milk

1 pound halibut, skinned and
cut into 1-inch cubes

1 tablespoon minced fresh thyme

1/3 cup minced fresh parsley

Freshly ground pepper, to taste

1. Heat a nonstick skillet, then add the corn. Sauté until the kernels are lightly browned and toasted, about 3 minutes. Stir in the salt, then remove the pan from the heat.

2. Cook the bacon in a heavy soup pot until crisp, about 5 minutes. With a slotted spoon, transfer the bacon to paper towels to drain. Pour off all but 2 teaspoons of the fat from the saucepan. Add the onion and sauté until soft but not brown, about 5 minutes. Add the potatoes and clam juice; bring to a boil. Reduce the heat, cover, and simmer until the potatoes are tender, about 20 minutes.

3. Add the corn, bacon, milk, halibut, and thyme to the soup pot. Simmer just until the halibut pieces are opaque in the center, about 5 minutes. Add the parsley and pepper, stir, and then serve.

*Per serving 220 Calories, 4 g Total Fat, 1 g Saturated Fat, 30 mg Cholesterol, 379 mg Sodium, 24 g Total Carbohydrate, 2 g Dietary Fiber, 21 g Protein, 162 mg Calcium.*

*POINTS per serving: 4.*

★ *American Way* To remove corn kernels from the cob, stand an ear of corn upright on a work surface and, with a sharp knife, cut downward along the cob.

# Mixed Greens with Toasted Hazelnuts, Blue Cheese, and Currants

MAKES 6 SERVINGS

*This flavorful salad highlights some of the best food produced in Oregon: fresh greens, hazelnuts, locally made blue cheese, and dried currants. Winter purslane, or miner's lettuce, is abundant in the fields and meadows of Oregon during the spring months. It was a favorite of Native Americans, as well as the Gold Rush miners who used it as a substitute for lettuce. This mix of peppery greens pairs perfectly with the hazelnut, which has thrived in Oregon since the early 19th century. In fact, in 1989, hazelnuts (known to locals as "filberts") were proclaimed the official state nut. Oregon produces about 98 percent of the nation's hazelnut crop.*

¼ cup hazelnuts

2 tablespoons extra-virgin olive oil

1½ tablespoons rice vinegar

1 tablespoon water

¾ teaspoon sugar

½ teaspoon salt

¼ teaspoon freshly ground pepper

8 cups assorted wild greens, or mesclun

¼ cup dried currants

2 tablespoons crumbled blue cheese

1. Preheat the oven to 325°F. Spread the hazelnuts on a baking sheet and toast them 7–10 minutes. Allow the nuts to cool slightly. Chop the hazelnuts and set aside.

2. To make the vinaigrette, combine the olive oil, vinegar, water, sugar, salt, and pepper in a small bowl. Whisk with a fork to blend.

3. Place the greens in a bowl, add the toasted hazelnuts and currants. Stir the vinaigrette and drizzle it over the greens; toss to combine. Top with the blue cheese.

*Per serving   140 Calories, 9 g Total Fat, 1 g Saturated Fat, 2 mg Cholesterol, 283 mg Sodium, 13 g Total Carbohydrate, 5 g Dietary Fiber, 4 g Protein, 53 mg Calcium.*

*POINTS per serving: 3.*

FLASHBACK>>1875

The Bing cherry is born in Oregon. It is the handiwork of a Chinese orchardman.

# Linguine with Cougar Gold Cheese and Grilled Walla Walla Onions

## MAKES 6 SERVINGS

*Walla Walla Sweets are grown in the dry central farmlands around Walla Walla, Washington. According to folklore, at the turn of the century, a French farmer who settled in Washington planted seeds of sweet onions from the island of Corsica. The Italian farmers who later settled in this area fell in love with the tasty onion and started developing their own strains.*

2 large Walla Walla onions, cut into
 1/2-inch–thick slices

1 pound linguine

1/3 cup minced fresh flat-leaf parsley

2 tablespoons minced fresh oregano,
 or 2 teaspoons dried and crumbled

2 tablespoons minced fresh thyme,
 or 2 teaspoons dried

1/2 teaspoon salt

Freshly ground pepper, to taste

3 tablespoons extra-virgin olive oil

1/2 cup coarsely grated Cougar Gold
 cheese

1. Spray the grill rack with nonstick cooking spray; prepare the grill. Or heat a nonstick ridged grill pan over medium-high heat. Spray the onion slices on both sides with nonstick spray. Grill the onions, turning once, until nicely browned, 5–7 minutes per side. Coarsely chop and set aside.

2. Cook the linguine according to package directions. Drain and place in a large serving bowl. Add the grilled onions, then sprinkle with the parsley, oregano, thyme, salt, and pepper. Add the olive oil and toss well to combine. Top the pasta with the cheese and serve immediately.

*Per serving 412 Calories, 11 g Total Fat, 3 g Saturated Fat, 10 mg Cholesterol, 262 mg Sodium, 64 g Total Carbohydrate, 4 g Dietary Fiber, 13 g Protein, 110 mg Calcium.*

*POINTS per serving: 8.*

★ *American Way* Substitute an aged white farmhouse cheddar if Cougar Gold is unavailable. Vidalia or Maui onions can be used in place of Walla Wallas.

*Linguine with Cougar Gold Cheese and Grilled Walla Walla Onions*

# Macaroni with Cougar Gold Cheese and Shiitake Mushrooms

MAKES 8 SERVINGS

*Cougar Gold cheese—an exceptionally high-quality cheddar—is made at the creamery of Washington State University in Pullman, Washington. Named after the school's mascot, the cheese comes in a can, where it is aged for about a year before being sold. It can be stored for many years, unopened, in the refrigerator, where it will age further and develop a more crumbly texture and sharper taste. The cheese melts into a creamy smoothness in sauces, and its unique nutty taste comes through perfectly. It is also an excellent grating cheese; use it as you would Parmesan.*

1 pound small pasta shells

1/2 cup water

1 tablespoon unsalted butter

3/4 pound shiitake mushrooms, stems discarded, cleaned, and sliced

1/2 cup quick-mixing flour (e.g., Gold Medal Wondra Flour)

4 cups fat-free milk

1 teaspoon salt

1/4 teaspoon hot pepper sauce

1 1/2 cups coarsely grated Cougar Gold Cheddar cheese

2 tablespoons Dijon mustard

1. Preheat the oven to 350°F. Spray a 9 × 13-inch baking dish with nonstick spray.

2. Cook the pasta according to package directions. Drain the pasta and rinse it under cold water. Drain well and set aside.

3. Bring the water and butter to a boil in a nonstick skillet. Add the mushrooms, cover, and cook 2 minutes. Uncover and cook, stirring, until the liquid evaporates and the mushrooms begin to brown, about 5 minutes. Set aside.

4. In a heavy saucepan, whisk the flour with 1 cup of the milk until smooth, then whisk in the remaining milk. Add the salt and pepper sauce. Cook over medium-high heat, whisking continuously, until the mixture boils. Continue whisking until the sauce thickens, about 2 minutes. Remove from the heat, add the cheese, and whisk until smooth. Stir in the mustard.

5. Combine the pasta, mushrooms, and sauce in a large bowl. Transfer the mixture to the baking dish and bake until bubbling and the top is lightly browned, about 45 minutes. Allow to cool slightly before serving.

*Per serving   403 Calories, 10 g Total Fat, 6 g Saturated Fat, 29 mg Cholesterol, 513 mg Sodium, 60 g Total Carbohydrate, 2 g Dietary Fiber, 18 g Protein, 322 mg Calcium.*

*POINTS per serving: 8.*

★ *American Way*  If you like, use oyster mushrooms or a combination of shiitakes and oyster mushrooms. Order Cougar Gold Cheese from the Washington State University Creamery throughout the year except July and August. Call 509-335-4014 or 800-457-5442, or visit their Web site at www.wsu.edu/creamery. If Cougar Gold is unavailable, you can substitute any aged white farmhouse cheddar.

# Scallop, Maui Onion, and Papaya Kebabs

MAKES 8 SERVINGS

*Pupus, the Hawaiian word for "finger food," originally was associated with sugar plantation workers who carried their lunches in little tin buckets. These lunches consisted of morsels of fish or chicken, eaten along with a bowl of rice. Now,* pupus *have come to denote hors d'oeurves or a sampler of tastes to whet the appetite. While these kebabs have all the hallmarks of* pupus, *they are a meal all their own.*

3 tablespoons pineapple juice

2 teaspoons olive oil

1 teaspoon low-sodium soy sauce

1 teaspoon grated peeled fresh ginger

1/8 teaspoon salt

1/8 teaspoon freshly ground pepper

2 pounds (about 32) large sea scallops

2 firm, ripe papayas, peeled, seeded, and cut into chunks

2 Maui onions, peeled, each cut into wedges

2 limes, cut into wedges

1. Spray a grill or broiler rack with nonstick spray; prepare the grill or preheat the broiler. Soak sixteen 12-inch wooden skewers in water for 10 minutes.

2. Combine the pineapple juice, olive oil, soy sauce, ginger, salt, and pepper in a zip-close plastic bag; add the scallops, squeeze out the air, and seal the bag; turn to coat the scallops. Set aside to marinate 15 minutes.

3. Thread each skewer, dividing the papaya, scallops, and onions equally to fill the 16 skewers. Discard the marinade.

4. In batches, grill or broil the kebabs, 5 inches from the heat, until the scallops are opaque in the center, about 4 minutes on each side. Serve the kebabs with the lime wedges.

*Per serving  229 Calories, 2 g Total Fat, 0 g Saturated Fat, 56 mg Cholesterol, 319 mg Sodium, 21 g Total Carbohydrate, 3 g Dietary Fiber, 30 g Protein, 82 mg Calcium.*

*POINTS per serving: 4.*

★ *American Way*  When outdoor cooking is not an option, the kebabs can be broiled. Be aware that the cooking time may vary slightly. If Maui onions are unavailable, substitute Vidalia or Walla Walla onions. The recipe is easily halved if you're not serving a crowd.

# POLYNESIAN TRADITIONS

More than a thousand years ago, the Hawaiian Islands were settled by Polynesians from the islands of Oceana further west. These immigrants brought taro and pigs, as the volcanic islands had little food to offer besides birds and seafood. Some speculate that coconut, another staple of the island's cuisine, was brought by those first immigrants or floated ashore and rooted on the fertile beaches. It is from these basic ingredients that Hawaiians were able to create their most famous feast, the luau. Similar to feasts celebrated in other parts of Polynesia, the luau centers around the Kaluha pig, which is roasted over hot rocks in a pit with some of the root vegetables that comprise the meal. Poi, a smooth paste made from the taro root, is often eaten plain with the fingers and serves as the base of a meal. A variety of fish dishes round out the menu.

The first European to spot the Hawaiian Islands was Captain James Cook, who landed there in 1778. But it was not until 40 years later, when whalers came to the islands because of their proximity to whale breeding grounds, that European foods were introduced to the area. In the early 19th century, missionaries brought New England fish stews, salt cod, and cornmeal to Hawaii. Shortly thereafter, Chinese immigrants brought Asian vegetables, Japanese brought soy and teriyaki sauce, seaweed, and noodles, Filipinos brought mung beans and fish sauce, and the Portuguese brought sweet bread, doughnuts, and bean soup. A state since 1959, Hawaii still offers visitors a taste of its traditional cuisine. In addition, upscale restaurant menus feature traditional and immigrant ingredients prepared in creative new ways.

# Alaskan Spot Prawns with Spaghettini

## MAKES 6 SERVINGS

*The icy cold waters off Alaska produce small, delicate-tasting shrimp called spot prawns. Riding along the swiftest currents, these succulent shellfish are caught by skilled fisherman using specially designed shrimp pots. They are sweet and have firm flesh, which makes them a perfect addition to a simple pasta dish.*

2 large garlic cloves, minced

1 pound spot prawns, peeled and deveined

1 cup bottled clam juice

1/2 cup dry white wine

1/4 teaspoon crushed red pepper

1/4 teaspoon salt

1 pound spaghettini

2 tablespoons extra-virgin olive oil

1/4 cup minced fresh flat-leaf parsley

1. Spray a large nonstick skillet with nonstick spray and set over medium heat. Add the garlic and sauté until lightly browned, about 2 minutes. Add the prawns and sauté until they just turn pink, about 2 minutes. Add the clam juice, wine, red pepper, and salt. Bring to a simmer, and cook until the prawns are just opaque in the center, then remove from the heat.

2. Meanwhile, cook the spaghettini according to package directions. Drain the pasta and place it in a warm serving bowl. Add the prawns with their sauce, then the olive oil and parsley. Toss to combine and serve immediately.

*Per serving 394 Calories, 7 g Total Fat, 1 g Saturated Fat, 95 mg Cholesterol, 282 mg Sodium, 58 g Total Carbohydrate, 2 g Dietary Fiber, 23 g Protein, 57 mg Calcium.*

*POINTS per serving: 8.*

★ *American Way* Small shrimp or rock shrimp can be used if spot prawns are not available.

### FLASHBACK >> 1867

Alaska is sold to the United States in a deal arranged by Secretary of State William Seward. The same year, thousands of miles away in New York, a chef at the famed Delmonico's restaurant creates Baked Alaska—ice cream enclosed with meringue and baked briefly in an oven—to celebrate the purchase, which is referred to as "Seward's Folly."

# Seared Ahi Tuna with Mango Salsa

## MAKES 6 SERVINGS

*Hawaiian cuisine makes great use of the fish and shellfish that are gathered from the surrounding ocean waters. Ahi tuna is a high-quality, lean, and delicious fish; it's perfectly partnered with tropical fruit salsa in this recipe.*

1 teaspoon olive oil

1/2 teaspoon ground cumin

1/2 teaspoon ground coriander

2 large firm, ripe mangoes, peeled, pitted, and diced

1/4 cup finely chopped red onion

1/4 cup chopped fresh cilantro

1 tablespoon fresh lime juice

1 jalapeño pepper, seeded and minced (wear gloves to prevent irritation)

2 teaspoons coarse salt

6 (5-ounce) ahi tuna steaks, about 1-inch thick

1/3 cup coarsely crushed black peppercorns

1. To make the salsa, mix the oil, cumin, and coriander in one bowl. Combine the mangoes, onion, cilantro, lime juice, jalapeño, and 1/4 teaspoon of the salt in another bowl. Add the oil-spice mixture to the mangoes and stir well to combine. Set aside at room temperature for at least 1 hour.

2. Spray the grill rack with nonstick spray; prepare the grill. Sprinkle the remaining salt on the tuna steaks. Place the pepper in a shallow dish or plate. Press each steak into the pepper until well coated on both sides.

3. Grill the steaks, covered, 5 inches from the heat, turning once, until an instant-read thermometer registers 120°F when inserted into the center of the steak, about 3 minutes on each side.

*Per serving* 225 Calories, 3 g Total Fat, 1 g Saturated Fat, 66 mg Cholesterol, 446 mg Sodium, 16 g Total Carbohydrate, 3 g Dietary Fiber, 35 g Protein, 55 mg Calcium.

*POINTS per serving: 4.*

★ *American Way* To make the coarsely ground pepper, pulse the pepper in a coffee grinder, or adjust the grind from fine to coarse on your pepper mill. If you don't have one, place whole peppercorns in a sealed heavy plastic bag and use a rolling pin or a heavy pan to coarsely crush the peppercorns. If a grill is not convenient, the tuna can be broiled, but the cooking time may vary slightly. The salsa is even better if allowed to sit for longer. Cover and refrigerate for up to 24 hours; allow to come to room temperature before serving.

# Chinook Salmon with Spring Vegetables in Foil

MAKES 4 SERVINGS

*The Columbia River, which divides Oregon and Washington, boasts some of the most spectacular salmon runs in the world, and is well known for the spring and fall runs of Chinook—or king—salmon. Fishing these runs was the livelihood for many of Oregon's Native American tribes, and, in some instances, still is today. The spring Chinook is prized for its firm, hearty red meat. This simple preparation, with asparagus and peas in a foil packet, brings out the best of the fish's flavors.*

4 leaves romaine lettuce

4 large cremini mushrooms, sliced

4 (6-ounce) skinless Chinook salmon
  fillets

1/8 teaspoon coarse salt

1/8 teaspoon freshly ground pepper

Pinch cayenne

1 pound asparagus, trimmed

1 pound fresh peas, shelled, or 3/4 cup
  thawed frozen peas

1/2 cup dry white wine

1/2 cup low-sodium chicken broth

1. Preheat the oven to 400°F. Spray four 12 × 12-inch foil rectangles with nonstick spray. Put the lettuce and mushrooms on the foil; top with salmon fillets. Sprinkle the salt, pepper, and cayenne. Arrange the asparagus over the fillets and scatter the peas over and around. Pour 2 tablespoons of wine and 2 tablespoons of broth over each fillet. Fold the foil into packets, making a tight seal.

2. Place the packets on a baking sheet. Bake until the salmon is just opaque in the center, about 20 minutes. Open the packets and carefully pull the lettuce leaves from under the mushrooms and discard. Serve, drizzled with any juices.

*Per serving   365 Calories, 18 g Total Fat, 4 g Saturated Fat, 113 mg Cholesterol, 146 mg Sodium, 8 g Total Carbohydrate, 4 g Dietary Fiber, 39 g Protein, 67 mg Calcium.*

*POINTS per serving: 8.*

★ *American Way*  This is a great dinner-party dish, since the recipe is easily doubled for serving a crowd and the packets can be assembled ahead of time. If Chinook salmon is not available, any other variety of salmon works fine in this recipe. The fish can be prepared to the point of baking and then refrigerated for up to 2 hours. Remove the packets from the refrigerator 30 minutes before baking.

# Stuffed Whole Red Snapper with Cilantro Pesto

### MAKES 6 SERVINGS

*In Hawaii, this traditional dish is called* laulau. *The old-timers wrapped fish, pork, chicken, or beef in the smooth, green leaves of the ti plant and cooked the meal in a grilling pit, called an* imu. *For this healthful, low-fat version, red snapper (*onaga *in Hawaiian) is stuffed with vegetables, then wrapped in ti leaves and steamed. A fish poacher or a heavy-duty roasting pan with a fitted rack is necessary for this recipe.*

### STUFFED SNAPPER

1 (3-pound) whole red snapper, cleaned

1/2 teaspoon coarse salt

1/4 teaspoon freshly ground pepper

3 large shiitake mushrooms, sliced

1 tomato, sliced

3 scallions, cut into 2-inch lengths

5 (quarter-size) slices peeled fresh ginger, cut into slivers

7 fresh or dried ti leaves or 2 (12 × 20-inch) sheets of foil

12 sprigs fresh cilantro

2 tablespoons reduced-sodium soy sauce

### CILANTRO PESTO

1 cup fresh cilantro leaves

1 large garlic clove, minced

1 tablespoon extra-virgin olive oil

1. Sprinkle the fish, inside and out, with the salt and pepper. Layer the cavity of the fish with the mushrooms, tomato, and scallions. Sprinkle inside the fish with half the ginger.

2. With a very sharp knife, cut the ribs from the ti leaves and discard. On a work surface, use the leaves to form a cross by overlapping 2 ti leaves horizontally, then 3 leaves vertically. Place the stuffed fish on top of the leaves. Sprinkle with the remaining ginger and scatter the cilantro sprigs around. Pour the soy sauce over the top. Lay 2 ti leaves horizontally on top. Fold the sides over the top to enclose the fish and tie the bundle tightly with string to secure. (Or, place the fish on 1 sheet of foil and place a second sheet on top; fold and crimp the edges together to make a packet.) Place the wrapped fish on a rack in a large pan over boiling water. Cover and steam until the fish is just opaque in the center, 20 minutes.

3. Meanwhile, to make the pesto, puree the cilantro leaves, garlic, and olive oil in a food processor or blender.

4. Carefully remove the fish from the poacher, unwrap it, and serve with the pesto.

*Per serving (with 1 tablespoon pesto): 175 Calories, 4 g Total Fat, 1 g Saturated Fat, 50 mg Cholesterol, 268 mg Sodium, 4 g Total Carbohydrate, 1 g Dietary Fiber, 29 g Protein, 60 mg Calcium.*

*POINTS per serving: 4.*

★ *American Way* Ti leaves are available fresh or dried in well-stocked Asian markets (if dried, they need only be soaked in hot water until they become soft and pliable). If you can't find ti leaves, use 2 sheets of aluminum foil. The pesto can be frozen in a plastic container or zip-close plastic bag for up to 1 month.

*Stuffed Whole Red Snapper with Cilantro Pesto*

# Pan-Roasted Copper River Salmon with Herbed Mayonnaise

MAKES 4 SERVINGS

*The Northwest's penchant for salmon reaches fever pitch in early May, when the first Copper River salmon begin arriving from Alaska. Each year these mighty salmon take on the two-hundred-mile run up the Copper, which makes them some of the richest tasting and most beautiful salmon you'll ever eat. When salmon is this good, simple cooking and a minimum of ingredients is all that is needed.*

¼ cup light mayonnaise

2 tablespoons minced fresh chives

1 tablespoon capers, drained and chopped

2 teaspoons fresh lemon juice

1 (1-pound) Copper River salmon fillet

½ teaspoon coarse salt

¼ teaspoon freshly ground pepper

1½ tablespoons vegetable oil

1. Preheat the oven to 450°F. Combine the mayonnaise, chives, capers, and lemon juice in a serving bowl; set aside.

2. Season the salmon with the salt and pepper. Heat a large, heavy-bottomed ovenproof skillet (preferably cast-iron) over high heat until almost smoking. Swirl in the oil, then add the salmon, skin side up. Cook 2 minutes. Using a broad spatula, turn the fillet and cook 2 minutes more. Transfer the skillet to the oven and roast until the salmon is opaque in the center, about 5 minutes. Serve the salmon with the herbed mayonnaise.

*Per serving   286 Calories, 18 g Total Fat, 4 g Saturated Fat, 84 mg Cholesterol, 409 mg Sodium, 4 g Total Carbohydrate, 0 g Dietary Fiber, 26 g Protein, 30 mg Calcium.*

*POINTS per serving: 7.*

★ *American Way*  Use any variety of salmon if you can't find Copper River salmon.

FLASHBACK >> 1993

Fishermen in Alaska bring in a record 191 million salmon, including 40 million sockeye from Bristol Bay.

# Beer-Braised Chicken Thighs with Morels

MAKES 6 SERVINGS

*Oregon has evolved into the capital of the microbrew industry, which is not surprising, considering it ranks second in the nation in the production of hops. What's more, Oregon boasts plenty of lush, damp forests filled with edible wild mushrooms, including the prized morel. This satisfying entrée combines the rich, dark flavors of a porter-style beer, the earthy taste of morels, and succulent dark chicken meat.*

⅓ cup all-purpose flour

2 teaspoons dried thyme

1 teaspoon paprika

1 teaspoon salt

6 (6-ounce) bone-in chicken thighs, skinned

2 tablespoons olive oil

1 onion, chopped

6 ounces fresh morel mushrooms, wiped clean and halved

1 (12-ounce) bottle porter-style beer

½ cup minced fresh parsley

Freshly ground pepper, to taste

1. Combine the flour, thyme, paprika, and salt in a shallow dish. Dredge the thighs in the flour mixture, coating them evenly; shake off the excess. Set aside.

2. Heat a large skillet. Swirl in the oil, then add the chicken. Cook, until the chicken is browned, about 3 minutes on each side. Transfer the chicken to a plate. Add the onion and mushrooms to the skillet and sauté until the onion is translucent and the mushrooms are lightly browned, about 5 minutes. Using a slotted spoon, transfer the mushroom mixture to another plate and set aside.

3. Return the chicken to the skillet, add the beer, and bring to a boil. Reduce the heat, cover, and simmer until the chicken is cooked through, 20–30 minutes.

4. Return the mushroom mixture to the skillet, then stir in ¼ cup of the parsley and the pepper; heat through. Serve the chicken with the sauce over the top and sprinkle with the remaining parsley.

*Per serving  192 Calories, 9 g Total Fat, 2 g Saturated Fat, 80 mg Cholesterol, 285 mg Sodium, 7 g Total Carbohydrate, 1 g Dietary Fiber, 21 g Protein, 32 mg Calcium.*

*POINTS per serving: 4.*

★ *American Way*  Black Butte Porter, a beer hand-crafted by Deschutes Brewery in Bend, Oregon, is a good choice for this recipe—but any hand-crafted porter will work. If morel mushrooms are unavailable, use 1 ounce dried morels, reconstituted; fresh cremini mushrooms would work too. Serve on a bed of egg noodles or fettuccine.

# Grilled Ellensburg Leg of Lamb with Apricot-Mint Compote

## MAKES 12 SERVINGS

*This dish combines some of the best of what Washington state has to offer. Ellensburg, Washington, a small town on the eastern side of the Cascade Mountains, is well-known for its succulent lamb. Farther east, in the Yakima and Wenatchee valleys, apricot orchards are abundant, and fields of mint are common.*

1 (3-pound) lean leg of lamb, butterflied and trimmed of all visible fat

3 tablespoons olive oil

6 large garlic cloves, minced

1 teaspoon coarse salt

1/4 cup dried oregano

1/4 cup dried rosemary, crumbled

1/2 cup finely chopped white onion

12 ripe apricots, pitted and chopped (about 3 cups)

2 tablespoons sugar

1/2 teaspoon table salt

1/4 cup chopped fresh mint

Freshly ground pepper, to taste

1. Place the lamb in a large shallow roasting pan. Combine the oil, garlic, and coarse salt in a bowl. Coat all sides of the lamb with the garlic mixture. Cover and set aside to marinate at room temperature for 1 hour. Coat one side of the lamb with the oregano and the other side with the rosemary.

2. Spray the grill rack with nonstick spray; prepare the grill. Grill the lamb 5 inches from the heat, turning once until an instant-read thermometer inserted in the thickest part of the lamb registers 120–130°F (medium rare), about 15 minutes for each side. Let stand 10 minutes before carving.

3. Meanwhile, to make the compote, spray a large nonstick skillet with nonstick spray and set over medium-high heat. Add the onion and sauté until soft, about 3 minutes. Add the apricots, sugar, and table salt and sauté until the apricots are tender, about 3 minutes more. Remove the pan from the heat and stir in the mint and pepper.

4. Cut the lamb into thin slices across the grain and serve with the apricot-mint compote.

*Per serving (2-ounce slice): 152 Calories, 6 g Total Fat, 2 g Saturated Fat, 50 mg Cholesterol, 173 mg Sodium, 7 g Total Carbohydrate, 1 g Dietary Fiber, 17 g Protein, 16 mg Calcium.*

*POINTS per serving: 3.*

★ *American Way*  You can serve this dish warm or at room temperature. If a grill is inconvenient, the lamb can be broiled, but the cooking time may vary slightly.

# Asparagus with Goat Cheese and Lemon Vinaigrette

MAKES 6 SERVINGS

*Depending on the weather conditions of any given season, Washington State ranks first or second in the nation in the production of asparagus (California is its leading competitor). But the proud Washington asparagus farmers will tell you that the firm, plump asparagus from their state is the result of an ideal growing situation: Eastern Washington has mineral-rich volcanic soil, mountain-fed irrigation streams, and warm days for vigorous growth. The cool nights promote the development of crisp stalks, vibrant color, and a unique flavor that is never bitter.*

2 pounds asparagus trimmed and fibrous stalks peeled

1 lemon

1¹/₂ tablespoons extra-virgin olive oil

¹/₈ teaspoon sugar

¹/₈ teaspoon salt

Pinch freshly ground pepper

¹/₃ cup crumbled aged goat's milk cheese

1. Cook the asparagus in a large pan of salted boiling water until crisp-tender, 3–5 minutes. Using tongs, transfer the asparagus to a large bowl of ice water. Cool the asparagus for 1 minute and then drain on layers of paper towels.

2. Remove the zest from the lemon using the fine side of a grater; set aside. Squeeze 2 teaspoons lemon juice and combine with the olive oil, sugar, salt, and pepper in a bowl. Mix with a fork until blended.

3. Drizzle the vinaigrette over the asparagus, sprinkle with the cheese, and garnish with the lemon zest. Serve immediately.

*Per serving   74 Calories, 6 g Total Fat, 2 g Saturated Fat, 7 mg Cholesterol, 73 mg Sodium, 3 g Total Carbohydrate, 2 g Dietary Fiber, 4 g Protein, 75 mg Calcium.*

*POINTS per serving: 2.*

# Golden Delicious Phyllo Apple Tart

MAKES 10 SERVINGS

*Apples are big business in the Pacific Northwest, with Washington accounting for 60 percent of the nation's fresh apple crop. Though the orchards were originally cultivated in the mild climes west of the Cascade Mountains, the spread of railroads and the improvements in irrigation and cold storage enabled the industry to blossom east of the mountains by the late 19th century. With a natural sweetness and firm but tender texture, the Golden Delicious is the perfect apple for this luscious tart.*

1 lemon

5 large Golden Delicious apples, peeled, cored, and cut into 12 wedges each

1/2 cup granulated sugar

1/2 cup packed brown sugar

1 teaspoon cinnamon

1/2 teaspoon freshly grated nutmeg

1/4 cup hazelnuts, toasted

1 tablespoon apple brandy or Grand Marnier

3 tablespoons unsalted butter

4 tablespoons apple jelly

1 tablespoon water

9 (12 × 17-inch) sheets phyllo dough, thawed according to package directions

1. Adjust the racks to divide the oven in half. Preheat the oven to 350°F. Remove the zest from the lemon using the fine side of a grater; set aside.

2. Combine 2 tablespoons lemon juice, apples, granulated sugar, brown sugar, cinnamon, and nutmeg in a large nonstick skillet. Simmer, stirring continuously to dissolve the sugar, until the apples are golden brown and tender, about 10 minutes. With a slotted spoon, transfer the apples to a bowl. Pour the syrup into a small bowl, cover, and refrigerate. Add the hazelnuts, lemon zest, and brandy to the apples. Stir to combine, then set aside to cool.

3. Combine the butter, 3 tablespoons of the apple jelly, and water in a microwavable bowl. Microwave on high until melted, about 30 seconds; stir to blend. Remove the phyllo sheets from the package, arrange in a flat stack, and cover with plastic wrap to retain moisture. With a pastry brush, lightly coat one sheet with the butter-jelly mixture, then fold it into thirds lengthwise, lightly coating each new surface as you fold it. Lay the strip in a 9-inch pie pan, with one end of the strip at the base of the side of the pan and the other end hanging over the opposite edge. Repeat with the remaining butter-jelly mixture and phyllo sheets, overlapping the strips in the pan in spoke-wheel fashion so that the entire inside surface of the pan is covered.

4. Spread the remaining tablespoon of jelly over the phyllo in the pan. Spoon the apples evenly over the jelly, then fold the overhanging portion of each strip of phyllo toward the center of the pan and twist to form a rosette. The phyllo will not cover the center of the tart and most of the filling will show.

5. Place the tart on a baking sheet to catch any overflow and bake in the center of the oven until nicely browned and crisp, about 45 minutes. Serve warm or at room temperature with a little of the cooled, reserved syrup drizzled over the top.

*Per serving* 257 Calories, 7 g Total Fat, 3 g Saturated Fat, 10 mg Cholesterol, 90 mg Sodium, 48 g Total Carbohydrate, 2 g Dietary Fiber, 2 g Protein, 26 mg Calcium.

*POINTS per serving:* 5.

*Golden Delicious Phyllo Apple Tart*

## America's Fruit Basket

Fruit trees thrive in mild winters, cool moist summers, and just the right dose of afternoon sunshine. And there is no place in America better suited to providing those requirements than the Pacific Northwest. Farmers in Washington and Oregon have capitalized on their perfect growing conditions by specializing in quality, tree-ripened fruit.

Mostly produced on small family farms, Northwest apples, peaches, plums, nectarines, apricots, and cherries are prized for their flavor, size, and perfect appearance, but this superior quality doesn't come easily. The area's farmers devote much effort to developing new and more flavorful fruits and to marketing specialty varieties developed elsewhere in the world. In addition to Granny Smith, Golden Delicious, Red Delicious, and McIntosh apples, Northwest orchards produce less familiar varieties such as Criterion, Gravenstein, Tydeman, and Newtown Pippin. A campaign among growers to promote variety-labeling means that we will soon recognize a wide variety of apples by their names—not just by identifications such as "cooking apple"— and use each in dishes for which it is best suited. Although other fruit from Washington and Oregon are less likely to be identified by variety, Bing and Ranier cherries, Redhaven and Elberta peaches, and Bartlett, Anjou, Bosc, and Comice pears are well known products of the area.

# All-American Cherry Pie

## MAKES 8 SERVINGS

*We'll never know if George Washington cut down a cherry tree to make a pie but our version is certainly easier to make than most. Our basic crust will help to keep the **POINTS** down, too. Serve this pie warm, with fat-free frozen vanilla yogurt, or light non-dairy whipped topping.*

### BASIC PIE CRUST

2 cups all-purpose flour

2 teaspoons sugar

1/4 teaspoon salt

1/3 cup plus 2 teaspoons cold unsalted margarine, diced

2/3 cup low-fat (1%) cottage cheese

1/2 cup plain low-fat yogurt

### FILLING

2 cans (20-ounce) light cherry pie filling

1 tablespoon fresh lemon juice

1. For the crust, combine the flour, sugar, and salt in a large bowl. With two knives, cut in the margarine until the mixture resembles coarse crumbs. Briefly drain the cottage cheese in a fine mesh sieve. Stir in the cottage cheese and yogurt until the mixture forms a soft ball. Gather the dough into a ball, divide it in half, and wrap each piece in plastic wrap. Refrigerate several hours or overnight.

2. Preheat the oven to 400°F. On a floured counter, roll out the dough to a 13-inch round. Fit the dough into a 9-inch pie plate, press to fit, and roll the dough over to form a rim. For the lattice top, roll out the second piece of dough into a 14-inch round, cut the dough into 1/2-inch strips, and place the strips on a baking sheet. Refrigerate both the bottom and the lattice.

3. Combine the cherry filling and lemon juice in a bowl. Scrape the prepared cherry pie filling into the prepared pie plate. Cover the cherries with a lattice top, sealing the edge. Trim and crimp the crust.

4. Bake the pie on a baking sheet, to catch any overflow, until the filling begins to bubble through the lattice, 45–50 minutes. Cool on a rack for 15–20 minutes and serve warm.

*Per serving* 323 Calories, 9 g Total Fat, 2 g Saturated Fat, 2 mg Cholesterol, 182 mg Sodium, 54 g Total Carbohydrate, 1 g Dietary Fiber, 6 g Protein, 46 mg Calcium.

*POINTS per serving:* 7.

★ *American Way* The secret of good pastry? Keep it cold, work quickly, and let it rest to relax the gluten before rolling it out. For best results, make the crust about 24 hours before you'd like to bake it.

# Coconut Bread Pudding with Chocolate Sauce

MAKES 8 SERVINGS

*Today, Hawaii is a paradise of tropical fruit, but surprisingly, most of the fruit grown here are not indigenous to the islands. For example, pineapple arrived from Brazil some 200 years ago. Though you might not think of bread pudding as a particularly Hawaiian dessert, combining coconut, coconut milk, pineapple, and a touch of chocolate will transport you to paradise without getting on a plane.*

1/2 cup sweetened shredded coconut

1 (20-ounce) can pineapple chunks in juice, drained

3 large eggs

2 large egg whites

1/2 cup sugar

1 teaspoon salt

2 1/4 cups fat-free milk

1 cup low-fat coconut milk

1 tablespoon vanilla extract

5 cups (3/4-inch square) French bread cubes

2 ounces bittersweet or semisweet chocolate, chopped

2 teaspoons cocoa powder

1. Preheat the broiler. Place the coconut in a baking pan and broil, 5 inches from the heat, until lightly browned, about 1 minute. Transfer the coconut to a plate to cool. Place the pineapple chunks in the baking pan in a single layer and broil until lightly browned, 2–3 minutes. Set aside to cool.

2. Preheat the oven to 350°F. Beat the eggs, egg whites, sugar, and salt in a bowl until combined. Blend in 2 cups of the milk, the coconut milk, and vanilla. Stir in the bread cubes and allow to sit for 10 minutes. Stir in the toasted coconut and pineapple; pour into a 7 × 11-inch glass baking dish. Bake until the pudding is puffed and brown, 40–50 minutes. Allow to cool slightly.

3. Meanwhile, combine the remaining milk, the chocolate, and the cocoa powder in a 1-cup glass measure. Microwave on High 45 seconds and then stir until well blended.

4. Serve the pudding drizzled with chocolate sauce.

*Per serving  283 Calories, 10 g Total Fat, 6 g Saturated Fat, 81 mg Cholesterol, 512 mg Sodium, 41 g Total Carbohydrate, 2 g Dietary Fiber, 8 g Protein, 131 mg Calcium.*

*POINTS per serving: 6.*

FLASHBACK >> 1880

Horticulturist John Kidwell arrives in Honolulu and spends over a decade developing and refining the production of high-quality pineapple that can be grown commercially. The first pineapple cannery opens in Hawaii in 1892.

*Coconut Bread Pudding with Chocolate Sauce*

# Huckleberry and Cranberry Pie

MAKES 10 SERVINGS

*The woods along the Kenai peninsula in Alaska are brimming with berries, including wild cranberries, raspberries, and huckleberries. Bears forage these delectable morsels for immediate gratification, but the locals gather buckets for creating delicious pies, cakes, preserves, and jam.*

2 cups all-purpose flour

2 teaspoons baking powder

3/4 cup sugar

1/2 teaspoon salt

3 tablespoons unsalted butter, frozen

3 tablespoons low-fat buttermilk

About 3 tablespoons ice water

1/2 small orange, unpeeled, seeded, and cut into pieces

4 cups huckleberries or blueberries

3/4 pound cranberries, picked over and stems removed

3 tablespoons cornstarch

2 tablespoons low-fat (1%) milk

1. To make the crust, combine the flour, baking powder, 1 tablespoon of the sugar, and salt in a bowl. With a coarse grater, grate the butter into the flour mixture. Using a pastry blender or 2 knives, combine until the mixture resembles coarse meal. Add the buttermilk and ice water and stir just until a dough forms, adding a bit more water if necessary. Wrap the dough in plastic and refrigerate for 20–30 minutes.

2. Meanwhile, to make the filling, coarsely grind the orange in a food processor or blender. Combine the chopped orange, huckleberries, cranberries, 1 2/3 cups of the sugar, and the cornstarch in a large nonstick saucepan; stir to combine. Bring to a boil and cook until the mixture has thickened and the sugar has dissolved, about 4 minutes. Remove from the heat and set aside to cool, about 20 minutes.

3. Turn the dough out onto a lightly floured counter and roll to a 12-inch round. Place the dough in a 9-inch round pie pan and gently press into place. Trim the edge, leaving no overhang, and refrigerate.

4. Gather together the scraps and roll out. Using a 1 1/4-inch decorative cookie cutter (such as a daisy, leaf, or star shape), make cut-outs. Reroll the scraps to make more cut-outs for a total of 30–35 pieces. Place the cut-outs in a single layer on a nonstick baking sheet and refrigerate.

5. Position a rack in the center of the oven. Preheat the oven to 400°F.

★ *American Way* If huckleberries are unavailable, blueberries work well.

6. Spoon the cooled berry filling into the chilled pie shell, mounding it in the center. Using a pastry brush, lightly coat the edge of the pastry with milk. Overlap the dough cut-outs along the outside of the pastry, pressing gently. Brush with milk and sprinkle with the remaining 1 tablespoon sugar. Place the pie on a baking sheet to catch any overflow and place in the oven. Bake until the crust is golden brown, about 50 minutes. Cool on a rack. Serve warm or at room temperature.

*Per serving   311 Calories, 4 g Total Fat, 2 g Saturated Fat, 10 mg Cholesterol, 246 mg Sodium, 66 g Total Carbohydrate, 2 g Dietary Fiber, 3 g Protein, 44 mg Calcium.*

*POINTS per serving: 6.*

# Index

Page references in *italics* refer to photographs.